PLEASE CHECK FOR CD

SCHOLASTIC

100 SCIENCE LESSONS

NEW EDITION

TERMS AND CONDITIONS

IMPORTANT - PERMITTED USE AND WARNINGS - READ CAREFULLY BEFORE USING

Licence

Copyright in the software contained in this CD-ROM and in its accompanying material belongs to Scholastic Limited. All rights reserved. © 2007 Scholastic Ltd.

Save for these purposes, or as expressly authorised in the accompanying materials, the software may not be copied, reproduced, used, sold, licensed, transferred, exchanged, hired, or exported in whole or in part or in any manner or form without the prior written consent of Scholastic Ltd. Any such unauthorised use or activities are prohibited and may give rise to civil liabilities and criminal prosecutions.

The material contained on this CD ROM may only be used in the context for which it was intended in *100 Science Lessons*, and is for use only in the school which has purchased the book and CD-ROM, or by the teacher who has purchased the book and CD-ROM. Permission to download images is given for purchasers only and not for users from any lending service. Any further use of the material contravenes Scholastic Ltd's copyright and that of other rights holders.

This CD-ROM has been tested for viruses at all stages of its production. However, we recommend that you run virus-checking software on your computer systems at all times. Scholastic Ltd cannot accept any responsibility for any loss, disruption or damage to your data or your computer system that may occur as a result of using either the CD-ROM or the data held on it.

SCOTTISH PRIMARY 1

YEAR R

Minimum specification:
- PC with a CD-ROM drive and 512 Mb RAM (recommended)
- Windows 98SE or above/Mac OSX.1 or above
- Recommended minimum processor speed: 1 GHz

For all technical support queries, please phone
Scholastic Custom...

O
507
ONE

Georgie Beasley

D0281712

05.08

Author
Georgie Beasley

Series Editor
Peter Riley

Editors
Jennifer Regan
Tracy Kewley
Kate Pedlar

Project Editor
Roanne Charles

Illustrator
Colin Shelbourn

Series Designers
Catherine Perera and Joy Monkhouse

Designer
Catherine Perera

CD-ROM developed in association with
Vivid Interactive

Published by Scholastic Ltd
Villiers House
Clarendon Avenue
Leamington Spa
Warwickshire CV32 5PR

www.scholastic.co.uk

Designed using Adobe InDesign.

Printed by Bell and Bain Ltd, Glasgow

23456789   7890123456

Text © 2007 Georgie Beasley

© 2007 Scholastic Ltd

British Library Cataloguing-in-Publication Data
A catalogue record for this book is available from the British Library.

ISBN 978-0439-94502-8

UNIVERSITY OF CHICHESTER

ACKNOWLEDGEMENTS

All Flash activities developed by Vivid Interactive.

Material from the National Curriculum © Crown copyright. Reproduced under the terms of the Click Use Licence.

Extracts from the QCA Scheme of Work © Qualifications and Curriculum Authority.

Extracts from the Primary School Curriculum for Ireland, www.ncca.ie, National Council for Curriculum and Assessment.

Every effort has been made to trace copyright holders for the works reproduced in this book, and the publishers apologise for any inadvertent omissions.

Post-It is a registered trademark of 3M.

This new edition of 100 Science Lessons follows the QCA Science Scheme of work but also meets many of the demands of the curricula for England, Wales, Scotland, Northern Ireland and Eire. The book is divided into six eight units which relate closely to the Early Learning Goals in the Curriculum Guidance for the Foundation Stage.

Each unit is divided into a number of lessons, ending with an assessment lesson. The organisation chart at the start of each unit shows the objectives and outcomes of each lesson, and gives a quick overview of the lesson content (main activities, group activities and plenary). The Early Learning Goals for the Foundation Stage for England, Wales, Scotland, Northern Ireland and Eire provide the basis for the lesson objectives used throughout the book, however, links to NC Levels 1 and 2 are suggested in the 'Outcomes' at the end of each lesson (for more details see 'Outcomes' below).

Lesson plans

There are detailed and short lesson plans. About 60 per cent of the lesson plans in this book are detailed lesson plans. The short lesson plans are closely related to them and cover similar topics and concepts. They contain the essential features of the detailed lesson plans allowing you to plan for progression and assessment.

The detailed lesson plans have the following structure:

CONTEXT

This section can be found at the start of each chapter. It gives a brief overview of the meaningful contexts through which each lesson can be delivered. Suggestions may be provided for obtaining and adapting resources and creating classroom displays. Links to other curriculum topics, may also be referred to, where appropriate.

OBJECTIVES

The objectives are stated in a way that helps to focus on each lesson plan and at least one is related to content knowledge and there may be one or more . When you have read through the lesson you may wish to add your own objectives. You can find out how these objectives relate to those of the various national curricula by looking at the relevant grids on the CD-ROM. You can also edit the planning grids to fit with your own objectives (for more information see 'How to use the CD-ROM' on page 6).

RESOURCES AND PREPARATION

The Resources section provides a list of everything you will need to deliver the lesson, including any photocopiables presented in this book. The preparation section describes anything that needs to be done in advance of the lesson, such as collecting environmental data.

As part of preparation of all practical work, you should consult your school's policies on practical work and select activities for which you are confident to take responsibility. The ASE publication Be Safe! gives very useful guidance on health and safety issues in primary science.

VOCABULARY

There is a vocabulary list of science words associated with the lesson which children should use in discussing and presenting their work. Time should be spent defining each word at an appropriate point in the lesson.

STARTER

This introductory section contains ideas to build up interest at the beginning of the lesson and set the scene.

MAIN ACTIVITY

These sections present a direct, whole class (or occasionally group) teaching session that will help you deliver the content knowledge outlined in the lesson objectives before group activities begin. It may include guidance on discussion, or on performing one or more demonstrations or class investigations to help the children understand the work ahead.

The relative proportions of the lesson given to the Starter, Main teaching activity and Group activities vary. If you are reminding the children of their previous work and getting them onto their own investigations, the group work may dominate the lesson time; if you are introducing a new topic or concept, you might wish to spend all or most of the lesson engaged in whole-class teaching.

GROUP ACTIVITIES

The Group activities are very flexible. Some may be best suited to individual work, while others may be suitable for work in pairs or larger groupings. There are usually two or more Group activities provided for each lesson. You may wish to them one after the other; use all together, to reduce demand on resources and your attention; or, where one is a practical activity, use the other for children, who complete their practical work successfully and quickly., or even as a follow-up homework task.

Some of the group activities are supported by a photocopiable sheet. These can be found in the book and on the CD-ROM. For some activities, there are also accompanying differentiated ideas, interactive activities and diagrams on the CD-ROM (for more information, see 'How to use the CD-ROM below).

The group activities may include some writing. These activities are also aimed at strengthening the children's science literacy and supporting their English literacy skills. They may involve writing labels and captions, developing scientific vocabulary, presenting data, explaining what they have observed, or using appropriate secondary sources. The children's mathematical skills are also developed through number and data handling work, in the context of science investigations.

ICT LINKS

Many lessons have this section, in which suggestions for incorporating ICT are given. ICT links might include: using CD-ROMS or the internet for research; preparing graphs and tables using a computer; using interactive activities and worksheets from the CD-ROM.

A CD icon is used to indicate where material from the accompanying CD-ROM is needed. This might be a differentiated version of a photocopiable worksheet, an interactive activity, the graphing tool or a diagram.

DIFFERENTIATION

Where appropriate, there are suggestions for differentiated work to support less able learners or extend more able learners in your class. Some of the photocopiable sheets are also differentiated into less able support, core ability, and more able extension to support you in this work. The book contains the worksheets for the core ability while the differentiated worksheets are found on the accompanying CD-ROM.

ASSESSMENT

This section includes advice on how to assess the children's work against the lesson objectives. This may include questions to ask or observations to make to help you build up a picture of the children's developing ideas and plan future lessons. A separate summative assessment lesson is provided at the end of each unit of work. .

PLENARY

Suggestions are given for drawing the various strands of the lesson together in this session. The lesson objectives and outcomes may be reviewed and key learning points may be highlighted. The scene may also be set for another lesson.

HOMEWORK

On occasions, tasks may be suggested for the children to do at home. These may involve using photocopiables or setting other appropriate activities to broaden the children's understanding of the topic being studied, as well as providing links between home and school experiences.

OUTCOMES

These are statements related to the objectives; they describe what the children should have achieved through the lesson.

The outcomes included in this section are closely related to the stepping stones and early learning goals found in the Knowledge and Understanding and Personal Development sections of the Foundation Stage curriculum guidance. They also link to the target setting process outlined in the Assessment for Learning tool kit.

The 'must' outcome links to the yellow, blue or green stepping stones and so steps one, two and three of the early years' profile; all children including nearly all those with learning difficulties are expected to reach the 'must' outcome by the end of the reception year. The 'should' outcome relates to the relevant part of the Early Learning Goals found either in the Knowledge and Understanding of the World or Personal Development sections. Nearly all of the children are expected to reach this outcome by the end of the reception year and relates to steps four to eight on the Foundation Stage Profile. The 'could' outcome provides more challenging goals for the more able children and links to Level 1 of the science National Curriculum and step nine on the Foundation Stage Profile, while the 'could even' outcome provides for any gifted and talented children needing the challenge of Level 2.

LINKS

These are included where appropriate. They may include links to subjects closely related to science, such as technology or maths, or to content and skills in subjects such as art, history or geography.

Relevant outcomes from Every Child Matters are referenced to make it easier to track how you are catering for these important aspects.

ASSESSMENT LESSON

The last lesson in every unit focuses on summative assessment. This assessment samples the content of the unit, focusing on its key theme(s); its results should be used in conjunction with other assessments you have made during the teaching of the unit. The lesson comprises two or more assessment activities, which may take the form of photocopiable sheets to work on or practical activities with suggested assessment questions for you to use while you are observing the children.

These lessons are intended to provide you with a guide to assessing the children's performance.

How to use the CD-ROM

SYSTEM REQUIREMENTS

Minimum specifications:
● PC or Mac with CD-ROM drive and at least 512 MB RAM (recommended)
● Microsoft Windows 98SE or above/Mac OSX.1 or above
● Recommended minimum processor speed: 1GHz

GETTING STARTED

The accompanying CD-ROM includes a range of lesson and planning resources. The first screen requires the user to select the relevant country (England, Scotland, Wales, Northern Ireland, Eire). There are then several menus enabling the user to search the material according to various criteria, including lesson name, QCA unit, National Curriculum topic and resource type.

Searching by lesson name enables the user to see all resources associated with that particular lesson. The coloured tabs on the left-hand side of this screen indicate the differentiated worksheets; the tabs at the top of the page lead to different *types* of resource (diagram, interactive or photocopiable).

PHOTOCOPIABLES

The photocopiables that are printed in the book are also provided on the CD-ROM, as PDF files. In addition, differentiated versions of the photocopiables are provided where relevant:
● green indicates a support worksheet for less confident children;
● red indicates the core photocopiable, as printed in the book;
● blue indicates an extension worksheet for more confident children.

There are no differentiated photocopiables for assessment activities.

The PDF files can be annotated on screen using the panel tool provided (see below). The tools allow the user to add notes, highlight items and draw lines and boxes.

PDF files of photocopiables can be printed from the CD-ROM and there is also an option to print the full screen, including any drawings and annotations that have been added using the tools. (NB where PDF files are landscape, printer settings may need to be adjusted.)

INTERACTIVE ACTIVITIES

The CD-ROM includes twelve activities for children to complete using an interactive whiteboard or individual computers. Each activity is based on one of the photocopiables taken from across the units. Activities include: dragging and dropping an insect's parts into the correct place; clicking on objects in the home to see if they light up; sequencing pictures for making porridge and sorting objects according to whether they light up, heat up, make sounds or move. *Note that the 'check' button should only be pressed, once the interactive task has been fully completed!*

GRAPHING TOOL

The graphing tool supports lessons where the children are asked to gather and record data. The tool enables children to enter data into a table, which can then be used to create a block graph, pie chart or line graph.

When inserting data into the table, the left-hand column should be used for labels for charts; the right-hand column is for numeric data only (see example below). The pop-up keypad can be used to enter numbers into the table.

DIAGRAMS

Where appropriate, diagrams printed in the book have been included as separate files on the CD-ROM. These include annotated diagrams for the you and the children to refer to when experimenting or making objects, such as a boat or a windmill. These can be displayed on an interactive whiteboard.

GENERAL RESOURCES

In addition to lesson resources, the CD-ROM also includes the planning grids for each unit, as printed in the book, and the relevant curriculum grid for England, Scotland, Wales, Northern Ireland and Eire. The curriculum grids indicate how elements of each country's National Curriculum are addressed by lessons in the book. The planning grids are supplied as editable Word files; the curriculum grids are supplied as Word and PDF files. Selection of a planning grid leads to a link, which opens the document in a separate window; this then needs to be saved to the computer or network before editing.

UNIT 1 Ourselves

Lesson	Objectives	Main activity	Group activities	Plenary	Outcomes
Lesson 1 Looking closely	• To develop sorting skills by looking carefully.	Sort a variety of fruits by colour, shape and size.	Look closely at the inside of fruits. Make fruit prints. Identify fruit segments. Set up a fruit shop.	Talk about the patterns made by the fruit prints.	• Can sort a range of fruits by colour, shape and size by looking closely. • Can sort fruits using other criteria.
Lesson 2 Describing fruit	• To develop sorting skills by touching and feeling. • To develop an idea of texture.	Talk about the textures of different fruits, developing vocabulary to describe them.	Sort fruits by texture. Make a fruit salad. Structured role-play in fruit shop.	Talk about the changes in the fruit when the fruit salad is made.	• Can find out about fruit by touching and feeling. • Can compare fruit before and after peeling, noting similarities and differences.
Lesson 3 How does it smell?	• To develop sorting skills by using the sense of smell.	Explore a variety of fruits using the sense of smell, developing the vocabulary to describe them.		Share a fruit salad and talk about the different smells.	• Can link the sense of smell to the nose. • Can identify fruit by using the sense of smell.
Lesson 4 Give me a drink!	• To know that we need to drink to stay alive. • To develop recording skills through sorting.	Make a list of favourite drinks.	Find out the most popular fruit drinks. Identify drinks that need to have water added. Get water ready to drink. Make fruit juice.	Talk about the importance of drinking healthy drinks.	• Know that they need to drink to stay alive. • Know that thirst is the body's way of saying 'Give me a drink'. • Can begin to organise information in graphical form.
Lesson 5 Feeding the senses	• To develop sorting skills by using the sense of taste.	Identify fruits by tasting, developing the vocabulary to describe them.		Share a fruit salad and talk about the different tastes.	• Can use the sense of taste to find out about fruit. • Can link the sense of taste to the tongue and mouth.
Lesson 6 Do not touch	• To learn that not all things are safe to touch, smell and taste.	Look for and examining 'danger' signs on empty cartons.	Add 'Do not touch' stickers to containers. Sort pictures of materials into 'safe' and 'not safe'. Identify 'danger' signs.	Look at cleaning materials and talk about their safety.	• Begin to learn how to keep themselves safe by knowing that not all things are safe to touch, smell and taste.
Lesson 7 All of the senses	• To learn which parts of the body are used to smell, touch, see, hear and taste.	Match the senses to pictures of a nose, hand, eye, ear and tongue. Label these body parts.		Reinforce safety issues relating to touches, smells and tastes. Talk about dangers to ears and eyes.	• Know which parts of the body we use to hear, see, smell and taste, and which main parts we use to feel and touch. • Have begun to think about how to look after our bodies and protect our hearing and sight.
Lesson 8 Touch and feel	• To learn that we can use our fingers and hands to touch and feel, and that we can use this sense to identify objects. To explore and describe a range of objects that have different shapes and textures.	Feely bag activity: identify an object by its shape and texture.	Feely bag activity: Record what they think they have touched. Print with objects of different textures.	Match the texture prints to the objects. Make a display of prints and objects.	• Can identify objects by feeling their shape and texture. • Can describe similarities and differences between objects. • Can talk about the materials from which different objects are made.
Lesson 9 Sorting sounds	• To learn to identify objects from the sounds they make.	Feely bag activity: identify an object from the sound that it makes.	Identify recorded sounds. Share a book with sound effects. Find pictures of things that make a sound. Play with percussion instruments.	Add sound effects to a familiar story.	• Know that they use their ears to hear. • Can recognise familiar objects from the sounds they make.
Lesson 10 The same or different?	• To begin to use their senses to identify similarities and differences.	Compare sound pots. Play a dominoes game with textures.	Repeat the 'texture dominoes' game. Match pairs of sound pots.	Play either game together, talking about the textures or sounds.	• Can begin to use more than one sense to explore a range of objects and to identify similarities and differences.

Lesson	Objectives	Main activity	Group activities	Plenary	Outcomes
Lesson 11 Touchy feely	• To explore using all five senses and to identify familiar objects. • To use of drawing to record findings in an investigation.	Use the senses to find out what is inside different parcels.	Identify food items using only the sense of taste.	Reveal the hidden items and foods. Talk about the senses used.	• Can explore a range of familiar objects using their senses. • Can talk about features and properties.
Lesson 12 Body parts	• To recognise and learn the names of parts of the body and be able to say what they are used for.	Learn songs to teach the parts of the body.	Make and solve body jigsaws. Fix 'people' jigsaws. Label body parts on a picture. Paint and label pictures of themselves.	Sing songs and rhymes about the parts of the body, with actions	• Can identify some external parts of the human body and recognise their names. • Can talk about what they are doing.
Lesson 13 Moving around	• To learn that we use different parts of our bodies to move in different ways.	Explore which body parts are used for moving in a PE lesson. Draw pictures of all the ways they moved.		Talk about all the ways the children moved and make a display with the pictures. Sing a movement song.	• Know that we can move in many different ways, using different parts of our bodies and sometimes more than one part at a time.
Lesson 14 Match the clothing	• To know that we all grow and change as we get older.	Look at photographs of the same person as a baby and as an adult. Compare the ways a baby and a toddler move.	Compare early and recent photographs of themselves. Look at baby clothes and toys. Match baby clothes to children's clothes. Sort baby clothes by type of item.	Make a display of the clothes and toys, reinforcing how we change as we grow older.	• Can sort and match items of clothing of very different sizes and explain how they would have fitted everyone at a certain stage in their life. • Know that we all change as we grow older.
Lesson 15 Helping ourselves	• To learn that we can all do many things for ourselves.	Talk to an adult visitor about care of a baby. List the things a baby can do and things the children can do. Paint self-portraits for display.		Make a display of faces and speech bubbles to show what a baby can do and what the children can do.	• Know what babies are and are not able to do for themselves. • Understand that as young children get older, they are able to do more things for themselves.
Lesson 16 Different faces	• To investigate similarities and differences between us.	Discuss the physical similarities and differences between two children.	Paint pictures of themselves. Play 'Spot the difference'. Play a 'Who am I describing?' game. Make a faces collage. Make handprints and footprints.	Ask the children to identify the subjects of some of their paintings.	• Know that we all have things about us that are the same and things that are different. • Can investigate similarities and differences through first-hand experience.
Lesson 17 Shapes and sizes	• To know that people come in different shapes and sizes. • To begin to order things according to size. • To begin to match objects and people according to size.	Compare the sizes of items in the context of the 'three bears' story.	Make beds for the three bears. Order soft toys by size. Make the three bears' cottage in the role-play area. Make the three bears' beds.	Talk about the different sizes of things in the three bears' cottage.	• Know the comparative language of size. • Can sort and match items according to size. • Have begun to classify things according to size.
Lesson 18 Tall and short	• To learn that we all grow. • To find out who are the tallest and shortest children in the class.	Compare the children's heights. Paint life-sized pictures of each other.		Organise the children into height order.	• Know that we all grow. • Know that some people grow taller than others. • Know that some people grow faster than others.

Assessment	Objectives	Main activity	Activities 2 and 3	Outcomes
Lesson 19	• To find out how many parts of the body the children can name. • To assess whether the children understand that we all grow and change as we become older. • To assess whether the children can identify simple similarities and differences between people.	Match labels to the correct body parts on the computer.	Order a set of pictures to show a person getting older. Draw pictures of themselves as babies and as they look now.	• Find out, recognise and identify some of the features of humans. • Understand the changes that occur in humans as we get older. • Look closely at similarities and differences between humans.

CONTEXT

Making a fruit salad

Lessons 1–5 of this unit are set in the context of making a fruit salad, and can be taught as a daily activity through the week. Lesson 6 goes on to look at hazardous substances that should not be touched, smelled or tasted. The activities can be included in a food topic, a healthy eating project and/or the making of a fruit shop role-play area. The children will be taught to explore the use of their senses through play activities, thus developing the early investigative skills of noticing similarities and differences and using them to sort and record. These ideas can be adapted for other food preparation activities, such as making sandwiches or vegetable fingers.

Lesson 1 ▪ Looking closely

Objective
● To develop sorting skills by looking carefully.

Vocabulary
pips, seeds, core, segments, peel, flesh, juice

RESOURCES ⊙

Main activity: Collection of fruit (enough to make a fruit salad for the children to share at snack time), including banana, pineapple, green and red apple, green and black grapes, pear, orange, kiwi fruit, peach and plum; tablecloth; sorting rings; card labels and a marker pen (optional); large bowl.
Group activities: 1 Cutting board; knife; sorting rings. **2** Green, red, yellow and orange paint; A3 paper. **3** Photocopiable page 35 (also 'Looking closely' (red) available on the CD-ROM); pencils. **4** Play fruit; baskets; table and tablecloth; magazines with pictures of fruit (or labels from tinned fruit); A3 paper; adhesive.
ICT link: Digital camera; different fruit segments and whole fruits; computer; printer.

PREPARATION

Choose types of fruit that look different in a number of ways: different shapes, colours, stems, peel and so on. Organise the tables for the focused Group activities. Spread the tablecloth in the centre of a carpeted area or over a large table. Organise the fruit and sorting rings in the centre, so that the children can see all the resources. Make enough copies of photocopiable page 35. Cut up some fruit into pieces (large enough for the children to handle) and put them in the bowl to share at the end of the lesson.

STARTER

Sit the children around the tablecloth. Show them the collection of fruit. Ask whether anyone can tell you the name of any of these fruits. Can they tell you the name of the kiwi fruit, pineapple and pear? Confirm the names of all the fruits.

MAIN ACTIVITY

Hold up the orange and ask the children to give you one word that describes what the orange looks like. Prompt them to mention the shape or the colour. Can they hold the orange in their hand so that it cannot be seen? Repeat this activity with the banana and one of the apples.

Ask the children whether they can put any of the fruits together

Differentiation
Support
Show the children 'Looking closely' (green) from the CD-ROM, which features pictures of more common fruit for them to match in the bowl.
Extension
Give the children 'Looking closely' (blue) from the CD-ROM, and encourage them to think of their own fruit to add to the bowl.

because they are the same colour. Put all the yellow fruits together, then the red, the green and so on, using the set rings. Now sort the fruits by size and by shape. Explain that you are sorting them into sets. You may wish to label the sets at this point. Tell the children that they have been using their sense of sight to sort the fruits, looking carefully to see the differences.

GROUP ACTIVITIES

1 With a group of six to eight children, cut the different fruits open one at a time and talk about what is inside. Discuss the peel, flesh, core and seeds. Tell the children that the seeds are called 'pips' in apples, pears, oranges and grapes, and 'stones' in plums and peaches. Ask the children questions such as: *Which is the juiciest fruit? How do you know? Can you see the juice?* Sort the fruits into sets by the colour of the pips, the appearance of the flesh, and whether or not we eat the peel.

2 With an adult helper, invite another group of four to six children to make fruit prints. This could be set in the context of making a frieze for the role-play area. Ask the helper to cut an apple, an orange and a banana horizontally across the centre, showing the shapes of the cross-sections and the star shape of the apple core. Let the children use green, red, yellow and orange paint to print fruit patterns, matching the colour of the paint to the colour of each fruit's peel.

3 Give the children a copy each of photocopiable page 35. Ask them to draw lines matching each whole fruit to a segment or slice in the bowl. Ask questions such as: *How can you recognise a segment of an orange? What do the kiwi fruit slices look like?*

4 Ask an adult helper to set up a fruit shop in the role-play area. Ask the less able children to sort the play fruits into baskets: one for each kind of fruit. Invite them to find pictures in magazines, or collect labels from tinned fruit to decorate their baskets and make posters for the shop.

ICT LINK

Use a digital camera to take photographs of different fruit segments and whole fruits, and print these off to make a domino game for the children to match the segments to their fruit.

ASSESSMENT

Note the children who can sort a range of fruits by colour, shape and size by looking closely at each fruit or segment. For more able children, note whether they sort by more complex criteria, such as whether they are citrus fruits or if they have stones or pips. Watch the children as they sort the fruit, and note those children who take the lead. Reorganise the groups to bring together the children not taking the lead, to see whether they are now able to complete the activity unaided.

PLENARY

Ask the children who took part in the fruit-printing activity to talk about the shapes they have made and the colours they have used. Do other children notice the star shape in the centre of the apple print and the shape of the orange segments? Are all the printed shapes circles? Which ones are? Would all the fruit prints be circles if they were cut across the middle?

Share the fruit salad by passing around the bowl and letting each child take a piece.

OUTCOMES

● All of the children *must* be able to look at living things to find out more about them.
● Most of the children *should* be able to investigate objects and materials by using their sense of sight, finding out about and identifying some features of fruits.

● Some children *could* communicate observations about the features of a range of fruits.
● A small number *could even* sort living things into groups using simple features and describe the basis for their groupings.

LINKS
ECM 1: Keeping healthy is covered in this and the following four lessons.
Across the curriculum: the skill of exploring using their senses is fundamental to the children's early learning in many areas of the Under-fives curriculum. The printing activity is closely related to Creative development, developing fine motor skills and physical development. The fruit shop activity is related to Mathematical development and developing knowledge and understanding of the world.

Lesson 2 ▪ Describing fruit

Objectives
● To develop sorting skills by touching and feeling.
● To develop an idea of texture.

Vocabulary
smooth, rough, prickly, sharp, squashy, hard, soft, sticky, juicy, wet

RESOURCES ◉
Main activity: Range of fruits with interesting textures, including an orange, apple, plum, pineapple, kiwi fruit and strawberry.
Group activities: 1 Sorting rings and labels. **2** Cutting board, knife and bowl; photocopiable page 36 (also 'Describing fruit – 1' (red) available on CD-ROM). **3** The 'fruit shop' role-play area from Lesson 1. 4 Pineapple; board and knife; photocopiable page 37 (also 'Describing fruit – 2' (red) available on CD-ROM); pencils.
ICT link: Digital camera; fruits; computer with word-processing program.
Plenary: Large sheet of paper.

PREPARATION
Write some of the set labels, using words that you want to introduce during the Group activities. Make copies of both photocopiable sheets.

STARTER
Sit the children in a circle so that they can see the fruit. Talk for a few minutes about the names of the fruits they can see.

MAIN ACTIVITY
Pass the apple around. Ask the children to touch it and think about how it feels. If they are able to, let them tell you what it feels like; otherwise, talk about its texture being hard and smooth as it is passed around the group. Next, pass the pineapple around and invite the children to comment on this fruit. They may say that it is heavy, prickly, hard and rough. Accept all responses, asking the children each time to say why they think that. The purpose is to find out what the children already know. Continue to pass around different types of fruit and talk about the textures until you are confident that the children understand what 'texture' means.

GROUP ACTIVITIES
1 Gather six to eight children around the sorting rings and fruit. Allow them to handle the fruit and talk about what they can feel. Ask them to put all the fruit that is smooth into one sorting ring and all the fruit that is not smooth into another. Label the rings 'smooth' and 'not smooth'. Sort the fruit again, using different criteria. Reinforce the learning objective: using the sense of touch to sort fruit.
2 Ask an adult helper to make a fruit salad with groups of up to six children. Brief the adult to talk about the juice and the 'squashiness' of the fruit. Give him or her a copy of photocopiable page 36: a list of prompt words to use with the children, describing what the fruit feels like. Ask the children: *Are*

Differentiation

Support
Introduce the language a word at a time. Ask an adult helper to pass around all the smooth fruit for the children to feel to help them understand what you mean by 'smooth'. Afterwards, pass the pineapple around and describe the texture to them while they handle the fruit. Repeat this with other fruits in your collection, and fill in 'Describing fruit – 1' (green) from the CD-ROM.

Extension
When the fruits have been sorted, ask the children to fill in 'Describing fruit – 2' (blue) on the CD-ROM, to talk about how fruits are similar and how they are different. They may want to talk about how the fruits look as well as how they feel – for example: *Does the pineapple look prickly? How do you know?*

the textures different now the fruit has been cut up? Why isn't the pineapple prickly any more? This will lead to a discussion about the differences between the way that fruit feels on the inside and on the outside.

3 Allow a group of children to play in the 'fruit shop' role-play area.

4 Spend time touching and smelling the pineapple when it is whole and when cut into rings. Complete photocopiable page 37 with the children.

ICT LINK
Take photographs of the outside and inside of your fruits. Insert these and descriptors (see photocopiable page 36) into a word-processing program and let the children use this to write sentences to describe the inside and the outside of their fruit.

ASSESSMENT
Note which children already have the vocabulary to describe texture at the beginning of the activity, so that you can extend this by comparing the fruit before and after peeling, noting similarities and differences. Set up a display of objects in the classroom with different textures for the children to explore, and note those who can sort using their sense of touch.

PLENARY
Look at two different fruits. List the things that are the same and the things that are different between the two fruits.

OUTCOMES
● All children *must* be able to look at living things to find out more about them.
● Most of the children *should* be able to investigate objects and materials by using their sense of touch, finding out about and identifying some features of fruits.
● Some *could* communicate observations about the features of a range of fruits by looking closely at similarities and differences.
● A small number *could even* sort living things into groups using simple features and describe the basis for their groupings.

LINKS
ECM 1: Keeping healthy.
Between units: there are links to the activities in Unit 4, where the children explore a variety of materials using their senses.

Lesson 3 ▪ How does it smell?

Objective
● To develop sorting skills by using the sense of smell.

RESOURCES
Collection of fruits, including orange, banana, apple and strawberry (other fruits with a distinctive and easily recognisable scent will do), each chopped up into a plastic cup with a paper cover held on with an elastic band; paper and pencils.

MAIN ACTIVITY
Talk to the children about how we smell things. Make sure they understand that we use our noses to smell. Emphasise the importance of not smelling things we are unfamiliar with: it might be dangerous. It is safe to do so in this lesson, because they will only be smelling familiar fruit to try to guess which is in each pot.

One at a time, pass the cups around the class and ask the children to guess what fruit is in each cup. Invite those who can to describe the smell,

Differentiation
Support
Children who need support,
and those who are still
unfamiliar with the names of
the fruits, may need to repeat
the activity in smaller groups
with an adult.
Extension
Ask children to make their own
pots (under supervision),
containing different fruits for
their friends to guess.

using words such as 'sweet' and 'tangy'. They could also use words and
phrases related to the names of fruits, such as 'orangey' or 'like a pineapple'.
(This is difficult for very young children, however, and is not essential.) As
each cup returns to you, remove the paper cover and pass the cup around
again so that the children can see whether they were right.

Set up a similar Group activity, using different fruits, for some of the
children to play during the day.

ASSESSMENT
Invite the children to record by drawing the fruits that they think are in each
pot. Keep these drawings as evidence of the children's ability to use their
sense of smell to identify fruit.

PLENARY
Share the fruit salad and talk about the different smells of the fruits.
Remind the children of the names of the different fruits.

OUTCOMES
● All of the children *must* be able to look at living things to find out more
about them.
● Most of the children *should* be able to investigate objects and materials
by using their sense of smell, finding out about and identifying some
features of fruits.
● Some *could* communicate observations about the features of a range of
fruits.
● A small number *could even* talk about their work linking the sense of
smell to the nose

Lesson 4 ▸ Give me a drink!

Objective
● To know that we need to
drink to stay alive.
● To develop recording skills
through sorting.

RESOURCES
Main activity: Fruit juices of different varieties (including orange, apple,
pineapple, blackcurrant, strawberry and grapefruit), containing no (or few)
additives and no added sugar; jugs, plastic cups.
Group activities: 1 Name cards for the children; a sheet of paper for each
fruit drink with a picture of the fruit in each corner (include a sheet for
water). **2** Paper, coloured pencils or crayons, sugar paper, adhesive. **3** Jugs,
tap water. **4** Juicer and fruit.
ICT link: Graphing tool on the CD-ROM.

PREPARATION
Check for any fruit allergies or dietary restrictions. Pour small quantities of
the fruit juices into jugs; include a jug of water.

STARTER
Show the children the
different fruit drinks and
the water. Explain that we
all need to drink if
we are to stay alive. Ask
the children whether they
are thirsty. Explain that
when they feel thirsty,
their body is telling them
that they need a drink.

MAIN ACTIVITY

Ask the children what drinks they like best. Do you like water? Make a list on the board or flip chart of all the fruit drinks the children like, using the names and sketches of the fruits. If different children choose the same drink, tally their responses alongside the fruit. Next, invite the children to choose and enjoy a small drink from the collection. Encourage them to try one that they are unfamiliar with, and to drink the water on its own also.

GROUP ACTIVITIES

1 Work with a group of eight to ten children. Ask them which drink they like best of the ones on offer. Display the sheets with pictures of the fruits on a table along with the name cards. Ask the children to point to the picture of the fruit from which their favourite drink is made (or to the water, if this is preferred). Challenge each child to take his or her name card from the group and place it on the sheet of paper representing his or her choice. Count and record how many name cards there are on each sheet of paper. Which drink did the group like best?

2 Ask an adult helper to talk to the children about all the kinds of drinks that need to have water added. The children should draw pictures of all the drinks they have thought of and stick them to a sheet of sugar paper: tea, coffee, squashes, powdered fizzy drinks and so on.

3 Organise small groups of children to fill jugs with water for snack time each day.

4 Use a juicer to make juice from real fruit.

ICT LINK 💿

More confident learners can use the graphing tool on the CD-ROM to create a block graph instead of a pictogram.

ASSESSMENT

Listen to the children's conversations as they talk about their favourite drinks. Question them to see whether they understand that when they feel thirsty, they need a drink.

PLENARY

Talk to the children about the fruit juices they have been drinking. Talk about the number of children who chose to drink water. Explain that it is very important to drink water at regular intervals, and not just fruit juices and other sugary drinks. Explain why: too much sugar is bad for your teeth, and sugary drinks can make you more instead of less thirsty. Encourage the children to drink a cup of water at this point, and reinforce the learning objective throughout the day by inviting them to drink water at regular intervals.

OUTCOMES

● All children *must* be able to develop an awareness of their own needs
● Most of the children *should* be able to recognise the importance of keeping healthy and that drinking plenty of fluid contributes to this.
● Some *could* communicate their findings in tables and graphs.
● A small number *could even* describe why animals need water to survive.

LINKS

ECM 1: Keeping healthy.
Between units: this lesson is linked to Unit 2, Lesson 4 on caring for pets.
Across the curriculum: the children recognising their own name links to communication, language and literacy; being aware of personal needs relates to personal development, and knowing how to keep healthy to physical development.

Lesson 5 ▪ Feeding the senses

Objective
● To develop sorting skills by using the sense of taste.

RESOURCES
Selection of fruits that have different tastes (ones that you know the children like), each cut up and placed in a sealed container. Be aware of any fruit allergies or dietary restrictions.

MAIN ACTIVITY
Talk to the children about how we taste things. Make sure they understand that we taste using the tongue and mouth. Emphasise the dangers of eating things that we are not used to, and tell the children that they should only play the following game with a trusted adult. Explain that they are going to guess what fruit they are eating without seeing it. Ask one child to close his or her eyes, then place a piece of fruit onto the child's tongue and invite him or her to eat it. Ask questions such as: *Is the fruit crunchy or soft? Is it dry or juicy? Is it sweet or sour?* Finally, ask the child whether he or she can identify the fruit using the sense of taste alone. Repeat the activity with other children, until they have all had a turn.

ASSESSMENT
Ask the children to draw the fruit they think they are tasting. Keep their drawings as a record.

PLENARY
Share the fruit salad at snack time, encouraging the children to describe the different tastes.

Differentiation
Support
Give children a piece of orange each and invite them to say what the fruit tastes like. Encourage the use of vocabulary as in the Main activity. Repeat this activity with several different kinds of familiar fruit before letting the children play the game (as above) with an adult helper.
Extension
Challenge the group with more exotic fruits that they will not easily recognise straight away. You may wish to introduce the children to these more unusual tastes before playing.

OUTCOMES
● All of the children *must* be able to look at living things to find out more about them.
● Most of the children *should* be able to investigate objects and materials by using their sense of taste, finding out about and identifying some features of fruits.
● Some *could* communicate observations about the features of a range of fruits.
● A small number *could even* talk about their work linking the sense of taste to the tongue and mouth.

Lesson 6 ▪ Do not touch

Objective
● To learn that not all things are safe to touch, smell and taste.

Vocabulary
safe, not safe, dangerous, poison, poisonous, hazard, acid, disinfectant, cleaner, chemicals

RESOURCES
Main activity: Photocopiable page 38 (also Do not touch - 1' (red) available on the CD-ROM); adhesive; collection of empty, washed containers of household cleaners, some of which have a range of signs on the packaging showing that we should not touch, taste or smell them. Include washing powder, dishwasher powder and tablets, polish, disinfectant and other cleaners that have a black cross on an orange background. Also include some items (such as spray polish and washing-up liquid) that do not have the cross, but nevertheless should only be used under supervision.
Group activities: 1 Photocopiable page 38 (also Do not touch - 1' (red) available on the CD-ROM); scissors. **2** Pictures of household

Differentiation

Support
Repeat Group activity 3 with children who need more support. Work with individuals or pairs to circle the signs on the pictures on 'Do not touch – 2' (green) on the CD-ROM, relating them to the actual bottles in your collection if possible.

Extension
Using 'Do not touch – 2' (blue) on the CD-ROM, challenge the children to consider other things that are not safe to touch, smell or taste, such as wild berries, alcohol, cigarettes and medicines, and add them to the blank boxes.

items (cut from magazines) that are and that are not safe to touch (see above – also shampoo, soap, bubble bath, food); two sheets of A3 paper.
3 Photocopiable page 39 (also 'Do not touch – 2' (red) available on the CD-ROM); coloured pencils.
ICT link: photocopiable page 38 (also Do not touch! 1' (red) available on the CD-ROM); pictures of different containers (see Group activity 2); digital camera; interactive whiteboard.

PREPARATION
Wash out all of the empty containers, and cut out magazine pictures for Group activity 2. You may wish to make these a permanent resource by mounting them onto card and laminating them. Make copies of the 'Do not touch!' stickers on photocopiable page 38. Send a letter to parents and carers to let them know you will be doing this lesson, so that they can reinforce the learning objective at home to give the children a consistent message.

STARTER
Show the children the collection of containers. Ask: *Do you recognise any of these? Do you have some of these in your cupboard at home?*

MAIN ACTIVITY
Select the washing powder container and point out the sign on the side. Can any of the children tell you what this sign means? It means that the contents of the container are dangerous and that we should never touch, smell or (worst of all) taste the contents. Explain the possible consequences of doing so (be sensitive to the children's feelings). Explain that the sign showing a black cross on an orange square means that what is inside the container is harmful if swallowed. It also means that it can irritate our eyes or skin if it gets into them or onto it. Stick one of the 'Do not touch' labels from page 38 on to the container. Look at a container that does not have symbol. Explain that it is OK to touch this one only if an adult is with them and has said it is safe. Repeat this activity with the other containers and photocopied labels and sort the containers into groups of safe/not safe to touch.

GROUP ACTIVITIES
1 Work with groups of six children to talk about the materials that were originally in the containers you have collected. Invite them to find the label on each container that tells them not to touch, smell or taste the contents. Give each child a copy of photocopiable page 38, and together add 'Do not touch' labels to the containers that contain materials that are dangerous.
2 Ask an adult helper to reinforce the message by talking to groups of up to four children about the pictures you have cut from magazines. Ask the children to place the materials that are safe to touch on one sheet of paper, and those that are not on another. Compare the numbers of pictures on each sheet of paper. Now ask the children whether any of the materials are safe to smell or taste. Do they decide that there are no pictures of things that are safe to smell or taste? Reinforce the message that it is never safe to smell or taste anything unless an adult they know has said it is safe to do so.
3 Give the children photocopiable page 39 and ask them to draw and colour in the sign on each picture that shows they should never touch the object. Ask them to draw on the back of the sheet items that they think they should never touch, and certainly never smell or taste.

ICT LINK
Set up the 'Do not touch' stickers and pictures of the containers. Take photographs of them with a digital camera and insert them into the software on the interactive whiteboard. During the main activity, as you talk

about each container, drag this onto the screen and drag and drop the 'Do not touch' sticker onto the container.

ASSESSMENT

It is important that the children learn that not all things are safe for them to touch, smell and (particularly) taste, and these issues must be handled sensitively. Note those children who do not yet understand the consequences of touching things without thinking first, and continue to reinforce this message in other activities.

PLENARY

Talk to the children again about the cleaning materials in your collection and how it is not safe to touch, smell or taste any of them. Explain that they are intended to kill germs, which means that they are poisonous and so can be harmful to people. Allow the children to talk freely about the tasks and what they have learned.

OUTCOMES

● All children *must* begin to learn how to keep themselves safe by knowing that not all things are safe to touch, smell and taste.
● Most of the children *should* be able to learn that some materials are dangerous.
● Some *could* communicate that some materials are dangerous and can damage our health.
● A small number *could even* use this knowledge to describe basic needs for survival.

LINKS

ECM 2: Staying safe.
Between units: the same learning objective is repeated in other contexts in lessons in Units 2 and 8.

CONTEXT 'Feely bag' activities

The next five lessons are about the senses, and are taught through activities involving the use of 'feely bags'. Make sure that you do not include items with sharp edges. Very young children enjoy these games, and they can be set up in the classroom as interactive displays for children to access throughout the weeks that follow.

Lesson 7 ◗ All of the senses

Objective
● To learn which parts of the body are used to smell, touch, see, hear and taste.

RESOURCES 💿

The song 'I've got a body' from *Spring Tinderbox* (A&C Black); large pictures of a tongue, ear, eye, nose and hand; card labels; paints and crayons in a range of colours; paper; adhesive; computer; 'Body parts' (green) from the CD-ROM (see Lesson 12 in this unit).

MAIN ACTIVITY

Teach the children the song 'I've got a body', adding verses about taste, touch, seeing and hearing. Ask the children to draw or paint pictures of their favourite flavours (for example, ice cream or pizza). Stick these onto a previously painted picture of a large tongue. Repeat the task with sounds we like to hear, favourite colours, favourite smells and things we like to touch. Stick the children's pictures onto large paintings of an ear, an eye, a nose and a hand respectively.

Ask the children to write labels for the parts of the body that we use to see, hear, smell, touch and taste. They can draw a body and attach the labels.

Extend children's thinking by talking about other parts of the body we can feel with. Can you feel anything with your feet? How do you know?

ASSESSMENT

In the group work, note which children draw the features in the correct order (starting with the eyes), which children copy from others and so on.

PLENARY

Reinforce the safety issues relating to touches, smells and tastes. Talk about the dangers to ears and eyes of loud noise and looking at the Sun.

OUTCOMES

- All of the children *must* value and contribute to their own well-being.
- Most of the children *should* be able to find out about and identify features of human senses
- Some children *could* know which parts of the body we use to hear, see, smell and taste, and which main parts we use to feel and touch.
- A small number *could even* have begun to think about how to look after our bodies and protect our hearing and sight.

Lesson 8 ▪ Touch and feel

RESOURCES

Main activity: Several feely bags, each containing a familiar object that has an interesting and distinctive surface for feeling (a ball of cotton wool, ceramic teapot, cup, toothbrush, hairbrush, metal spoon, sticklebrick, tennis ball, teddy bear, metal saucepan, wooden spoon, handkerchief); an ice cube and a rubber ball.
Group activities: 1 As for Main activity. **2** Paper and pencils. **3** Collections of similar objects for printing (such as cotton reels, toy car wheels, cotton wool balls, train track pieces, Lego bricks); thickly mixed paint in a range of colours, polystyrene trays, sponges, paper, aprons.
ICT link: Describing words and photographs of a range of objects with interesting textures; computer or interactive whiteboard.

PREPARATION

Mix paint in a range of colours to a fairly thick consistency for printing.

STARTER

Pass an ice cube around the group of children and ask them to say what it feels like. Encourage them to use words such as 'slippery', 'cold', 'hard', 'smooth' and 'icy'. Shrieks may also be included! Ask them whether it is easy to hold the ice cube, whether it fits inside their hand and whether it has a recognisable shape. The answers may change as the activity goes on. Repeat this activity with a rubber ball. Ensure that children understand that they should never hold ice directly from the freezer as it can burn.

Differentiation

Support

Pass a teapot around the group, pointing out the different parts that they can feel. Ask them whether they can feel the shape of the teapot's handle and spout. *Can you hold the teapot in your hand?* Now place the teapot inside a bag and ask the children to feel the things you have talked about. Model the description for them.

Extension

Children can move quickly to the independent group task. Afterwards, ask them to make a game for their friends: putting several objects inside a bag and challenging their friends to identify the one they are describing by touch. Ask them why they chose the objects they did.

MAIN ACTIVITY

Explain to the children that you have several bags, with an object hidden inside each one. Say that you are going to play a game together: you are going to ask someone to guess what the object inside the bag is just by using the sense of touch, without looking. Pass the bag to a child who you know will be able to say a little about the object in the bag. Ask him or her to say something about it. *Do you know what the object is? How do you know? Does it have a special shape that helps you to say what it is? Does the object fit inside your hand? Does it have a handle? How does it feel? Is it smooth or rough? Hard or soft?* Continue with another object and a different child, until a few children have had a turn at guessing an object.

GROUP ACTIVITIES

1 Repeat the Main activity with a group of six children, giving all the children an opportunity to guess a new object inside each bag.

2 Allow one group to play the game independently by giving them a bag containing several different objects for them to guess. Ask them to draw pictures of all the objects they think are inside the bag and label each with the material from which they think it is made. At the end of the activity, remove the objects to see whether the children have guessed them all correctly. Use an additional adult helper for this if possible.

3 Organise a group to try printing with a range of objects (see Resources).

ICT LINK

Set up describing words and photographs of a range of objects with interesting textures onto the computer or interactive whiteboard. Ask the children to select, drag and drop some describing words onto the screen for their friend to choose the photo of the matching object.

ASSESSMENT

Observe the children as they feel the object in the bag. Are they thinking about the shape and texture? Note those children who understand easily, and move them on to the extension task (making a game). Continue to focus on the children who are not yet able to describe the object in terms of their sense of touch, even though they may be able to identify it.

PLENARY

Look at the children's prints together. Ask the other children whether they can guess which object has made each print from its shape and texture. Make a display of the prints and objects for the children to match during the week. Challenge some children to find the ones they think have the same or different textures, and ask them to explain why.

OUTCOMES

● All children *must* be able to examine objects to find out more about them
● Most of the children *should* be able to investigate objects and materials by using their sense of touch.
● Some *could* find out about and talk about the materials from which different objects are made.
● A small number *could even* describe similarities and differences between the properties of materials.

LINKS

ECM 3: Enjoying and achieving.
Between units: this lesson can be taught within the set of lessons in Unit 4 based on the 'hardware store' role-play area, which develops the vocabulary of materials and their properties.
Across the curriculum: identifying an object from one face of its shape begins to develop the children's geography skills.

Lesson 9 ▪ Sorting sounds

Objective
● To learn to identify objects from the sounds they make.

Vocabulary
tinkle, swish, crackle, rattle, high, low, loud, quiet, soft

RESOURCES
Main activity: Feely bags containing a hand bell, doorbell, baby's rattle, container (with a tight-fitting lid) full of water, full packet of crisps, drum, beater and other easily recognisable musical instruments.
Group activities: 1 Cassette or CD with a number of sounds made by different objects recorded on it; cassette or CD player. It is easy to make your own tape or CD, but several commercial sound-matching games are available. **2** Audio story book, computer. Talking books for use on a computer are produced by Sherston Software and by Oxford University Press (to support their Oxford Reading Tree scheme). You can pick up a variety of books from bookshops that have high-quality sound effects. **3** Shopping catalogues; scissors. **4** Selection of percussion instruments, strikers and scrapers.
Plenary: Big Book versions of *Can't You Sleep, Little Bear?* by Martin Waddell (Walker Books) or *We're Going on a Bear Hunt* by Michael Rosen (Walker Books).

PREPARATION
Place the objects inside separate bags and put them where you intend to do the Main activity well before the lesson. This will ensure that the children do not hear any of the objects being moved before the activity begins.

STARTER
Put your hand inside a bag and find a bell. Ring the bell while it is still inside the bag, and ask the children to say what is making the sound. Do they find this easy?

MAIN ACTIVITY
Explain that you have other objects inside the bags that make different sounds. Invite the children to guess what is making the sound as you move each object inside its bag. Talk about the kind of sound each object makes. Is it loud or quiet? Say that another word for 'quiet' is 'soft'. Does the object crackle or splash? Is it a high sound or a low sound? Does any sound remind them of what the object is used for? For example, why does a bell make a loud noise?

GROUP ACTIVITIES
1 Ask an adult helper to play a tape or CD of sounds to a group of four children. Can they guess what objects are making the sounds? Reinforce the idea that the children are using their ears to listen carefully and identify what is making the sound.
2 Ask another adult helper to share a sound book (see Resources) with pairs of children.
3 Work with a group of six to eight children, cutting pictures of items that make sounds (such as an alarm clock, a drill, a car, a microwave oven, a cuckoo clock) from shopping catalogues and talking about the sounds these items make.
4 Give the children a small selection of percussion instruments, strikers and scrapers, and let them investigate the different sounds that can be made with these.

ASSESSMENT
During the Main activity, invite the children to record what they think is making each sound in the bags (or ask an adult helper to record their comments). Use this record to plan additional play activities (if necessary) to reinforce the learning objective.

Differentiation

Support

Ask an adult or older child to pair up and help in the sound matching game. Give the adults clear guidance before the task to help them ensure that the children are learning the vocabulary associated with sound.

Extension

Give the group a bag containing several different percussion instruments. Ask the children to take turns to make a sound while the rest of the group guesses what the instrument is.

PLENARY

Read out the story of *Can't You Sleep, Little Bear?* or *We're Going on a Bear Hunt* (see Resources). Invite the children to join in with the sound effects, using body percussion and the instruments from Group activity 4.

OUTCOMES

● All children *must* explore the different sounds of instruments and show an awareness of change.
● Most of the children *should* be able to investigate and listen closely to the sounds they make and how they can make these change.
● Some *could* recognise that sound comes from a variety of sources and name some of these.
● A small number *could even* compare the loudness and pitch of sounds.

LINKS

EMC 3: Enjoying and achieving.
Across the curriculum: give the children opportunities to add sound effects to a poem or song in creative development activities. Also give them a range of percussion instruments and invite them to create a musical composition of loud, soft, high and low sounds. Link the lesson to literacy by asking them to join in reading either of the books used in the Plenary session.

Lesson 10 ▫ The same or different?

Objective
● To begin to use their senses to identify similarities and differences.

Vocabulary
similar, same, different, scratchy, tinkly, high, low, rattle, loud, quiet.

RESOURCES
Main activity: Domino cards with matching textures, pictures and colours and matching sound pots (see Preparation).
Group activities: Additional sets of the resources used in the Main activity.

PREPARATION
Make pairs of sound pots from lidded plastic cups and a range of materials, including small bells, rice, dried peas, nails and sand. Make a set of domino cards containing a mixture of textures, colours and pictures: divide each rectangular card shape into two and stick a textured material on one half and a colour or picture on the other. Continue until you have a set that will allow you to complete a circuit by matching the ends.

STARTER
Introduce the sound pots to the children. Shake two of the pots in sequence, making sure that they do not have the same sound. Ask the children to say whether the sounds are the same or different. Why are the sounds different? Is one sound louder than the other? Does one pot make a different kind of sound? Is it more tinkly? Can anyone guess what is making this sound?

MAIN ACTIVITY
Shake two more pots and ask the children about these sounds. Use questions (as above) to make them think about how the sounds are the same and how they are different. Next, introduce the domino cards to the children. Invite a child to feel one of the textures (with his or her eyes closed if this will help). *What does the material feel like? Can you find a card that has the same texture?* Place this card at the end of the first domino. Talk about the pictures or colours at the other ends of the cards. Can the children find matching colours or pictures by looking? Invite them to say why they chose the card they did. You should now have a texture at each end of the row of dominoes. Invite the children to find a matching texture to place at each end, and to say why they chose the cards they did. How are the two textures the same or different?

GROUP ACTIVITIES
1 Play the matching domino game with a group of six to eight children, either all together (as above) or by distributing the cards to give each child a more limited choice. Carry on until the set is complete.
2 Allow one group to play with the sound pots, trying to match them up.

ASSESSMENT
Make a note of those children who are confident about using their senses to explore the sounds, textures and pictures, and those who have the vocabulary they need to explain their choices.

PLENARY
Play the dominoes game at the end of the session, if most of the children are able to match up the various features of the dominoes. Otherwise, play the matching game with the sound pots.

OUTCOMES
● All of the children *must* explore textures and sounds to find out more about them.
● Most of the children *should* begin to use more than one sense to explore a range of objects and to identify similarities and differences.

Differentiation
Support
Use commercial domino sets to focus on matching textures or pictures separately. Talk to the children about how the pictures are different and how they are the same.
Extension
Extend children's thinking by asking them to make their own sound pots matching game for their friends to play.

- Some *could* communicate observations of materials and sounds in terms of their properties.
- A small number *could even* describe similarities and differences between sounds and materials.

LINKS
ECM 3: Enjoying and achieving.
Between units: this lesson links to the work on materials in Unit 4.

Lesson 11 ◗ Touchy feely

Objectives
- To explore using all five senses and to identify familiar objects.
- To use drawing to record findings in an investigation.

Vocabulary
shape, same, similar, smell, texture, see, hear, touch, feel, taste

RESOURCES
Main activity: Several boxes of different sizes; familiar object for each box, including two teapots, cup, bell, orange, teabag, teddy bear; wrapping paper; tissue paper; adhesive tape; further set of boxes with familiar objects to be used for ongoing assessment.
Group activity: Food samples for the children to taste and identify, including cheese, chocolate, apple, tomato, cucumber and orange; plate; tea towel; paper; pencils.

PREPARATION
Place an object inside each box and wrap the box with wrapping paper. Make sure that the smells of the orange and teabag come through by punching a few holes in each box. Provide a hole in the side of one box large enough for the children to feel the teddy bear. Wrap the cup and one of the teapots directly in tissue paper so that their shapes can easily be seen.

Check for any food allergies or dietary restrictions when selecting the food samples. Cut the food items into bite-sized pieces, place them on a plate and cover them.

STARTER
Show the children the teapot wrapped in tissue paper, and ask them what they think is wrapped inside the parcel. *How do you know?* Prompt them to recognise and identify the handle and spout. Sing the rhyme 'I'm a little teapot' to reinforce the features of a teapot. Place the second, unwrapped teapot alongside the first one to show that the shapes are the same or similar. Talk about this if necessary.

MAIN ACTIVITY
Allow the children to play with the other parcels. Observe closely to see which children use their senses to try to discover what is inside each parcel. Listen to their conversations and talk about what they can feel, smell, hear and see. Do they have the vocabulary to describe the texture and shape that helps them to identify the teddy bear? Can they use their sense of smell to identify the orange? Who can recognise the bell by using their sense of hearing? After about five minutes, ask the children to talk about what they think is inside the parcels. Does anyone disagree?

GROUP ACTIVITY
With groups of four children, explain that you are going to explore the tastes of some food items. They should try to guess what the food items are, but keep their guesses secret until all the children have had a chance to taste the items. Ask the children to close their eyes, and place a piece of apple on each child's tongue. Now say: *Open your eyes*, and ask the children to draw a picture of what they think the food item was. Make sure that they have no opportunity to copy each other. Repeat the process for all the food items. At the end of the activity, talk about the children's pictures. Tell them that you

Differentiation

Support
Provide the children with objects that are more easily recognisable; ask prompt questions to lead them to the answer if necessary.
Extension
Include some objects that are more difficult to recognise; encourage the children to discuss their ideas with each other.

want to keep their 'recordings' because the pictures show how well they have investigated the different tastes.

ASSESSMENT

Leave a set of wrapped parcels on the side for the children to interact with during the week. This will allow you to note which children are able to develop their exploration skills, and to assess whether you need to organise additional activities to reinforce the learning.

PLENARY

Gather the children together and show them the what is inside each of the parcels and the food items they tasted. Ask the children who had guessed correctly to say which senses they used to get the answer right.

OUTCOMES

● All children *must* find out more about objects by using their senses.
● Most of the children should be able to investigate a range of familiar objects using their senses.
● Some *could* talk about what they see, hear, touch, smell and taste in terms of the features and properties.
● A small number *could even* identify the materials from which the objects are made.

LINKS

Across the curriculum: this activity develops the children's speaking and listening skills.

CONTEXT

The Baby Clinic or Health Centre

The next five lessons are set in the context of a 'Baby clinic'. Set up a baby clinic in the role-play area, to include dolls, other toys and baby clothes. Make sure that there is a display space close to this area for the children's photographs and pictures.

Lesson 12 ◗ Body parts

Objective
● To recognise and learn the names of parts of the body and be able to say what they are used for.

Vocabulary
head, hands, fingers, arm, leg, foot, feet, toes, eyes, mouth, nose, ears, lips, tongue, neck, back, bottom, stomach

RESOURCES ◉

Main activity: The songs 'I've got a body' from *Tinderbox* (A&C Black) and 'I have two ears' by Gill Daniell from *Count Me In* (A&C Black).
Group activities: 1 Pictures of people cut from magazines; adhesive sticks; card; scissors. **2** jigsaws of people **3** photocopiable page 40 (also 'Body parts' (red) available on CD-ROM). **4** Paper and paints in a range of colours; card labels; Post-it Notes; felt-tipped pens for the extension activity.
ICT link: 'Body parts' (red) available on the CD-ROM.

PREPARATION

Set up the painting activity for the children to access. Brief adult helpers about the intended learning outcome of the Group activity they are supporting.

STARTER

Teach the children the song 'I've got a body' from *Tinderbox*. Make up additional verses for stamping, walking, clapping, clicking (fingers) and nodding.

Differentiation 💿
Support
Use 'Body parts' (green)
available on the CD-ROM,
which includes simple
vocabulary to match to
different body parts.
Extension
Challenge the children to
continue as far as they can
with the labelling activity,
using 'Body parts' (blue) on
the CD-ROM, which includes
additional vocabulary.

MAIN ACTIVITY

Ask the children which part of the body they use to clap, stamp, walk and so on. Use the song
'I have two ears' to reinforce these ideas (or repeat 'I've got a body'). Now ask them to point to another part of the body. Can they say what it is called, how many of it they have, and what they can do with it/them? Sing this as another verse. Continue with this until the children cannot think of any more body parts or become restless.

GROUP ACTIVITIES

1 Organise a group of four children to make people jigsaws by cutting pictures of people from magazines, mounting them on card and cutting off the arms and legs ready to reassemble. Talk with the children about what they use each part of the body for.

2 Allow one group of children to work on people jigsaws from a commercial source.

3 Adult helpers can work with pairs of children to label body parts by completing photocopiable page 40.

4 Ask the children to paint pictures of themselves. Display the finished paintings with labels attached to the relevant parts of the body.

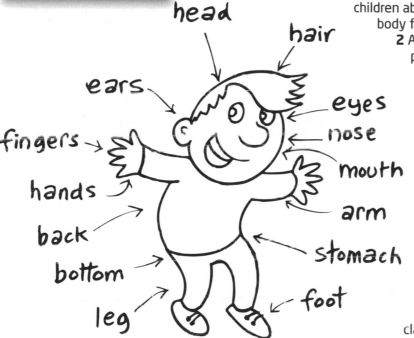

ICT LINK 💿
Show 'Body parts' (red) from the CD-ROM on the whiteboard. Use the line tool to link connect the labels to the different body parts as a class activity.

ASSESSMENT
Note those children who are able to name most of the external parts of the body, and are attaining Level 1 in this aspect of science. Note those children who can recognise and point to different body parts and features, attaining the relevant Early Learning Goal.

PLENARY
Sing a variety of songs and number rhymes about the body, using appropriate actions to accompany the words.

OUTCOMES
● All children *must* be able to describe simple features of the body.
● Most of the children *should* be able to identify some features of the body.
● Some *could* identify some external parts of the human body and recognise their names.
● A small number *could even* to recognise that people grow.

LINKS
Between units: this lesson links with those in Unit 2 on the body parts of animals.
Across the curriculum: the learning in this lesson can be reinforced through physical development activities that involve using hands, fingers, arms, legs, feet and toes. The parts of the body can be used as a context in which to develop counting activities.

Lesson 13 ▪ Moving around

Objective
● To learn that we use different parts of our bodies to move in different ways.

RESOURCES
Large space for the children to move in; balancing apparatus; mats; benches; low tables; skipping ropes; stilts, hoops; stepping-stones; paper; digital camera; coloured pencils or crayons. Specialist PE equipment may be necessary to meet the needs of individual children.

MAIN ACTIVITY
Do your established warm-up activity for physical development activities. Tell the children that they are going to move in lots of different ways, using different parts of their bodies. Invite them to move using their feet and legs: encourage and develop skipping, creeping, hopping, walking, jumping and running movements. Develop the theme by getting the children to move in different directions and to use hands as well as feet.

Move on to a range of apparatus including balance beams, low tables, mats and benches. Give the children a range of small equipment including skipping ropes, hoops, stilts and stepping-stones. Invite them to use the equipment to move in different ways, using different parts of their bodies.

Ask the children to record all the different ways they can move by drawing pictures. Use their pictures to make a wall frieze.

ICT LINK
Take photographs of the children and use them for a discussion about the range of different ways they moved during the lesson. Discuss how their movements are the same as or different from those animals make.

ASSESSMENT
Note those children who can distinguish a number of different ways of moving, and who are beginning to use different body parts to improve the quality of their movements (for example, outstretched arms for balancing).

PLENARY
Talk about all the ways that the children moved as you add their pictures to your frieze. Finish by singing one of your favourite movement songs.

OUTCOMES
● All children *must* know that we can move in many different ways using different parts of our bodies.
● Most children *should* know that sometimes we move more than one part at a time.

Differentiation
Support
Children could use one type of equipment or one piece of apparatus at a time and develop their activities over a series of six lessons. Talk about one kind of movement during each lesson to focus learning and make the objective more specific (for example, balancing in week 1, skipping in week 2, jumping in week 3).
Extension
Make the apparatus more challenging. You could develop an obstacle course, adding and changing items in each lesson to encourage the children to use different parts of the body and move in different ways. For example, the course could be constructed to develop balancing one day and crawling, jumping and climbing the next; or using a horizontal ladder (or plank) one day and a sloping ladder the next.

Lesson 14 ▪ Match the clothing

Objective
● To know that we all grow and change as we get older.

Vocabulary
change, different, small, smaller, tiny, bigger, taller, same

RESOURCES 💿
Main activity: Pictures of yourself as a baby and at present; if possible, items of clothing and toys that belonged to you and the children as small children; video footage of a baby and toddler (if available).
Group activities: 1 Pictures of the children as babies and at the present time; A3 paper; speech bubbles cut from white paper; adhesive; felt-tipped pen; display board. **2** Collection of baby clothes and toys. **3** Collection of girls' and boys' clothing; photocopiable page 41 (also 'Match the clothing' (red) available on the CD-ROM); pencils. **4** Several baskets.
ICT link: 'Match the clothing' interactive available on CD-ROM.

PREPARATION
Take photographs of all the children, either using a digital camera or in time to have the film developed before the lesson. Send a letter home asking parents and carers for photographs of the children when they were babies, and for some of their baby clothes and toys.

STARTER
Look at the collection of baby clothes, toys and photographs with the children. Give them some time to handle the items carefully. Talk about the toys. Does anyone have a younger brother or sister at home who has the same toys? Ask the children who they think wears the clothes. Would they fit them still, or have they grown too much?

MAIN ACTIVITY
Show the children a photograph of yourself (or another teacher or child) as a baby. Ask them how the person in the photo looks. Are they sitting, lying or standing? How big are they? Do they have hair, teeth? Now show them a photo of yourself now. Look at the same person now. Has anything changed about that person? What has changed? Make a list of all the things that have changed: the differences between the two pictures.

Show the children a video of a baby and a toddler, and ask them to say how the movements have changed. Talk about how the toddler moves. Are we safer on our feet now? Why is this? Explain that we gain a better balance as we get older.

GROUP ACTIVITIES
1 Work with groups of four children. Talk about how they look in their baby photographs and how they look now, using the photographs they have brought from home and those taken recently in school. The children can write how they have changed in the speech bubbles, or you can scribe for them. Fold a sheet of A3 paper in half and add the titles 'Me as a baby' and 'Me now'. Stick the photographs on either side of the sheet and add the speech bubbles in the appropriate places. Fix the sheet to the display board with 'Look how I've changed!' in huge letters at the top. Repeat the activity until all the children have done it.
2 Ask an adult helper to talk to groups of six children about the collections of baby clothes and toys. They should talk about the size and style of the clothes, and encourage the children to identify fabrics and fastenings. Would the clothes fit them? Why not? Who would wear them? Can they name the toys? Can they say how the baby plays with them?
3 Give the children matching sets of baby and children's clothes to sort into pairs. Ask them to match the items on photocopiable page 41 (for example, the baby dungarees match to the trousers).
4 Allow a group of four children to play in the role-play area, sorting the baby clothes into items of the same type (socks, pullovers and so on) in different baskets.

ICT LINK
Use 'Match the clothing' interactive on the CD-ROM.

ASSESSMENT
Make a note of the children who can sort and match items of clothing of very different sizes and, in addition, those who can explain how they would have fitted everyone at a certain stage in their life. Note those children who understand that we change as we get older through growing, playing and

doing more complicated things. This will give you assessment information to use in planning the next lesson, which might include looking at finer differences between age groups (such as wrinkles and grey hair).

PLENARY

Make a display of all the baby things collected for this lesson, talking about the differences and reinforcing the children's awareness that we all change as we grow.

OUTCOMES

- All children *must* be able to notice that some things are the same and some are different.
- Most of the children *should* be able to look closely at similarities and differences.
- Some *could* communicate observations of people.
- A small number *could even* recognise that all living things grow.

LINKS

Between units: this lesson links to the lessons in Unit 2 on animal growth.
Across the curriculum: the children can read the story *Once There Were Giants* by Martin Waddell (Walker Books) as part of a literacy activity. They can sort items of clothing into pairs as part of a numeracy lesson.

Lesson 15 ◖ Helping ourselves

Objective
- To learn that we can all do many things for ourselves.

RESOURCES

An adult accompanied by a baby; things for the baby (a baby bath, warm water, a towel, feeding equipment); a warm draught-free place; paper; pencils; paints; scissors; large picture of a baby; large speech bubble.

MAIN ACTIVITY

Introduce the adult and baby. Give the children time to ask questions and talk about the baby. Invite the adult to bath, dress and feed the baby if possible. Talk to the children about what is happening, and point out all the things that the adult has to do for the baby because the baby is unable to do these things for him- or herself. Invite the children to ask questions about what the baby is and is not able to do.

Talk to the children about whether they are now able to do some of these things for themselves. Make a list of the things they can now do, and invite them to record what they have discovered by drawing pictures and placing them alongside the correct words in the list. Add to the list during the week as you note more things that the children can do for themselves.

Ask the children to draw a speech bubble and write in it what they can do now that they have grown up. Ask them whether these are things that they could do as a baby.

Ask the children to paint pictures of their own faces. Let them dry and then cut them out to include in a display.

Differentiation
Support
Act as a scribe to support the children as they produce a similar list, and work with groups of four to question them and relate their ideas back to what they saw when the baby was bathed
Extension
Ask children to extend the list beyond what you have recorded together by writing a long list of all the things that they can do now.

ASSESSMENT

Watch the children during the Main activity and note those who ask questions. Does the question have an obvious answer?

PLENARY

Stick a picture of a baby to the centre of a display board, and invite the children to contribute to a speech bubble saying what the baby is able to do by him- or herself. Then add the children's face pictures and speech bubbles, reading them out loud as you do so.

OUTCOMES

● All children *must* be able to know what babies are and are not able to do for themselves.
● Most of the children *should* have a developing awareness of what they can and cannot do.
● Some *could* understand that as young children get older, they are able to do more and more things for themselves.
● A small number *could even* give reasons for their views.

Lesson 16 ▪ Different faces

Objective
● To investigate similarities and differences between us.

Vocabulary
freckles, hair, long, short, fair, blonde, dark, brown, green, blue, fat, thin, spectacles, tall, short, similar, similarities, different, differences

RESOURCES 💿
Group activities: 1 Paint and crayons in a range of colours including skin tones; paper; paintbrushes; a large wall area for display. **2** Photocopiable page 42 (also 'Different faces' (red) available on CD-ROM); pencils. **4** Range of collage materials including disposable plates, eye-coloured circles, hair-coloured wool; scissors; PVA glue. **5** Paint; polystyrene trays; bowl; sponge; water; soap; a towel.
ICT Link: *My World* computer program; computer; interactive whiteboard.

PREPARATION
Mix skin-tone paints and other colours if your children are not yet mixing their own colours. Cut some of the wool into different (life-sized) lengths for hair.

STARTER
Tell the children that you are going to make a display together to show all the things that are the same about them, and all the things that are different. Ask two children who have some similar features and some contrasting features to act as models for the Main activity.

MAIN ACTIVITY
Ask the two 'models' to stand at the front of the class. Ask the other children to look very carefully at one of them. What can they tell you about the colour of this child's hair and eyes, how tall the child is, how long the child's hair is and so on? Repeat the task with the second child. Now ask the class to look carefully at both of the children. *Can you see anything about them that is the same? For example, do they have the same colour hair or eyes? Can you see any differences between them?*

GROUP ACTIVITIES
1 Ask an adult helper to work with groups of four children as they paint pictures of themselves. The children should pay particular attention to the colour of their eyes, skin and hair, and be sure to paint their hair to an appropriate length. The helper needs to add the child's name to each painting, with a sentence saying whether the child is tall or short for his or her age. (If they are able to, the children should write these sentences.)
2 The children should complete photocopiable page 42 independently by drawing or colouring around the differences in different colours and adding more features to each face to make them different from each other.
3 Work with a group of six to eight children, chosen to show clear similarities and differences in their features and size. Describe one child in the group to the other children, and invite them to guess who you are describing. Invite a child to do the same if possible.
4 Set up a table with collage materials for the children to make plate faces. These can be used to make a border to the display.
5 Organise an adult helper to help the children make handprints and footprints using the resources listed above.

ICT LINK

Ask the children to 'make a face' using the *My World* computer program. Import two faces at a time on to the interactive whiteboard for the children to note the similarities and differences.

ASSESSMENT

Photocopiable page 42 is intended for the children to complete independently if possible. Keep these sheets as a record of the children's ability to identify differences. For differentiation, use 'Two faces' (green) or (blue) from the CD-ROM, depending on their level of skills.

Group activity 3 provides an opportunity to assess which children can use an understanding of similarities and differences to help identify the person described.

PLENARY

Enlarge a copy of photocopiable page 42 and talk about the differences between the two children. Show the children one or two of the paintings, covering up the name, and ask them to say who is in the picture and how they know.

OUTCOMES

- All children *must* be able to show an awareness of difference.
- Most of the children *should* be able to look closely at similarities and differences.
- Some *could* talk about the different features of human faces in terms of eye colour, hair colour and size.
- A small number *could even* recognise that we all grow.

LINKS

Across the curriculum: this lesson can be linked to creative development by allowing the children to mix their own skin tone and other colours using red, blue, yellow, white and black paints. Links to personal and social development can be made by allowing the children to talk about and accept the physical differences between us.

CONTEXT

Goldilocks and the Three Bears

The next two lessons make use of the traditional story of 'Goldilocks and the Three Bears'. Other familiar stories are linked to the theme of size, including 'The Three Billy-Goats Gruff' and *The Enormous Crocodile* **by Roald Dahl (Puffin).**

Lesson 17 ▪ Shapes and sizes

Objectives
● To know that people come in different shapes and sizes.
● To begin to order things according to size.
● To begin to match objects and people according to size.

Vocabulary
Large, big, bigger, biggest, small, smaller, smallest, middle-sized

RESOURCES
Main activity: Copy of 'Goldilocks and the Three Bears'; Father Bear's plate, dish and spoon and Baby Bear's chair and bed (see Group activity 3).
Group activities: 1 Collection of recycled materials; PVA glue; scissors. **2** Collection of soft toys of various sizes. **3** Collection of items including spoons, dishes, plates, cups and chairs; beds and pillows in three different sizes (for example, for a doll, baby and adult); large, medium and small teddy bears; a table. **4** Toy beds and pillows in three different sizes.
ICT link: *My World* computer program; computer.

STARTER
Read the story of 'Goldilocks and the Three Bears'. Spend a few moments going over the story to make sure the children are familiar with it.

MAIN ACTIVITY
Talk to the children about the different sizes of the three bears and their belongings. How do we know which are Father Bear's plate, dish and spoon? Let the children choose these and give them to the biggest bear. Which are Baby Bear's chair and bed? Again, let the children place these by the smallest bear.

Choose and compare two items of the same type (for example, two chairs). Ask the children to show you which is smaller and which is bigger. *Is it the same in our houses? Do we have bigger clothes than our younger brothers and sisters, but smaller clothes than Mum or Dad? Do we have a bigger chair and a bigger bed than a baby has? Why do you think that is?* Explain that as we get older we grow, and that we all come in different shapes and sizes – just like the three bears.

GROUP ACTIVITIES
1 Ask a group of children to use the recycled materials to make beds for Father, Mother and Baby Bear.
2 Give the children a range of soft toys and let them play with these before putting them in order according to their size. Talk to each child to establish the reason for his or her order. It could be according to girth, height or weight.
3 Organise a three bears cottage role-play area for the children to set up the bears' breakfast table.
4 Ask a group of children to make the three bears' beds, using the correct-sized pillows, sheets and blankets for each bed.

ICT LINK
Use the *My World* computer program to build a picture of the rooms in the three bears cottage.

ASSESSMENT

This lesson deals with the very earliest classification skills of matching and ordering similar objects by size. It is important that you let the children decide on the criteria for their ordering (height, weight and so on). Note the children who are able to match items to the bears correctly according to size. Give the children who cannot do this additional sorting and matching activities to reinforce learning.

PLENARY

Talk to the children about the breakfast table and beds. *How do we know which sheets and pillow to use? Does the biggest bear fit in the smallest bed? Why not?*

OUTCOMES

- All children must be able to show an awareness of patterns
- Most of the children should be able to look closely at patterns.
- Some could sort and match items by size.
- A small number could even classify objects by size.

LINKS

Between units: this lesson links well with the porridge-making activity in Unit 4, Lesson 11.
Across the curriculum: there are several links to numeracy activities in the Goldilocks story, and good opportunities to develop vocabulary for describing size.

Lesson 18 ▪ Tall and short

Objective
● To learn that we all grow.
● To find out who are the tallest and shortest children in the class.

RESOURCES
Large sheets or rolls of paper; pencils; paints in a range of colours; Blu-Tack.

MAIN ACTIVITY
Talk to the children about how tall they are. Ask three children to stand side by side and compare heights. Use the words 'tallest', 'shortest', 'taller' and 'shorter'. Ask the children who they think is the shortest person in the room. Do they know who is the tallest?

Explain that you are going to investigate how tall people are. Put the children into groups of up to four, and give each group a name. Ask them to use large sheets of paper on the floor to draw around each child in turn, then paint pictures of themselves inside the outlines. When they have finished, fix each group's paintings to the wall with Blu-Tack in order of size, and add the group's name. Later in the lesson, mix up the pictures or mix up pictures from different groups; then ask each group to restore the correct height order.

ASSESSMENT
Ask the children questions, including. *Who is the tallest/shortest in your group? Who is taller/shorter than Fred?* Make a note of their answers.

Differentiation
Support
Allow children to compare two people only. Emphasise that one is 'taller than' or 'shorter than' the other, and continue until they are able to complete this simplified task. If necessary, help them to learn the concept by asking them which of two objects (such as bottles) is taller or shorter.
Extension
Ask the children to think about whether they think the tallest person is the heaviest and the shortest person is the lightest. Find out by weighing to see if they were right.

PLENARY
Organise the class into height order by asking all the children to stand in a line with a taller child behind them and a shorter child in front. At various times during the day and the week, repeat this activity until you are sure that the children understand it and can do it independently. Change the order of your line from time to time, so that you have the shortest child at the front some days and the tallest child on others. You may also say: Line up all those who are taller than Fred, and so on.

OUTCOMES
● All children *must* be able to notice we are all different heights.
● Most of the children *should* know that some people are taller than others
● Some *could* say that some people grow faster than others.
● A small number *could even* respond to suggestions about how to find out whether the tallest person is the heaviest.

Lesson 19 ▪ Assessment

Objective
● To find out how many parts of the body the children can name.
● To assess whether the children understand that we all grow and change as we become older.
● To assess whether the children can identify simple similarities and differences between people.

RESOURCES 💿
Starter: Large picture of a child; Post-it Notes, felt-tipped pen; Blu-Tack.
Assessment activities: 1 Computer and 'Body parts' editable on CD-ROM (see 'Body parts' Lesson 12 from this unit); printer. **2** Photocopiable page 43 (also 'Assessment – 1' (red) available on CD-ROM); scissors, adhesive sticks; paper. **3** Photocopiable page 44 (also 'Assessment – 2' (red) available on CD-ROM); pencils.
ICT links: 2 'We all grow' interactive available on the CD-ROM. **3** Digital camera; computer; printer.

PREPARATION 💿
Write some of the names of parts of the body on to Post-it notes. Set up the computer with the 'Body parts' (red) from the CD-ROM. Make one copy per child of each of the two photocopiable sheets.

STARTER

Work with a group of eight children. Ask them to point to and name a part of their own body that they know. Write the name on a Post-it Note and stick it on to a large picture of a child displayed on the wall beside you. Continue until the children have named as many parts as they can. If you start with children who need more support, each group that follows can be challenged to think of less obvious parts of the body.

ASSESSMENT ACTIVITY 1 ●

Ask an adult helper to work with pairs of children on the computer, using 'Body parts' (red) from the CD-ROM. Use the tools to draw lines to connect the body parts to the correct labels. Alternatively, use the highlighter to block the words, then ask the children to label as many parts of the body as they can, from memory, using the pencil tool. The adult can act as a reader, and help the children to add their names and print out their labelled pictures.

ASSESSMENT ACTIVITY 2 ●

Ask the children to complete photocopiable page 43. Cut out the pictures and arrange them in the correct order to show a person getting older. As an extension, ask the children where their own and their teacher's pictures would go in the sequence.

ICT LINK ●

Using 'We all grow' interactive from the CD-ROM on the Interactive Whiteboard or computer, drag and drop the pictures into the correct order of how we look as we grow older.

ASSESSMENT ACTIVITY 3

Ask the children to complete photocopiable page 44. These activities ask them to draw pictures of themselves as babies and as they look now.

ICT LINK

Use a digital camera to take photographs of the children and scan and load these into a computer with photographs of when they were babies and toddlers. Write a sentence or two about how they have changed over the years. Print off a copy and extend the activity by asking some children to add a picture of how they think they will look when they get older. These could be made into a 'Growing up' classroom display.

PLENARY

Talk through a completed worksheet in Assessment activity 2 and/or 3 and talk with the children about how they know the person in each picture is getting older. What changes have taken place? Use the interactive activity from the CD-ROM as a starting point for discussion.

ASSESSMENT OUTCOMES

On completion of these lessons and Assessment activities, you should know which children have attained the scientific aspects of the following early learning goals in knowledge and understanding of the world:
- All children *must* be able to describe simple features of humans.
- Most of the children *should* be able to identify some features of humans.
- Some *could* identify some external parts of the human body, and recognise their names and similarities and differences.
- A small number *could even* recognise that people grow and that we change as we get older.

Looking closely

◼ Match the fruit.

before

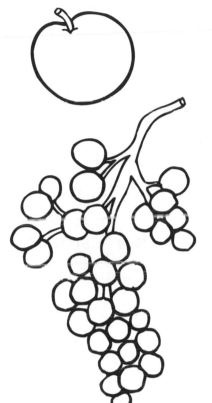

after

Illustration © Colin Shelbourn

Describing fruit – 1

 rough spiky, knobbly, hard, yellow, green, brown, not soft, not round

 rough, squeezable, orange, round, sour

 hard, green or red, blemishes, not soft or squeezable, smooth, round, crunchy, sweet, sour

 soft, juicy, not hard, smooth, sweet

 spongy, green, furry, soft, itchy, oval

 yellow, smooth, long, thin, bendy, spongy, hard or soft

 soft, spongy, green or purple, small, round, smooth, juicy

◼ Can you think of any words to describe what they taste like?

_____

_____

_____

_____

_____

Illustration © Colin Shelbourn

◖SCHOLASTIC

Describing fruit – 2

Does it have a smell?

_____

What does it look like? Does it look prickly? How can you tell?

_____

_____

Is it good to touch? Why or why not? _____

_____

Does it have a smell? What is it like? _____

Would you like to eat it? _____

_____

Illustration © Colin Shelbourn

Do not touch – 1

Illustration © Colin Shelbourn

Do not touch – 2

■ Draw and colour in the correct colour warning signs onto each product.

oven cleaner	dishwasher powder
bleach	washing powder

Illustration © Colin Shelbourn

Body parts

■ Cut out the labels. Stick each label next to the correct body part.
Add some more labels of your own.

head	leg	foot	hand
arm	finger	body	neck

■SCHOLASTIC

Match the clothing

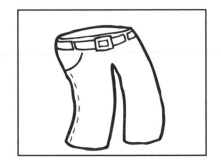

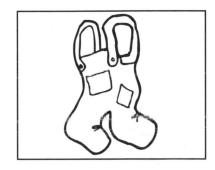

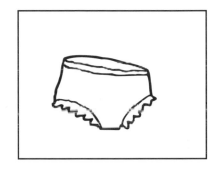

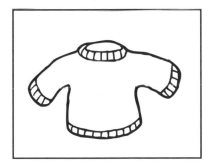

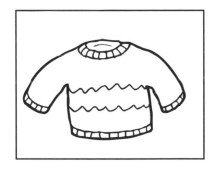

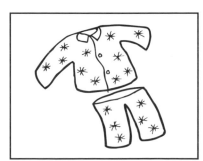

Illustration © Colin Shelbourn

Illustration © Baz Rowell/Beehive Illustration

Different faces

■ Look at the two faces. What makes them different? Give each face a different hair colour. Give each face the same colour eyes.

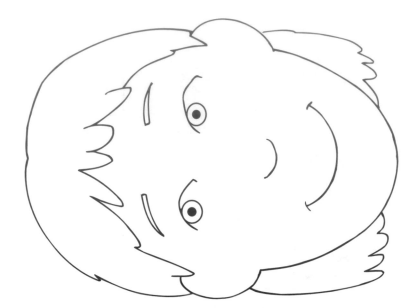

■ Add more features to each face to make them different from each other.

■SCHOLASTIC

Assessment – 1

PHOTOCOPIABLE

Assessment – 2

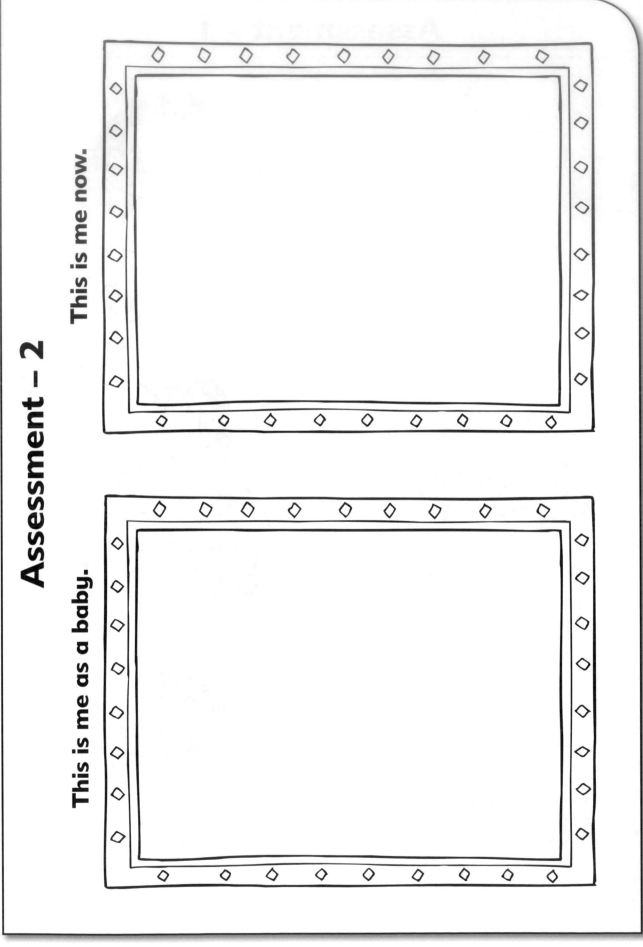

This is me now.

This is me as a baby.

SCHOLASTIC

UNIT 2 — Animals and plants

Lesson	Objectives	Main activity	Group activities	Plenary	Outcomes
Lesson 1 Animals around the world	• To learn that there are many different kinds of animal in the world.	Identify some familiar animals and look at their features.	Sort animals by colour and habitat. Sort animals by sounds they make. Paint pictures of animals. Play with toy sets, for example a farm or Noah's Ark. Develop imaginative play using the water tray. Play an animal sound matching game.	Look at one of the completed animal sets and talk about where in the world they live.	• Can identify animals not previously known. • Know which animals live with us in our homes and which live on farms, in the sea, in the wild and in other countries. • Talk about animals in terms of their size, their colour and the sounds they make.
Lesson 2 Counting animals' legs	• To learn that different animals have different numbers of legs.	Sort animals by the number of legs they have.	Group animals with two, four, six and eight legs on a pictogram. Draw the correct numbers of legs on pictures of animals. Solve animal jigsaws.	Look at the finished pictograms and talk about the animals in each column.	• Have begun to develop the skill of sorting. • Can record findings in a pictogram. • Understand that some animals have the same number of legs, some have no legs and very few have an odd number of legs.
Lesson 3 Young and old	• To notice differences and similarities between adult animals and their young.	Play a game to match young and adult animals.		Talk about differences between adult animals and their young.	• Have begun to notice the similarities and differences between young and adult animals. • Know that baby animals grow into adult animals of the same kind.
Lesson 4 Caring for our pets	• To learn about the ways that we need to care for our pets. • To recognise items associated with pet care.	Look at a collection of items used in pet care and identify the purpose of each one.	Set up a vet's in the role-play area. Make a large picture of fish in an aquarium. Paint pictures of favourite pets. Make pictures of pets with collage materials. Make a pet shop in another role-play area.	Make a display of the children's pictures and the pet care items.	• Know how to care for different kinds of pets. • Know that animals need food and water to stay alive. • Know that pets need exercise and the correct type of food.
Lesson 5 How do animals move?	• To learn that animals move in different ways.	Create a dance using different movements that animals make.		Read the story of 'The Hare and the Tortoise' or sing 'Caterpillars Only Crawl'.	• Know that a particular animal can move in different ways. • Know that some animals move only on the ground, and that some also fly. • Know that how animals move depends on whether they have legs or wings.
Lesson 6 Animals with shells	• To learn that some animals have shells.	Look closely at living snails in a tank.		Read 'The Hare and the Tortoise'. Compare the tortoise shell with the snail shell.	• Can recognise a shell on an animal. • Can talk about how shells are used.
Lesson 7 Ants, beetles and ladybirds	• To learn that insects always have six legs. • To learn that some insects have wings and can fly.	Play a game to build up a picture of an insect.	Play the game in small groups. Create a habitat for model insects. Make model insects. Make ladybirds. Make butterflies.	Discuss the model insects and their features.	• Can talk about insects' colour, number of legs and ability to fly. • Can recognise name common insects.
Lesson 15 Looking at leaves	• To learn that different plants have different kinds of leaves.	Make lists of similarities and differences between leaves in a collection.	Sort leaves. Describe their features. Print leaf patterns. Make close observational drawings of leaves.	Repeat from Lesson 12, focusing on leaves.	• Know that leaves come in different sizes, shapes and colours. • Know the features of leaves.
Lesson 16 Looking at flowers	• To learn that different plants can have different kinds of flowers.	Explore flower and stems and paint and make model flowers.		Look closely at a flower and consider the role of the pollen.	• Can recognise some features of a flower. • Learn that a flower's petals are the same colour and shape.

Lesson	Objectives	Main activity	Group activities	Plenary	Outcomes
Lesson 8 Incey, Wincey Spider	• To learn that spiders have eight legs.	Talk about spiders and spiders' webs.	Make model spiders. Make a spider's web. Trace or thread a spider's web pattern.	Make a display together of the spiders and webs.	• Know that all spiders have eight legs. • Know that spiders spin webs to catch their prey.
Lesson 9 Living in water	• To learn that some animals live in water.	Look at models of animals that live in the sea. Sort them by whether they have legs.	Make fish pictures. Compare sea animals. Make model sea animals. Play with sea creature models..	Complete a display together.	• Find similarities and differences between sea animals. • Can sort animals according to whether they have legs. • Can record findings. • Know some animals that live in the sea.
Lesson 10 Identifying animals	• To recognise the features of some animals, such as shape and size. • To sort familiar animals according to number of legs and where they live • To identify an animal from the sound it makes.	Make a pictogram of animals according to the number of legs they have.	Sort animals by the colour or pattern of their coat. Match animal sounds to pictures.	Suggest criteria for sorting.	• Can name animals; identify them from the sound they make; identify how many legs they have; sort them by features. • Can record information in pictograms.
Lesson 11 Growing plants	• To learn that there are many different green plants. • To learn that most green plants have stems, leaves, roots, flowers and seeds.	Make posters for the garden centre role-play area. Look carefully at seeds.		Display the children's posters in the garden centre.	• Know that plants grow from seeds. • Can recognise and identify the stem, leaves, roots, flowers and seeds of a range of flowering plants.
Lesson 12 Exploring plants with the senses	• To explore plants using the senses of touch, sight and smell.	Explore the scents and textures of plants, developing vocabulary.	Explore the textures and scents of plants. Plant seeds and plantlets in a role-play.	Talk about favourite plants and the reasons.	• Use different senses to find out about plants, noticing their features.
Lesson 13 Comparing plants	• To identify similarities and differences between two plants.	Note the similarities and differences between two plants.		Note the similarities and differences between another two plants.	• Develop observational skills by noticing things that are the same and things that are different. • Can identify a flower, stem, leaves and root.
Lesson 14 See my sunflowers grow	• To learn that seeds grow into plants.	Plant sunflower seeds in pots.	Plant seeds individually, water them and monitor their growth. Look at foods made from sunflowers. Explore compost, pots and garden tools. Role-play.	Talk about the care of their seeds and the recording of results.	• Know how to plant and care for seeds. • Know that plants need water. • Know that seeds grow into plants.
Lesson 17 Fruit and veg	• To learn that some plants are safe to eat and others are not.	Sort a range of fruits and vegetables. Consider which parts we eat.	Sort things that are and are not safe to eat. Role-play a greengrocer's shop. Make soup or salad.	Share the soup or salad.	• Know that certain parts of a plant can be eaten. • Know that not all plants can be eaten.
Lesson 18 Why do we eat?	• To learn that we need to eat in order to stay alive.. • To record information in the form of charts and graphs.	Make a 3-D and pictorial graph of favourite vegetables.	Make graphs. Make a vegetable snack. Make a model of a healthy meal. Print with vegetables..	Collate the graphs and interpret the results.	• Know that we need to eat in order to stay alive. • Know that eating certain vegetables is good for you. • Know that information can be recorded as a graph.

Assessment	Objectives	Activities 1 and 2	Activities 3 and 4	Outcomes
Lesson 19	• To assess the children's ability to name the parts of a flowering plant. • To assess the children's ability to notice similarities and differences between plants, and to sort plants according to noticeable features.	Name and label the parts of a flowering plant. Cut out labels and attach them to the correct parts of a plant picture.	Ring the differences between two plant pictures. Sort pictures of plants into sets by whether they have flowers, leaves, stems.	• Can recognise and identify the flower, petals, stem, leaves and roots of a flowering plant. • Know that plants need water to live.

CONTEXT

Where animals live

Lessons 1-5 are concerned with places where animals live: a farm, home, pet shop or wildlife park. The children are given opportunities to think about where animals live, both in domestic contexts and in the wild. A computer and TV are used to support the activities.

Lesson 1 ▶ Animals around the world

Objective
● To learn that there are many different kinds of animal in the world.

Vocabulary
the names of all the animals in your picture collection; stripes, spots, fur, feathers, big, small

RESOURCES
Main activity: Video/DVD showing different animals; set of large pictures of different animals; CD-ROM such as *Amazing Animals* (Dorling Kindersley). Choose pictures relevant to the experience of your children, and some that will extend their learning further.
Group activities: 1, 2 and 4 Set of toy or model animals for the children to play with and sort (these could be a farm, Noah's Ark or zoo animal set); pictures of the same animals to cut out; scissors; adhesive sticks; paper. **3** Paper; paint in a range of colours. **5** Water tray. **6** Cassette recorder and animal sound matching game (either purchased or made in school).
ICT link: *Amazing Animals* CD-ROM.
Plenary: The anthology *Apusskidu*, edited by Beatrice Harrop (A&C Black).

PREPARATION
Watch the video and familiarise yourself with the content of the CD-ROM. Put the large pictures into a sequence, starting with the animals with which you think the children are familiar. To provide a collection of animal pictures for cutting out, you can either take various pictures of each type of animal from magazines or use templates to produce identical pictures. You may wish to start this series of lessons by visiting a local farm that is set up to receive young children as visitors. Please follow your school's policy about visits, especially those involving farms and animals.

STARTER
Talk to the children about their pets. Does anyone have an animal living with him or her at home? Do any of the children live on a farm? If so, use them as a resource for the introduction. Otherwise, show the children the video and CD-ROM of different animals. Talk about some of the animals seen. *Are they big or small? What colour are they? Do any have stripes, spots, fur or feathers? What sounds do they make?* If the children have touched any of these animals, talk about how the animal's coat felt.

MAIN ACTIVITY
Choose your first picture. Ask the children whether they can name the animal. Continue doing this, using pictures of relatively familiar animals, until it is clear that most of the children know the names of the animals being shown. Start to talk about the familiar features of these animals: their size, the sounds they make, their colours and any markings. Now show the children pictures of about six new animals, telling them the animals' names as you do so.

GROUP ACTIVITIES
1 Work with groups of four to six children, talking about the toy animals in your collection. Sort the animals by their colour and then by whether they live with us in our homes, on a farm, in the sea or in the wild (in our country or in other countries). Allow the children to record their 'Where they live' sets

by cutting and sticking pictures of the animals on to headed pieces of paper.

2 Ask an additional adult to work with groups of four to six children, sorting the toy animals according to the sounds they make.

3 Ask the children to choose an animal they are not familiar with and paint a picture of it independently. Display the pictures in the classroom. You may wish to display these in the context of a story such as 'Noah's Ark'.

4 Let groups of four children take it in turns to play with the toy animal set, such as farm or zoo animals or Noah's Ark. Ask them to arrange the set to make a complete model.

5 Put models of animals that live in water in a water tray for the children to play with.

6 Set up an animal sound matching game for the children to play independently: a recording of an animal sound is played, and the children point to a picture of each animal as they hear it.

ICT LINK
Sort the pictures on the *Amazing Animals* CD-ROM into sets according to whether the animals live on land or in water; in homes as pets or in the wild; in this country or another country.

ASSESSMENT
Assess whether the children are learning the vocabulary necessary to describe the animals in your collection, by listening to their conversations and noting those children who are able to talk about the animals in terms of their features, as well as their names and where they live. This will provide you with information concerning the appropriate content and level of the work in the next lesson.

PLENARY
Look at the completed farm, zoo or Noah's Ark and talk about the way the children have organised the animals to make their model. Reinforce the idea that there are many different kinds of animals and that they all live somewhere in our world. Sing 'The Animals Went in Two by Two' (from *Apusskidu*) and other animal songs that you already know.

OUTCOMES
● All children *must* be able to find out about animals not previously known.
● Most of the children *should* be able to talk about animals in terms of their size, their colour and the sounds they make.
● Some *could* recognise and identify a range of common animals.
● A small number *could even* sort animals into groups and recognise that animals are found in different places.

LINKS
Across the curriculum: this lesson can be linked to work on communication, language and literacy. Read the children stories and poems to reinforce the names of different animals, such as *The Pigs in the Pond* by Martin Waddell (Walker Books). Talk about whether the animals are really like those in the stories and poems. For example, would real tigers behave like the one in *The Tiger Who Came to Tea* by Judith Kerr (Collins)? When choosing texts you may wish to avoid stories that give the animals a human dimension.

Lesson 2 ▪ Counting animals' legs

Objective
● To learn that different animals have different numbers of legs.

Vocabulary
the names of the animals in your collection; no, none, zero, two, four, five, six, eight, legs

RESOURCES ◉
Main activity: Pictures and models of several different kinds of animals (a cat, dog, sheep, cow, pig, horse, duck, hen, elephant, giraffe, bird, spider, octopus, insect, snake, snail, tortoise, whale, shark, starfish, worm and fish; these can be bought from any good educational supplier).
Group activities: 1 Enlarged (A3) copy of photocopiable page 74 (also 'Counting animals' legs – 1' (red) available on CD-ROM); Blu-Tack; photocopiable pages 74 and 75 (also 'Counting animals' legs –1 and 2' (red) available on CD-ROM) ; scissors; adhesive. **2** photocopiable page 76 (also 'Counting animals' legs – 3' (red) available on CD-ROM); pencils. **3** Range of animal games and jigsaws.
ICT links: 'Counting animals' legs' interactive available on CD-ROM.

PREPARATION
Make enlarged copies of photocopiable page 74 to use for demonstration and for the children.

STARTER
Sit the children in a circle around the collection of animal models and pictures. Show these to the children, and pass the models around so that the children can play with them. Find out whether the children know the names of all the animals in your collection. Keep those that the children are familiar with, and either teach them the names of some of the others or remove them from the activity at this stage.

MAIN ACTIVITY
Choose a familiar animal, such as a dog or cat. Show the children a model or picture of that animal and ask them what they can see. Ask questions such as: *What colour is the animal? Are all cats the same colour, or can they be different colours? How many legs does the animal have? Do all cats have four legs?* Ask the children to find all the other animals that have four legs in your collection.

Now ask the children to choose another animal. Discuss the number of legs, the animal's size and the colour and pattern of its coat. Again, ask the children to find all the animals that have the same number of legs. Continue with other animals in your collection until you are sure the children are looking carefully at the number of legs.

GROUP ACTIVITIES
1 Work with a group of six children at a time, looking at the models and pictures of animals. Ask the children to find all the animals that have four legs and put them together in a row or line. Repeat the activity with the animals that have two, six and eight legs. *Do any of the animals have one, three or seven legs? How many animals have five legs? Do any have no legs?* As you sort the animals, tell the children their names (if they do not already know them). Show the children the enlarged copy of photocopiable page 74. To one of the numbered columns, attach a picture of an animal with the same number of legs (for example, a beetle in the column labelled '6'). Give each child a copy of photocopiable page 75. Ask them to cut out the pictures of animals, sort them according to the number of legs, then stick them down on to a copy of photocopiable page 74 to make a large pictogram. Discuss any pictures that they cannot place. Ask them to add to the pictogram with their own drawings over the next few days. Show them how to label the pictogram appropriately.
2 Talk to the children about odd and even numbers in a numeracy lesson. Give them copies of photocopiable page 76, which contains pictures of

Differentiation

Support
Give them 'Counting animals' legs' 1 and 2 (green) on the CD-ROM, which include a smaller chart and animals with only two, four, six or eight legs for children to sort. Continue the support activity using 'Counting animals' legs – 3' (green) from the CD-ROM, for children to draw the correct number of legs on to different animals.

Extension
Give the children 'Counting animals' legs' 1 and 2 (blue) on the CD-ROM, which include a larger chart and animals which the children might not be familiar with, for them to sort. Continue the extension activity using 'Counting animals' legs – 3' (blue) from the CD-ROM, children draw on the correct number of legs on to different animals. How will the children draw the legs on to the millipede?

different animals without legs. Ask them to draw on the legs. They will soon realise that the legs are placed in pairs, on opposite sides of the body. Many animals have four or six legs, and very few animals have an odd number of legs (for example, a starfish has five).

3 Allow groups of four children to play with the different animal games and jigsaws you have provided.

ICT LINK

Using 'Counting animals' legs' interactive on the CD-ROM, count the number of different animal legs and drag the pictures on to the correct column of the chart to make a pictogram.

ASSESSMENT

Make a record of the investigative skills the children have developed, including sorting animals by their number of legs. Note those who are able to talk about what they have done. Keep the children's pictograms as evidence of their ability to make simple recordings of their findings.

PLENARY

Talk about the children's pictograms. *How many animals have we found with four legs, six legs, no legs, eight legs, five legs? How many animals have more than four legs? Are there more animals with four legs than with eight legs?*

OUTCOMES

● All children *must* be able to talk about different animals during their play.
● Most of the children *should* be able to talk about things that are the same and different in the context of the different colourings and number of legs that animals have.
● Some *could* communicate what they see when looking at the different animals, especially the number of legs.
● A small number *could even* sort animals according to the number of legs and use the information to make a pictogram to show what they have found out.

LINKS

Across the curriculum: this lesson provides a good context for counting and sorting activities.

Lesson 3 ▸ Young and old

Objective
● To notice differences and similarities between adult animals and their young.

Vocabulary
the names of all the animals in your picture collection; stripes, spots, fur, feathers, big, small

Differentiation

Support
Talk to children in smaller groups, and discuss one kind of animal in each activity session. Allow them to make a display showing the adult animal correctly matched to its young. Add words to describe the similarities and differences between young and adult animals.

Extension
Introduce pictures of other familiar animals to extend children's knowledge and ask them to match the adult animals to their young.

RESOURCES
Photographs of the children's pets; pictures of adult cats and dogs and of puppies and kittens.

MAIN ACTIVITY
Ask the children who have a dog, cat, puppy or kitten at home to talk about it. Invite them to tell you their pet's name, its colour, what it likes to do and so on. If they have a photograph of their pet, ask them to bring this in and pass it around the group. Discuss the pets' names. Sometimes a name is chosen because of an animal's colour or because of other features. This may provide opportunities to develop speaking and listening skills.

Show the children a picture of an adult dog. Talk about the features of the dog. Ask questions such as: *How many legs does it have? What is its colour?* Next, show the children a picture of a puppy. *Does the puppy look the same?* Talk about all the ways the puppy looks the same and all the ways it looks different. Repeat the activity with the pictures of the cat and kitten.

ASSESSMENT
Most children will note the differences in the animals' size, colour and shape, and the fact that the numbers of eyes, ears and legs are the same. Note those children who are able to notice less obvious differences, such as the texture of the coat or the shape of the head.

PLENARY
Talk to the children about what they have found out about young and adult animals. Look at pictures of an adult dog or cat and the corresponding young animal; agree on and ring the differences between them.

OUTCOMES
● All children *must* be able to find out more about the animals they know.
● Most of the children *should* be able to notice the similarities and differences between young and adult animals.
● Some *could* recognise young and adult animals by their features.
● A small number *could even* know that baby animals grow into adult animals of the same kind.

Lesson 4 ▸ Caring for our pets

Objectives
● To learn about the ways that we need to care for our pets.
● To recognise items associated with pet care.

Vocabulary
soft, fluffy, small, bigger, feed, groom, wash, exercise

RESOURCES
Main activity: Collection of items that are used in pet care. Include brushes for grooming; food and water dishes and bottles, food items (such as carrots, fish food, greens and pet food containers); leads, collars and name tags; pet toys and pet homes (such as sleep baskets and fish tanks). Someone may be able to bring in a pet passport.
Group activities: 2 and 3 Paints in a range of colours; paper. **4** Range of collage materials; scissors; adhesive; paper. **5** Photographs of the children's pets.
ICT link: Word-processing package to make posters.
Plenary: Display surface and display board; cardboard boxes of different sizes; pieces of fabric; stapler.

Differentiation
Support
Look first at kittens and then at puppies. Be very specific about the needs of these pets, and ask the children what is meant by 'exercise'. Talk through a puppy's need to go for long walks and a kitten's need to have clean fur.
Extension
Make a pictogram to show the variety of pets owned by the children in the class. Find out from this information which is the most popular kind of pet.

PREPARATION

Cover a display board with suitable backing paper. Organise several cardboard boxes along the surface in front to create different display heights, and cover them with fabric (stapled in place). Ask the children to bring in items used in pet care and photographs of their pets (see Resources). Make sure that any pet food containers shown are well washed out, empty and safe. Invite a child or parent to talk to the class about a pet and show a photograph of it (see Starter).

STARTER

Tell the children that you are going to think about all the things that are needed to look after different kinds of pets. Ask a child or parent to talk about a pet. Encourage him or her to explain what the pet eats, where it lives, how often it has to be fed, watered and washed or groomed. Alternatively, talk about your own pet if you have one. Show a photograph of the pet being talked about if possible.

MAIN ACTIVITY

Show the children some of the things in your pet care collection. Ask whether anyone can say what each item is used for. Talk about the need to feed different pets the correct food. For example, rabbits, hamsters and guinea-pigs need plenty of greens to eat, and water should also be available, especially on hot days. Talk about the importance of exercise when showing a dog's lead or a hamster's exercise wheel. Encourage the children to talk about the ways that pets play.

GROUP ACTIVITIES

1 Talk to groups of six children about the care of different pets. Set up a role-play situation where the children are taking their pet to the vet with a variety of complaints, such as toothache or being overweight. Ask the children how the pet can be cured, encouraging them to refer to the correct type of food and exercise.
2 Organise a group of ten children to make a large painting of some tropical fish or goldfish in an aquarium. Talk about the pets and other animals that live in water: fish, frogs, newts and so on.
3 Give the children paints in a range of colours and ask them to make pictures of their favourite pets for the display.
4 Set up a table with collage materials and ask an additional adult to help the children make pictures of rabbits, hamsters, cats and dogs.
5 Make a pet shop role-play area with the photographs and various pet care items. Ask the children each to find everything that a particular pet needs to keep it healthy.

ICT LINK

Use a word-processing package to make posters for the role-play area.

ASSESSMENT

Note whether the children find the correct or incorrect things for their pet in the pet shop. For example, do they choose cat food for a rabbit, or a dog lead for a cat?

PLENARY

Make the display together. Staple the children's pictures and photographs to the display board, and display the pet care items on the boxes. Add appropriate labels.

OUTCOMES

- All children *must* know they need to care for their pets.
- Most of the children *should* know how to care for different kinds of pets.

- Some *could* talk about their own pets and how they look after them.
- A small number *could even* explain that pets need exercise to be healthy and food and water to stay alive.

LINKS
ECM 2: Keeping healthy
Between units: this lesson is linked to Unit 1, Lesson 5 on how humans stay healthy and need food and water to stay alive.
Across the curriculum: the graph of favourite pets (see extension) links to data-handling in the context of numeracy.

Lesson 5 ▸ How do animals move?

RESOURCES
Video clips of various animals moving; cassette or CD player and recording of *Peter and the Wolf* by Prokofiev, or any music that can be used to suggest the different movements of animals (such as *The Carnival of the Animals* by Saint-Saens); pictures and models of animals (see Main activity); a copy of Aesop's fables or *Harlequin* edited by David Gadsby and Beatrice Harrop (A&C Black).

MAIN ACTIVITY
Before the lesson, show the children video clips of different animals moving and introduce some vocabulary that describes the animals' movements such as 'crawl', 'hop', 'run'.

Show the children a picture of a cat and play the relevant extract from *Peter and the Wolf*. Talk about the way the cat moves, using the words 'walk', 'run', 'jump' and 'creep'. Ask the children: *Does the cat move quickly or slowly, or both? Does it move close to the floor? Can it fly? Can it swim? Does it jump?* Let the children move to the music in their own way; afterwards, for a short time, let them evaluate and improve their performance. Repeat the activity for the other animals depicted in the music (including the flying bird, the duck and the wolf), using the words 'fly', 'swoop', 'hop', 'walk' and 'hover'. If you use other music, adapt the selection of animals as appropriate.

ASSESSMENT
Working with small groups, show the children pictures of animals and ask them to depict (by describing or acting out) each animal's movement. Include a spider, snake, kangaroo and snail as well as more familiar animals such as a dog, cat, bird and rabbit.

PLENARY
Read Aesop's fable 'The Hare and the Tortoise' to the children, or sing 'Caterpillars Only Crawl' from *Harlequin*.

OUTCOMES
- All children *must* know that animals move in different ways.
- Most of the children *should* know that a particular animal can move in more than one way.
- Some *could* know that some animals move only on the ground, and that some also move in the air.
- A small number *could even* know that the way animals move depends on whether they have legs or wings.

CONTEXT Stories and rhymes

The next five lessons can be taught through the context of stories and rhymes, many of which are traditional and/or will be familiar to the children. They can also be used for text-level work in literacy lessons.

Lesson 6 Animals with shells

Objective
● To learn that some animals have shells.

RESOURCES
Glass tank half-filled with compost and leaves, with some small twigs and wood from branches placed on the top; collection of live snails; pictures of other animals that have a shell; paper; pencils; paints; copy of Aesop's fables.

MAIN ACTIVITY
Collect some snails from the school grounds the day before this lesson, and place them in the prepared tank.

Talk to the children about the snails. Explain that you found them all in the school grounds – and that once the children have finished looking at them, you will return them to the place where they were found. Explain the need to take great care of the snails while they are in your classroom. Talk about how the snails are moving. *Do they have any legs?* Talk about the shell and what the snail uses it for. Ask a child to point to the shell. *Why does the snail always carry it around?* Show the pictures and talk about other animals that have shells, including crabs, mussels and tortoises. *Do they all use the shell in the same way?* (They all use it to hide in, but some have a shell that closes entirely and others do not.) Ask the children to point to the shell of each animal in your pictures. Ask them to draw and paint pictures of the snails and other animals that have a shell.

Differentiation
Support
Support children by giving them many opportunities to observe the snails and talk about what they can see (particularly the shell). Tempt the snails to eat and place food a little way away, so that the snail has to move to reach.
Extension
Challenge children to look more closely at the pictures of various shelled animals. Make simple comparisons between the size, shape and colour of the different shells.

ASSESSMENT
Note whether the children's pictures represent the shell accurately. Note those children who can talk about the shape and size of the shell and the way that the animal hides in it when it is disturbed.

PLENARY
Read 'The Hare and the Tortoise' from Aesop's fables. Talk about the tortoise shell and how it is similar to and different from the snail shell.

OUTCOMES
● All children *must* be able to recognise a shell on an animal.
● Most of the children *should* be able to look closely at the different shells and say whether each belongs to a snail or not.
● Some children *could* say which shell belongs to which animal.
● A small number *could even* talk about how shells are used by different animals.

Lesson 7 Ants, beetles and ladybirds

RESOURCES
Main activity: Dice with numbers 1-6; photocopiable page 77 (also 'Ants, beetles and ladybirds -1' (red) available on the CD-ROM); adhesive; card; commercial pictures and models of insects, including an ant, ladybird, wasp

Objective
● To learn that insects always have six legs.
● To learn that some insects have wings and can fly.

Vocabulary
head, legs, six, body (thorax, abdomen), eyes, antenna

and bee.

Group activities: 1 Photocopiable pages 78 and 79 (also 'Ants, beetles and ladybirds – 2' (red) and 'Ants, beetles and ladybirds – 3' (red) available on CD-ROM); adhesive; card. **2** Sand pit or sand tray; wood and stones. **3** Recycled and collage materials; scissors; PVA glue. **4 and 5** paints; card; black sugar paper; scissors; adhesive; Ladybird diagram available on CD-ROM; interactive whiteboard or computers.

ICT link: 'Ants, beetles and ladybirds' interactive available on the CD-ROM for use with the interactive whiteboard or on individual computers.

PREPARATION
Make six copies of photocopiable page 77, glue them to thick card and cut out the legs, body and head of the ant. Make similar insects from copies of photocopiable pages 78 and 79 to extend the game. Change your dice so that it has two '1' faces by blanking out five of the spots on the '6' face.

STARTER
Show the children the models and pictures of insects. Talk about the colour, shape and features of each one. Can the children see the eyes, legs and wings? Ask them why some insects can fly and others cannot. Do they know it is because some insects have wings and others do not? Sort the insects into those that can fly and those that cannot. Next, show the children a large model or picture of an ant. Talk about its head, eyes, body and legs. Count the legs together. Show the children the antennae and their position on the head.

MAIN ACTIVITY
Sit the children in a circle and play the dice game together, using your ant picture and body parts from the photocopiable sheet. The children should take turns to throw the dice. Each number corresponds to a different part of the body: 5 gets the thorax and abdomen, 4 the head, 3 an antenna, 2 an eye and 1 a leg. The children throw the dice and pick up the matching feature to build the ant. Play several times, letting the children take it in turns to place the features into position.

GROUP ACTIVITIES
1 Ask an adult helper to play the dice game, using photocopiable pages 78 and 79 with a group of four to six children. The helper should reinforce how many legs the beetle and ladybird have.
2 Put stones, pieces of wood and some of the model insects into the sand pit or sand tray,
and invite the children to make a home for the insects. Talk about which insects can fly and which cannot.
3 Use a range of collage and recycled materials to make models of different insects with the children. You may wish to suspend these from the ceiling or among large leaves arranged on a display board.
4 Make large ladybirds with the children from card, red paint and black paper dots. Display the Ladybird diagram from the CD-ROM on the whiteboard to show children how to cut down the centre almost to the end of each one, and open the wings slightly (see diagram below). Glue a piece of black sugar

Differentiation
Support
Support children by letting them play the game using 'Ants, beetles and ladybirds' 1, 2 and 3 (green), available on the CD-ROM, which feature fewer parts for the children to fit together.
Extension
Play the game using 'Ants, beetles and ladybirds' 1, 2 and 3 (blue) available on the CD-ROM which include more animal parts to put together. A few children may be ready to learn the names of the three major insect body parts – the head, thorax and abdomen – in which case you can play the game with the number 6 getting the abdomen and 5 getting the thorax.

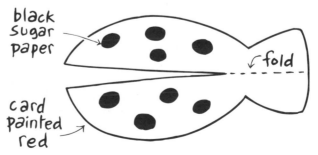

paper under the opened wings on the body.

5 Use paint and the folding technique (as above) to make butterflies with the children.

ICT LINK

Let the children use 'Ants, beetles and ladybirds' interactive from the CD-ROM on the Interactive Whiteboard or computer to build up pictures of an ant, beetle and ladybird.

ASSESSMENT

Note those children who are able to talk about the different insects in terms of colour, size and number of legs, and those who know which insects can fly and which cannot.

PLENARY

Display the model insects that the children have made. Ask one or two to talk about their model, explaining how they made it and why they painted it the colour they have. Count the number of legs on each model and identify those that can fly.

OUTCOMES

- All children **must** be able to comment on the features and pattern of ants, beetles and ladybirds.
- Most of the children **should** be able to recognise, identify and name common insects and look closely at similarities, differences and patterns.
- Some **could** talk about the features according to their colour, number of legs and whether they can fly.
- A small number **could even** know that insects have certain features and know where these are located.

LINKS

Across the curriculum: read the children stories and rhymes about common insects, including *The Bad-Tempered Ladybird* by Eric Carle (Puffin) and the traditional nursery rhyme 'Ladybird, Ladybird, Fly Away Home'.

Lesson 8 ▫ Incey Wincey Spider

Objective
- To learn that spiders have eight legs.

Vocabulary
web, spider, eight legs, body

RESOURCES

Main activity: Picture of a spider; large picture of a spider's web (see Preparation); black tissue paper; adhesive tape; pipe-cleaners; blue paper circles; black wool or cotton thread.
Group activities: 2 Sequins and offcuts of shiny paper; adhesive; glitter pens. **3** Art straws; adhesive. **4** Photocopiable page 80 (also 'Incey Wincey Spider' (red) available on the CD-ROM); pencils (or card, hole punch and wool).
ICT link: Digital camera; printer; computer; internet access; 'Incey Wincey Spider (red) from the CD-ROM.

PREPARATION

Use white paint on black paper to make a large picture of a spider's web (A2 or the size of the display board).

STARTER

Sing 'Incey Wincey Spider' together, adding actions to the words. Talk about what happens to the spider in the song. Ask: *Have you ever washed a spider down the bath plughole at home? Can you think of another way to get the spider out of the bath?*

MAIN ACTIVITY

Show the children a picture of a spider. Count the number of legs together.
Talk about the children's perceptions of spiders (be sensitive to any children
who have a fear of spiders). Explain that you are going to make a large
display of spiders for the classroom. Show them your picture of a spider's
web, and talk about the reason why spiders spin webs. Say that some
children will help to decorate the web so that it sparkles as if on a frosty
morning (see Group activity 2). Show the children how to make spiders by
screwing up an A3 piece of black tissue paper into an oval shape and fixing
in the ends with sticky tape. Use eight pipe-cleaners (or strips of black sugar
paper) to make the legs, fixing them to the body with sticky tape before
adding two blue paper circles for eyes. Attach a length of black wool or
cotton to suspend the spider from the ceiling.

GROUP ACTIVITIES

1 Work with groups of four to make a spider in the same way as the Main
activity, until every child has made a spider.
2 Ask an adult helper to work with a group of children, decorating the spider's
web by gluing sequins and offcuts of shiny paper to the white lines on the
web. Some children may wish to use glitter pens to add circles of colour along
the lines.
3 Work with groups to make spider's webs by winding black cotton or wool
around circular constructions of art straws (see illustration). Suspend the
webs among the spiders.
4 Use photocopiable page 80 as a tracing activity, or make it into a
threading activity by mounting copies on card and punching holes at the
intersections for the children to thread wool through.

ICT LINK

Use a digital camera to take
photographs of spiders' webs in the
local environment. Print these off and
add them to your display. Look on the
Internet for pictures of different
spiders. Use them to talk to a group of
more able children about the
similarities and differences.

Display 'Incey Wincey Spider' (red)
from the CD-ROM on an interactive
whiteboard. Use the drawing tool to
complete the web as a whole-class
activity.

ASSESSMENT

Note which children know that spiders
have eight legs, and are able to add
eight legs to their spider models.

PLENARY

Make the display together. Staple the
finished web to a display board before
fixing some spiders onto the web and
suspending others from the ceiling,
interspersed with the wool and straw
webs. Use some webs and spiders, along with the threading cards, to make a
frame for the finished picture. Reinforce the fact that spiders have eight
legs.

OUTCOMES
● All children *must* be able to recognise and name a spider.
● Most of the children *should* know that all spiders have eight legs and be able to add them to a model of a spider..
● Some children *could* know that spiders spin webs in which to catch their prey.
● A small number *could even* describe what different spiders look like and name the similarities and differences between them.

LINKS
Between units: this lesson can be linked to the creation of the Little Miss Muffet display in Unit 6, Lesson 1.
Across the curriculum: the children have opportunities to develop manual skills when completing the spider's web sewing card and web-winding activities.

Lesson 9 ◖ Living in water

Objective
● To learn that some animals live in water.

Vocabulary
whale, octopus, crab, fish, starfish, dolphin, shark, sea, waves, salt, salty

RESOURCES
Main activity: Display board; blue and green paper; blue and green crêpe or tissue paper; adhesive; white paint; copy of *The Rainbow Fish* by Marcus Pfister (North-South Books); pictures and models of animals that live in the sea; goldfish in a tank; salt; water; a beaker.
Group activities: 1 Fish shapes cut from paper; scissors; offcuts of coloured paper; PVA glue. **2** Paper; coloured pencils. **3** Recycled materials; adhesive; scissors. **4** Water tray; blue food colouring; ice cubes or lumps.
Plenary: Paper labels, thin cotton.
ICT link: Computer; printer; internet access.

PREPARATION
Cover a display board with blue and green paper, and staple strips of blue and green crêpe and tissue paper across the top to represent waves. Add touches of white paint to the tops of the 'waves'.

STARTER
Read the story *The Rainbow Fish* by Marcus Pfister. Talk to the children about all of the fish mentioned in this story. Show the children the goldfish in your tank, and talk about their features.

MAIN ACTIVITY
Show the children the model animals in your collection. Tell them that all of these creatures live in the sea. Find out which children have been to the seaside. Explain that sea water is like other water, but is salty. You may wish to show those who have never been to the seaside what 'salt water' is by dissolving some table salt in a beaker of water.

Sort the animals into two groups: those that have legs and those that do not. Ask: *What do you notice about the animals that have no legs?* (They have fins and a tail.) *How are they different from those that have legs?* (Those with legs do not have fins.) *How many of the animals have eyes?* (All of them.)

Talk about how these animals manage to live in the water. For example, explain that fish need to be in the water all of the time: they will die on land. Other animals, such as dolphins and whales, need to go to the surface of the water every so often to take a large breath of air. Ask the children whether they know of any other animals that live in the sea.

Differentiation
Support
With children who need
support, it is best to take one
animal at a time, asking the
children to make a model or
draw a picture of each one as
you talk about its features.
Extension
Extend children's knowledge
by talking to them about other
kinds of water environment,
such as rivers and ponds. Talk
about some of the animal life
in these environments.

GROUP ACTIVITIES

1 Organise the children into groups of six to make pictures of fish. Give each child a paper fish shape, and show the children how to cut and stick circles and stripes to make colourful fish like the ones in the story. The finished fish pictures can be stapled to the display.

2 Work with groups of four or six children to talk about the similarities and differences between the animals that live in the sea. Ask the children to compare two of the animals and record what they notice by drawing them.

3 Ask an adult helper to work with the children, making other model animals to go in your display (such as an octopus, dolphin, whale, starfish, crab or shark).

4 Add blue food colouring and cubes or lumps of ice to the water in the water tray to encourage imaginative play with the collection of sea creature models.

ICT LINK

Find pictures of fish on the internet. Print and cut these out and add them to the display.

ASSESSMENT

In the Plenary, hold up various pictures of animals and ask children to say whether they live in the sea or not. Note those children who can distinguish between marine creatures and similar land-living animals such as a snail or a woodlouse.

PLENARY

Finish the display together, adding labels for the animals' features (fins, claws and so on). Attach some model animals to thin cotton and suspend them in front of the display to create a 3-D effect. Place your pictures of animals in front of the display for the children to sort every day into two groups.

OUTCOMES

● All children *must* know which animals live in water.
● Most of the children *should* be able to find similarities and differences between animals that live in the sea.
● Some *could* record by drawing what they have found out.
● A small number of children *could even* sort animals according to whether they have legs.

LINKS

Across the curriculum: this lesson links well with creative development. Let the children paint and collage pictures of fish. In a dance lesson, create a dance about the movement of fish using the music 'Aquarium' from The Carnival of the Animals by Saint-Saëns. The children could also compose a musical accompaniment to their dance, or to a poem, using pitched and non-pitched percussion instruments.

Lesson 10 ▪ Identifying animals

Objectives
● To recognise the features of some animals, such as shape, size, colour and pattern.
● To sort familiar animals into sets according to their number of legs and where they live.
● To identify an animal from the sound that it makes.

Vocabulary
the names of the animals in the sets; pattern, coat, spots, stripes, sound, sea, shor, colour.

RESOURCES
Main activity: Set (Set A) of pictures of familiar animals, including a dog, cat, cow, pig, fish, bird, spider, snake, ladybird, ant and worm; paper; pencils.
Group activities: 1 Set (Set B) of pictures of animals that have a distinctive colouring and/or pattern, such as a tiger, elephant, horse, monkey, rabbit, leopard, zebra, giraffe, spotted and stripy fish, butterfly and ladybird (you may wish to include cows, dogs and pigs with spots); set (Set C) of pictures of animals that live in different environments, including a whale, dolphin, crab, starfish and snail. **2** Audio tape/CD (and player) with different animal sounds; matching set (Set D) of pictures.

PREPARATION
Organise the Group activities around the classroom, depending on the number of adult helpers you have available. Prepare a chart for the pictogram in the Main activity.

STARTER
Show the children the animal pictures in Set A. Ask them to name the animals. Ask questions such as: *Can you tell me how many legs each of the animals has? Can you tell me any other animals with the same number of legs? Can anyone show me how this animal moves? Why can't the snake walk?* (Because it doesn't have legs.)

MAIN ACTIVITY
Ask the children to organise the pictures in Set A into a pictogram according to the number of legs each animal has. Invite them to add to the collection of animal pictures by drawing some of their own. This makes the activity open-ended and allows the children to show you how well they understand the concept.

GROUP ACTIVITIES
1 With groups of up to six children, sort the pictures in Set B according to the colour or pattern of the animal's coat. Which children recognise that the elephant has no distinctive coat markings? How many can name another animal that has no distinctive coat markings, such as the hippopotamus, the rhinoceros or the lion? Go on to sort the pictures in Set C according to where the animals live: in the ground, on the shore, in the sea and so on.
2 Play an audio tape or CD of animal sounds, and ask the children to identify which animal is making each sound by holding up the matching picture from Set D.

ASSESSMENT
Keep the children's pictograms from the Main activity. Note those children in Group activity 1 who can separate the stripy animals from the spotted ones; and those who know, or can predict sensibly, where an animal lives (for example, a whale lives in the sea rather than in rivers or on the shore). In Group activity 2, see who can identify the animals by name as well as by pictures.

PLENARY
Show the children pictures of four animals in turn and ask them to suggest the criteria they could use for sorting. Use this as a stepping stone to follow up activities where the children decide for themselves the criteria they will use for sorting the picture.

Differentiation

Support
Provide a smaller sample of pictures of animals for the children to organise into a pictogram.
Extension
Provide pictures and sound of more unusual animals.

OUTCOMES

● All children *must* be able to identify the names of familiar animals.
● Most of the children *should* be able to identify familiar animals from the sound they make.
● Some *could* identify how many legs various types of animal have.and record the information in pictograms.
● A small number *could even* sort animals by visible features.

CONTEXT Role-play

The next eight lessons involve the use of the role-play area as a farmer's market, greengrocer's shop or garden centre. Many of the play activities suggested in these lessons are set within this last area, and provide the starting points for other learning activities suggested under Links.

Lesson 11 ▬ Growing plants

Objectives
● To learn that there are many different green plants.
● To learn that most green plants have stems, leaves, roots, flowers and seeds.

RESOURCES

Lots of empty seed packets and some containing a few seeds (make sure they have not been dressed with insecticide); pot plants; flowers; vegetables; a picture of a tree; books about plants, including *The Tiny Seed* by Eric Carle (Puffin); posters showing plants; collection of other items (such as a trowel, flowerpots, watering can, seed trays, sieve, seed compost, various seeds) that can be bought from a garden centre; paper; pencils; paints and brushes. You may wish to link this lesson to a visit to a local garden centre.

MAIN ACTIVITY

Explain that you are going to set up a garden centre in the role-play area. Show the children what you already have for this. Talk about the kinds of things you will find at the garden centre. Together, make posters of things that can be bought from the garden centre – particularly plants and flowers.

Talk about the roots, stems, leaves and flowers on the plants before asking the children to draw and paint pictures of some of the plants.

Tell the children that the plants always make seeds, so that more plants of the same kind will grow. Show them the seed packets. Talk about the pictures on the packets, then show the children some of the seeds. *Does the seed look anything like the picture?* Allow them to marvel at the fact that such a large and beautiful plant grows from such a small and simple seed. Read *The Tiny Seed* by Eric Carle.

ASSESSMENT

From the children's drawings, note whether they have included all the parts of the plant or flower and drawn them in the correct places.

PLENARY

Display the children's pictures and posters around the role-play area. Arrange some of the plants and other items you have collected in the 'garden centre'.

OUTCOMES

- All children *must* be able to show an awareness of change.
- Most of the children *should* know that plants grow from seeds, and should be able to ask questions about why seeds grow.
- Some *could* recognise and identify the stem, leaves, roots, flowers and seeds of a range of flowering plants.
- A small number *could even* recognise that plants produce seeds which grow into more of the same plant.

Lesson 12 ▪ Exploring plants with the senses

Objective
- To explore plants using the senses of touch, sight and smell.

Vocabulary
spiky, smooth, tickly, soft, dry, thick, thin, long, short, rough, textured, smell, scent, sharp, shiny, dull, sweet, spicy, sneeze, (aroma, perfume)

RESOURCES

Main activity: Cactus (not too spiky!); Christmas pine; spider plant; rosemary plant; ornamental garden grass; holly; ivy; laurel; mint plant; lemon plant; curry plant; lavender; heather; flowers with textured stems (such as carnation, rose, busy lizzie and daffodil) and distinctive smells (such as freesias, pineapple broom and orange blossom); an orange; mint sauce; curry powder; pineapple juice; lemon juice.
Group activities: plant pots; compost.

PREPARATION

Cut some of the thorns from the rose stem. Check for any allergies, and make sure that any children liable to be affected do not come into contact with the plants. Check your Local Authority list of plants that should not be used.

STARTER

Show the children all the plants in your collection and talk about what one or two of them look like. Talk about the size, shape and colour of the leaves, stem, flower (if any) and roots (if visible). Put the plants into sets according to whether they have leaves, then whether they have flowers.

MAIN ACTIVITY

Ask the children if they have ever seen any of the plants before. Can they name any of them? Can they describe what it might be like to touch any of the plants (for example, the cactus)? Can they describe what the plants might smell like?

Differentiation

Support
Explore three plants with a group of children who need support, encouraging them to use all their senses. List everything they say about their discoveries. Use this recording to assess their knowledge and use of language.

Extension
To extend, organise children into one group and work with them on making observational drawings. Ask them to focus closely on the leaves and their position on the plants. Sort the pictures into sets: plants with leaves and plants without.

Choose one or two of the plants that smell, and pass them one at a time around the group for the children to smell. Ask the children what these smells remind them of. Pass around the items whose smells match the plants: curry powder with the curry plant, mint sauce with the mint, pineapple juice with the pineapple broom and so on. Encourage the children to think of words to describe the smells: 'sweet', 'spicy', 'makes you sneeze' and so on.

Repeat the activity with plants that have different textures, such as the Christmas pine and busy lizzie, and talk about how they feel. Encourage the children to think of words to describe textures: 'thick', 'thin', 'long', 'short', 'tickly', 'soft', 'rough', 'smooth' and so on.

GROUP ACTIVITIES

1 Work with groups of four children to explore the texture of some of the plants in the collection. This will allow you to keep an eye on the rose and cactus touching, which could be a problem if not supervised closely. Ask the children to put the plants into sets according to their texture. Encourage them to use words such as 'hard', 'spiky', 'prickly' and 'smooth'.

2 Ask an adult helper to work with a group of children to explore various plants and plant-derived items by using the sense of smell. The helper should discuss the scent made by each plant with the children, asking them whether these scents remind them of anything before passing the items around for them to smell.

3 Allow a group of children to plant seeds (in pots or trays), set out the plants and buy and sell them in the 'garden centre' role-play area. A parent helper would be useful to support this activity.

4 If your spider plant has small plantlets, plant these in pots for the children to look after in their 'garden centre'.

ASSESSMENT

Note those children who use their senses to explore and find things out about the plants in your collection (see Differentiation). Note those children who are beginning to make simple comparisons between features of different plants, such as leaf shape or scent.

PLENARY

Ask one group to choose their favourite plant from the collection. Can they say why this is their favourite? Encourage them to talk about what they can see, feel and touch. Reinforce the learning objective: *we can find out about plants by using our senses.*

OUTCOMES

● All children *must* be able to find out more about plants by looking closely, touching and smelling.
● Most of the children *should* be able use the senses of sight, smell and touch to find out about a range of plants, noticing their features, shape, size and colour; make lists and drawings with support.
● Some children *could* name the visible parts of plants and record this in pictures.
● A small number *could even* make observations and compare different plants.

LINKS

ECM 4: Making a positive contribution to the community.
Between units: this lesson links to work on looking after plants in Unit 3.

Lesson 13 ▪ Comparing plants

Objective
● To identify similarities and differences between two plants.

RESOURCES
Flowering plant (such as a chrysanthemum); non-flowering plant (such as a spider plant or Christmas pine); magnifying lenses; prepared drawing of two plants for comparison (see Differentiation). Check for any allergies, and make sure that children liable to be affected do not come into contact with the plants. Internet access; computer; printer.

MAIN ACTIVITY
Show the children the non-flowering plant and talk about its shape, size and colour. Note the shape, size and colour of the leaves. *Are they long or short, fat or thin? Are they dark green or light green? Do they have straight or curved edges?* Repeat this activity to describe the flowering plant. Ask the children to point out things about the two plants that are the same. (For example, they both have leaves, roots and stems; they are both growing and need looking after.)

Ask groups of children to look carefully at the two plants. First of all, they should look at the features that are different – for example, one has flowers and the other does not; one has several colours (flowers, leaves and stem) and the other is mostly green. They should use magnifying lenses to look carefully at the leaves. Note down all the differences that the children describe, such as the length, breadth, shape and colour of the leaves.

ICT LINK
Use the internet to find pictures of plants from around the world that are very different in the way they look. Use these to decorate the garden centre and to note down similarities and differences

ASSESSMENT
Ask an adult helper to write down what the children say as they point out the similarities and differences between the plants. Focused observation of children working independently will provide a good opportunity for this. Also see Differentiation.

Differentiation
Support
For support, choose two different plants and only look for things that are different about them. Ask the children to show the differences by colouring a prepared drawing of the two plants under your direction. You could use bowls of bulbs, such as yellow daffodils and purple crocuses – this will give the children clear differences of colour and size to focus on, and it will be easy for them to notice and colour the differences.

Extension
Talk to the children about whether all plants have seeds, a flower, stem, roots and leaves. Let them choose their own plants to repeat the activity independently. Use their recordings for assessment purposes.

PLENARY
Repeat the activity with another two different plants, either chosen by you to reinforce a particular point picked up during the lesson (through assessment) or chosen by the children. The children may need to pick out different plants from a wider selection for each feature they notice, and some will need to repeat the same idea with different plants.

OUTCOMES
● All children *must* be able to notice that plants have different parts.
● Most of the children *should* be able to develop observational skills by noticing things that are the same and things that are different.
● Some *could* know that plants have seeds, a flower, stem, leaves and root but not necessarily all at the same time.
● A small number *could even* observe and compare a range of different plants.

Lesson 14 ▸ See my sunflowers grow

Objective
● To learn that seeds grow into plants.

Vocabulary
sunflower, seed, plant, plant pot, seed compost, grow, growth

RESOURCES ◉
Main activity: Sunflower seeds; sunflower head (optional); plant pots; seed compost; lollipop stick.
Group activities: 1 Felt-tipped pens; sunny spot in the classroom; digital camera. **2** Paper; pencils. **3** Sand tray; water; some pots, trowels and forks. **4** Other plant seeds.
ICT link: Collection of foods made with sunflower seeds (such as margarine, oil, cake); digital camera; computer.
Plenary: Photocopiable page 81 (also 'See my sunflowers grow' (red) available on CD-ROM); pencils.

PREPARATION
The best time for planting these seeds is in March or April. Avoid planting them close to the holidays, when the children will miss the first signs of growth.

STARTER
Show the children the sunflower head, if you have one. Alternatively, show and pass around the sunflower seeds. Wonder at how many seeds have grown from just one tiny seed.

MAIN ACTIVITY
Give each child a sunflower seed and talk about the colour, shape and size of the seeds. Show the children how to press a seed into seed compost in a plant pot. Explain why you are planting two in each pot. (In case one doesn't grow.) Talk about how the children will need to care for the plant when it begins to grow. Write your name on a lollipop stick and show the children how to stick this into the pot. Discuss where would be a good place to put the pot so that you can keep an eye on the plant and look after it.

GROUP ACTIVITIES
1 Rotating groups of four children, allow every child in the class to plant two sunflower seeds. Write each child's name on a lollipop stick and add it to the pot before placing it in a sunny position. The children should water their seeds regularly and monitor the growth of the plants during the next few weeks, transplanting them when necessary to larger pots and to outside. A digital camera is ideal for recording growth. The children should monitor the plant growth with adult support.
2 As the children finish planting their seeds, ask an additional adult to help the children make a record of what they did.
3 Fill the sand tray with slightly damp seed compost and a selection of pots, trowels and forks for the children to explore. This will give them experience of handling compost and of filling containers.
4 Allow a group of four children to play in the 'potting shed' (role-play area), planting other seeds. Make sure they use seeds that have not been dressed with insecticide.

ICT LINK
A group could look at a collection of foods made with sunflowers, take photographs of these, and use a computer to resize and organise them to make a frame for a recording sheet.

ASSESSMENT
Group activity 2 can be used to assess the children's knowledge of how to plant seeds. Skilful questioning will allow you to find out which children know the conditions for growth, such as the need for water. If an adult

Differentiation

Support
Organise children who need support into pairs, so that you can give them individual attention.

Extension
Challenge children to plant their seeds in different places (for example, in an area of the school garden) and to monitor the growth to see whether the seeds grow better outdoors or indoors in pots. Allow the children to record the growth, so that they have evidence on which to reach a conclusion.

helper supervises this activity, give him or her a prompt sheet with suitable questions to ask.

PLENARY

Show the children the row of plant pots and explain the need to water the seeds every day. Talk about how much water each plant needs. Tell the children that they are going to watch how well the seeds grow over the next few weeks. You may wish them to count the days until the first sign of growth, or to record which seed grows first. Give the children photocopiable page 81 to use for recording the growth of their seeds. For differentiation, use 'See my sunflowers grow' (green) or (blue) from the CD-ROM depending on their level of ability, for recording the growth of their seeds.

OUTCOMES

● All children *must* be able to notice patterns and change.
● Most of the children *should* be able to ask questions about how seeds grow.
● Some *could* talk about what they are doing and why, and know that seeds grow into plants.
● A small number *could even* plant and care for seeds and know that plants need water.

LINKS

ECM 4: Making a positive contribution to the community.
Between units: this lesson links to Unit 3, Lesson 4.
Across the curriculum: the children develop their dexterity through handling and planting small seeds.

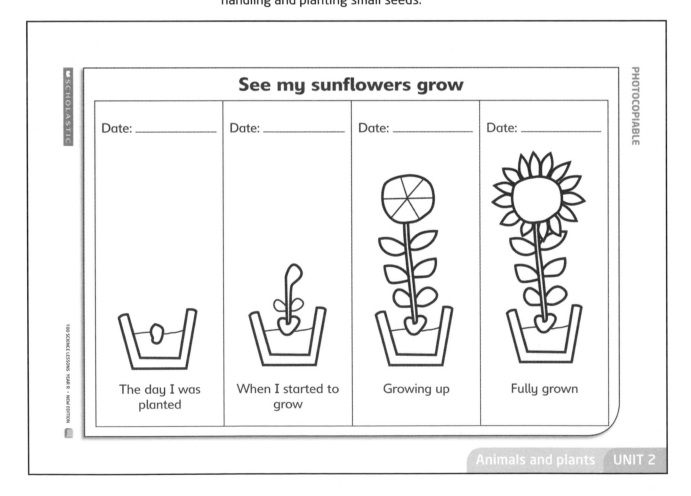

See my sunflowers grow

Date: _____   Date: _____   Date: _____   Date: _____

The day I was planted | When I started to grow | Growing up | Fully grown

Animals and plants UNIT 2

Lesson 15 ▪ Looking at leaves

RESOURCES
Main activity: umbrella plant; Christmas pine; large sheets of paper (or flipchart); marker pen.
Group activities: 1 Laurel bush; holly bush; spider plant; cheese plant and yucca plant. (If it is autumn you can use a collection of leaves from the local area instead, and discuss colour as an attribute.) **2** A3 paper; pencil. **3** Clay; paints and wax crayons in suitable colours for leaves; large picture of a tree; adhesive. **4** Paper; pencils.
ICT link: Digital camera; different types of leaves; computer; printer.

PREPARATION
Draw three very different leaves on a sheet of A3 paper for Group activity 2.

STARTER
Place your umbrella plant and Christmas pine in the centre of the group, so that they can all see the leaves. Invite the children to gently feel the leaves on each plant. Make a note of their descriptions of how the leaves on each plant feel. Look at and feel the underside of the leaves. Ask the children whether the leaves on the two plants are the same or different, and to describe the similarities and differences.

MAIN ACTIVITY
Divide a large sheet of paper (or flipchart page) into two halves, with the headings 'The same' and 'Different' at the top. List all the things about the leaves that are the same (green, attached to branches, more than one leaf growing at each point) and the things that are different (one is sharp, the other is smooth; one is thin, the other is fat). If necessary, to help the children understand the process, repeat the activity with two more plants.

GROUP ACTIVITIES
1 With a group of children, look at the leaves on your plants (or the collection of leaves) closely and decide on a criterion for sorting. Sort the leaves into two types – for example, with spikes and without spikes; long and short; shiny and dull.
2 With another group, look closely at the leaves and talk about their features (such as veins, edges, top side and underside). Look at the three drawings one by one, and ask the children to describe the leaves. Encourage them to use their own words. Scribe the children's descriptions on each sheet of paper.
3 Ask the children to make prints (with paint), wax crayon rubbings and clay models of the leaves using colours appropriate to the season, then cut them out and add them to a large picture of a tree with branches.
4 Ask the children to make close observational drawings of the leaves. Display these with the plants (or leaves) in a corner of the classroom.

ICT LINK
Take pictures of the different types of leaves using a digital camera. Load the pictures onto the computer, and ask the children to make a recording frame by selecting and dragging leaves from the picture selection and arrange them around the edge of their paper before printing it off to use to record their descriptions.

ASSESSMENT
Collect the children's descriptions and drawings and keep them as evidence. On each one, note the child's contribution to Group activity 1 and whether he or she can sort the leaves according to given criteria.

PLENARY

Ask the children to say which is their favourite plant and why. Is it because of the shape and colour of the leaves? Do they make the plant look pretty?

OUTCOMES

● All children *must* be able to explore the leaves noticing and commenting on pattern, shape and colour.
● Most of the children *should* know that leaves come in different sizes, shapes and colours.
● Some *could* know the features of leaves including veins, edges, top side and underside.
● A small number *could even* record their observations using some scientific vocabulary.

LINKS

Between units: this lesson links closely with all those that develop the observational skill of identifying similarities and differences. You may choose to select these lessons to develop this skill progressively.

Lesson 16 ▸ Looking at flowers

Objective
● To learn that different plants can have different kinds of flowers.

RESOURCES

Flowering pot plants and bunches of flowers (some of the same kind but with different-coloured flowers), including a lily; some non-protected wild flowers, including a dandelion and a daisy; paper; paints in various colours; scissors; tree with blossom (or a picture of one); collection of recycled materials, including drinking straws, garden canes and wires.

MAIN ACTIVITY

Look at the flowers in your collection. Pass them around for the children to look at and handle. Ask them to look at the stem and describe what they see and feel. *Is the stem hard or soft? Can you squeeze it thinner? Is it thick or thin?* Explain that a stem is sometimes called a stalk. *What do you think the stem is used for?* If necessary, compare a plant stem to a drinking straw: *Water and other nutrients come up through it.*

Look at all the flowers and ask the children to identify all the colours they can see. Look at one particular flower, such as a tulip or poppy, and look closely at the petals, stem and centre. *Is the flower all the same colour, or is the inside a different colour?* Sort the flowers according to their colour. *Are any colours not here?* (Brown, grey, black.) *Is one colour more common than the others?* Next, look closely at the petals. *What shape are the petals? Are they all the same size?* Investigate the number of petals on each flower. *Which flower has the most/least petals? Is there a number that is counted most often (for example, six)? Does the same kind of flower always have the same number, shape and size of petals? Are all the petals in the same flower always the same colour?* (Yes.)

Organise Group activities with adult support:
1 The children can paint large pictures of the flowers using bright colours, cut them out when dry and add them to a display.
2 Look at a tree with blossom (or a picture of one). Explain that the trunk is the stem of the tree. Discuss the purposes of the trunk. Ask: *Does this tree have flowers? What do they look like?* Explain that the flowers on a tree are called 'blossom'.
3 Ask the children to use recycled materials to make flowers and plants that match ones in your collection. For example, they could attach petal shapes to straws to make dandelions, or use garden canes and petals for carnations. Talk with them about why they chose particular materials.

ASSESSMENT
Keep the children's work (see Differentiation) as a record of their understanding. Note those children who know that a flower is made up of petals and an inside bit, and those who can recognise the stem.

PLENARY
Look closely at a lily and talk about the petals and the inside bit. Show the children the pollen (take care not to make them sneeze and stain their clothes). Discuss how bees collect the pollen and spread it from flower to flower, helping the plant to make seeds.

OUTCOMES
- All children **must** be able to notice and comment on shape and colour of petals.
- Most of the children **should** be able to recognise things that are the same and things that are different and identify some features of flowers.
- Some **could** understand that different flowers have different numbers and shapes of petals.
- A small number **could even** recognise some features of a flower (even if they are unable to name them) and learn that all the petals on the same flower have the same colour and shape.

Lesson 17 ◗ Fruit and veg

Objective
- To learn that some plants are safe to eat and others are not.

RESOURCES
Main activity: Collection of fruit and vegetables including a tomato, carrot, potato, lettuce and the fruits used in Unit 1, Lesson 1; sorting rings.
Group activities: 2 Pictures of foods that are not safe to eat (such as toadstools and wild berries) and of other fruits and vegetables (including sweetcorn, cabbage, cauliflower, peas and cucumber). **4** Equipment to make soup or salad; cooking bowls and spoons or plates.
Assessment: paper; coloured pencils.

PREPARATION

Take the children to visit the local supermarket or greengrocer's if there is one nearby. Look at the variety of fruit and vegetables that are being sold. Set up a 'greengrocer's shop' in the role-play area.

STARTER

Talk about the range of fruit and vegetables seen at the greengrocer's or supermarket. Ask the children which they do and do not like to eat. Explain that we all have different tastes and like to eat different things. All the things sold at the greengrocer's and supermarket are safe to eat (as long as they are fresh and have been washed). Other things can be found growing that are not safe to eat, such as toadstools (which look like ordinary mushrooms) and deadly nightshade berries (which look like blackcurrants). Tell the children that they should never eat anything unless an adult they know has said it is safe for them to do so.

MAIN ACTIVITY

Show the children the fruits and vegetables in your collection. If the children are able to name any of these, encourage them to do so. If not, tell them the names. Ask them to sort the collection into sets of the same colour, so that they can see the range of colours more clearly. Now hold up each fruit or vegetable in turn and ask whether we eat all of it. Make two piles in sorting rings: those that we eat all of (such as a carrot) and those that we only eat part of (such as an orange).

GROUP ACTIVITIES

1 Ask an adult helper to repeat the Main activity with groups of up to six children in order to reinforce the learning objective and make sure the children understand whether we eat all or part of each fruit and vegetable.
2 Show the children pictures of things that we should not eat and things that are safe to eat. Ask them to sort the pictures into two piles: things that are safe to eat and things that are not. Reinforce the idea that it is only safe to eat something if an adult we trust has said it is safe.
3 Allow groups of four children to 'buy' and 'sell' the fruit and vegetables in the 'greengrocer's shop' role-play area.
4 Make soup or salad with some of fruits and vegetables in your collection.

ASSESSMENT

Ask the children to draw a picture of all the things in the collection that are safe to eat. Some children could label the items (fruit, vegetable) and their parts (seed, leaf and so on).

PLENARY

Share the soup or salad with the children.

OUTCOMES

● All children *must* be able to find out more about vegetables and fruits.
● Most of the children *should* know that certain parts of a plant can be eaten and that not all plants can be eaten.
● Some *could* identify features of vegetables.
● A small number *could even* sort vegetables into groups according to the part that we eat.

LINKS

ECM 1: Keeping healthy and **ECM 2:** Staying safe.
Across the curriculum: this lesson can be linked to any healthy eating project that you have running in your school. Reinforce the children's awareness of the importance of a healthy diet.

Differentiation
Support
Talk to children in groups of three or four about the more familiar vegetables. For example, ask them how they like their potatoes cooked. *Do you like baked potatoes, chips, roast potatoes, boiled potatoes? Do we ever eat the skin of the potato, or do we always take it off?*
Extension
Challenge children to talk about which parts of fruits and vegetables we eat - for example, the seeds of pea plants, the leaves of cabbage plants and the seeds, flesh and skin of tomatoes. Ask them to identify, in turn, the vegetables and fruits of which we eat the seeds, leaves, flowers and roots.

Lesson 18 ▸ Why do we eat?

Objective
● To learn that we need to eat in order to stay alive.
● To record information in the form of charts and graphs.

Vocabulary
vegetables, carrots, sweetcorn, peas, potatoes, cabbage, cauliflower, broccoli, green, orange, white, brown, yellow, column, chart, graph, best, favourite

RESOURCES
Main activity: Collection of vegetables (carrots, potatoes, cabbage, peas, broccoli, cauliflower and sweetcorn); pictures of these vegetables; large blank chart; the song 'Paintbox' from *Harlequin* edited by David Gadsby and Beatrice Harrop (A&C Black).
Group activities: 2 Plates; round-bladed knives. **3** Paper plates; adhesive; pictures of different foods. **4** Paper; paint in various colours.
Plenary: Graphing tool on CD-ROM.

PREPARATION
Draw a chart on a large sheet of paper with one column for each vegetable in your collection. Cut out pictures of each of these vegetables, and make several photocopies that the children can colour and stick to the chart. Talk to the children as they play in the 'greengrocer's shop' role-play area for several days before you intend to carry out this lesson, so that you can find out all the vegetables that they do and do not like. Teach them the song 'Paintbox'.

STARTER
Sing the song 'Paintbox' with the children. Talk to them about what they usually eat for dinner. How many of them like to eat burgers, chips, vegetables? Explain that we need to eat in order to stay alive. Show the children the collection of vegetables and tell them that you are going to make a chart to show which vegetables they like to eat.

MAIN ACTIVITY
Place one piece of each vegetable at the bottom of each column on the chart: a pea, a small carrot, a cabbage leaf, small pieces of broccoli and cauliflower and so on. Ask one of the children to say which vegetable he or she likes the best. Be prepared for someone to answer with a vegetable that is not part of your collection! If you have done your homework, this shouldn't happen (see Preparation). Invite the child to place the vegetable that he or she likes the best in the correct column. Ask the other children to help by explaining if necessary. Repeat the activity with a few other children.

GROUP ACTIVITIES
1 Repeat the activity with groups of six children, taking turns to place their favourite vegetable on a chart. When the chart is finished, ask them to replace each of the vegetables with a picture to represent it and stick their picture into place. Count how many pictures there are in each column, and invite the children to say which is their group's favourite vegetable.
2 Ask an adult to help the children cut up some of vegetables to enjoy at snack time. Carry out a risk assessment and check for allergies first. Talk about how eating vegetables is good for us and helps to keep us healthy.
3 Give each child in a group a paper plate, an adhesive stick and pictures of food and vegetables. Ask the children to make a picture of the dinner they would like to have today. They can then take this home to show their parents or carers.
4 Set up a printing table so that the children can print with potatoes and carrots. Talk about the shapes they have made (circles and ovals).

Differentiation

Extension
Organise the children to do Group activity 1 together and include the choices of all the children in the class. As you remove the vegetable replace it with a cube of the same colour – for example orange for carrots, yellow for corn, light green for peas and so on. Transfer the information on to a block graph together, using the graphing tool on the CD-ROM, and then invite the children to record the information individually on their own graph, preferably using a computer generated graphing program.

ASSESSMENT
During the Plenary session, note those children who are able to record their choices on the chart unaided. As you talk to the children during the activity, use focused questions to find out which children understand that we need to eat to stay alive.

PLENARY ⊚

When all the groups have recorded their favourite vegetable choices on separate charts, repeat the activity with all the children together. Using the interactive whiteboard and suitable graphing package, ask each child in turn to select a picture of his or her favourite vegetable and stick it in the correct column. When the chart is finished, count up how many there are in each column and invite the children to say which is the class's favourite vegetable. Write 'Our favourite vegetable' as a title and print off the chart to display in the 'greengrocer's shop' role-play area.

The information gathered by the class could be converted into a block graph using the graphing tool on the CD-ROM.

OUTCOMES

● All children *must* be able to find out more about vegetables.
● Most of the children *should* know that we need to eat in order to stay alive.
● Some *could* know that eating certain vegetables is good for you, and be able to draw a simple pictogram with some support to record their favourite vegetables.
● A small number *could even* record their findings on a block graph.

LINKS

ECM 2: Keeping healthy.
Between units: this lesson links with several lessons in Unit 1.
Across the curriculum: the QCA design and technology Scheme of Work has a Year 1 unit called 'Eat more fruit and vegetables', which could follow on from this lesson. This lesson also provides a context for handling data aspects in numeracy.

Lesson 19 ▪ Assessment

Objectives
● To assess the children's ability to name the parts of a flowering plant.
● To assess the children's ability to notice similarities and differences between plants, and to sort plants according to noticeable features.

RESOURCES ⊚

Assessment activities: 1 Plant that has a stem, leaves and a flower; Post-it Notes, felt-tipped pen. **2** Photocopiable page 82 (also 'Assessment - 1' (red) available on the CD-ROM); scissors; adhesive. **3** Photocopiable page 83 (also 'Assessment - 2' (red) available on the CD-ROM); pencils. **4** photocopiable page 84 (also 'Assessment –3' (red) available on the CD-ROM); scissors; adhesive; paper; pencils; sorting rings; labels.

ICT links: 1 Assessment - 1 (red) on the CD-ROM. **2** 'Assessment - 2' (red) on the CD-ROM. **4** 'Parts of a plant' interactive from the CD-ROM; interactive whiteboard or computer.

Plenary: Two different plants, or pictures of them,

ASSESSMENT ACTIVITY 1

Show the children the plant and ask them whether they can name any of the parts. Write their suggestions on Post-it notes and invite the child who made each suggestion to put the label on the correct part. Group the children according to ability for this activity, then set them off on the following Assessment activities.

ASSESSMENT ACTIVITY 2 ⊚

Give the children a copy of photocopiable page 82 and ask them to cut out the labels and stick them to the correct parts of the flower picture.

ICT LINK ⊚

Use the 'Parts of a plant' interactive as a means of discussing the answers to Assessment 1.

Display 'Assessment – 2 (red) on an interactive whiteboard and use the drawing tool to circle the differences between the two plants.

ASSESSMENT ACTIVITY 3
Give the children a copy of photocopiable page 83. Ask them to ring the things that are different between the plants.

ASSESSMENT ACTIVITY 4
Give the children a copy each of photocopiable page 84 and ask the children to cut out the pictures and sort them into the following labelled sets:
● plants that have flowers and plants that do not; plants that have leaves and plants that do not.
For differentiation, give the children 'Parts of a plant 3' (green) or (blue) from the CD-ROM, depending on their level of skills, and encourage them to sort the pictures into the following sets:
● (a): plants that have flowers and plants that do not.
● (c): plants that have flowers and plants that do not; plants that have leaves and plants that do not; plants that have stems and plants that do not.
 Challenge the children to think of their own criteria for sorting the plants.

PLENARY
Talk about the differences that the children have noticed between the two plants from Assessment activity 3. Display pictures of two plants or show the children two plants and talk about how they are different. Refer to the shape, colour, size and features to compare each plant.

ASSESSMENT OUTCOMES
● All children *must* know some features of plants.
● Most of the children *should* recognise similarities and differences between different plants.
● Some *could* sort plants into sets by observable criteria.
● A small number *could even* think of their own criteria for grouping plants.

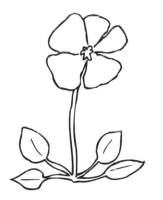  

PHOTOCOPIABLE

Counting animals' legs – 1

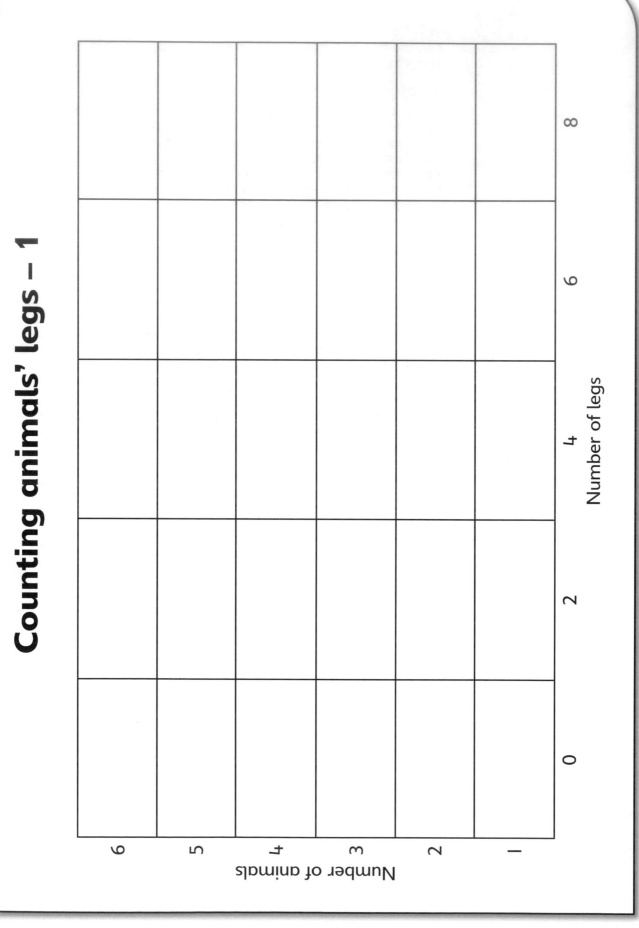

Number of animals

Number of legs

0   2   4   6   8

1   2   3   4   5   6

Counting animals' legs – 2

Illustration © Colin Shelbourn

Counting animals' legs – 3

Illustration © Colin Shelbourn

▶SCHOLASTIC

Ants, beetles and ladybirds – 1

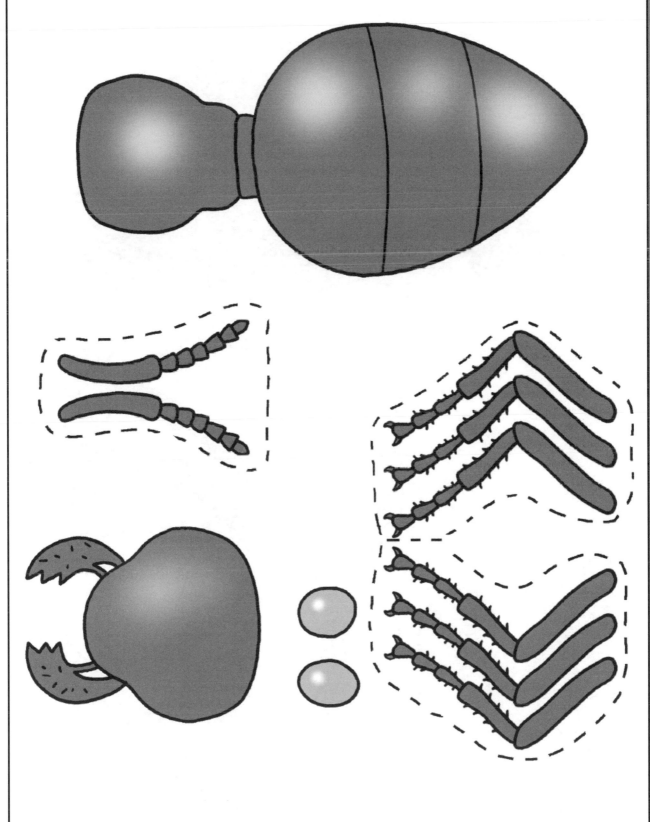

Illustration © Colin Shelbourn

Ants, beetles and ladybirds – 2

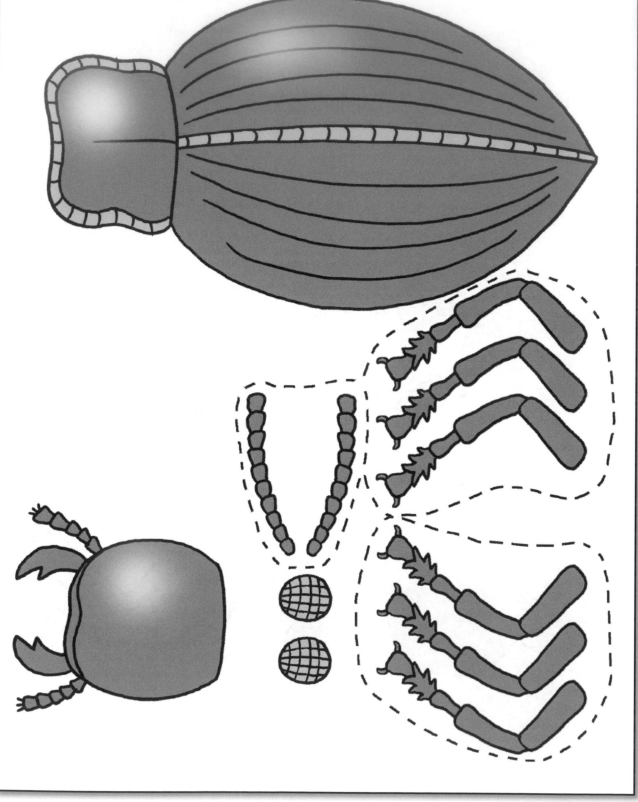

Illustration © Colin Shelbourn

◢SCHOLASTIC

Ants, beetles and ladybirds – 3

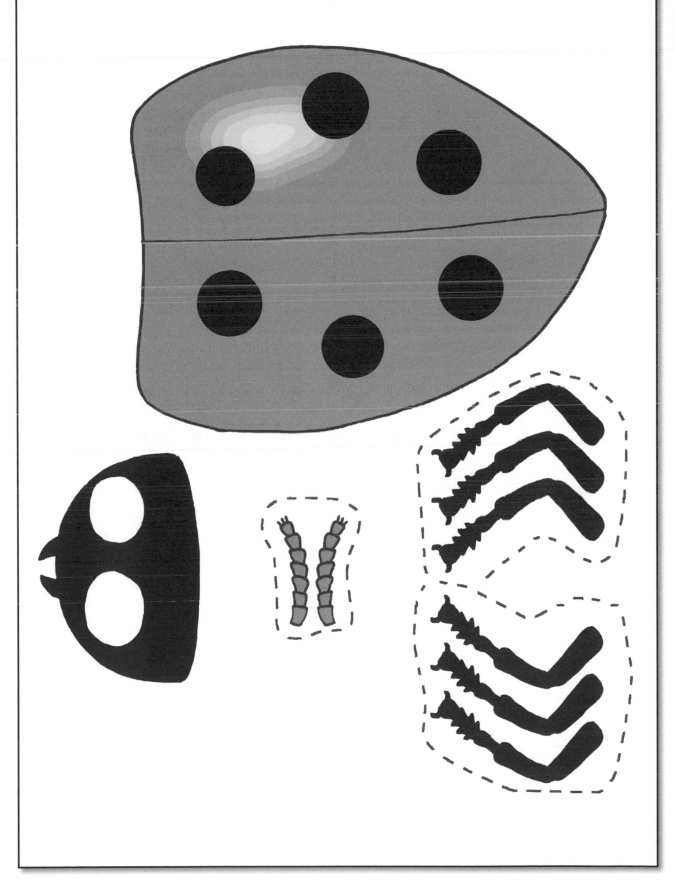

Incey Wincey Spider

■ Draw the spider's web by joining the dots correctly.
Start at the ▲.

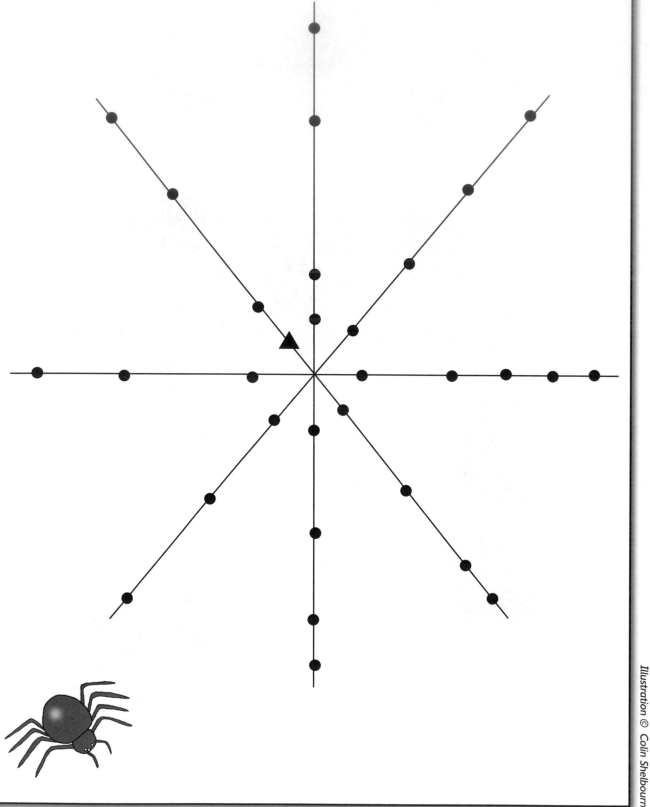

■SCHOLASTIC

Illustration © Colin Shelbourn

See my sunflowers grow

Date: _____

The day I was planted

Date: _____

When I started to grow

Date: _____

Growing up

Date: _____

Fully grown

Assessment – 1

■ Match the words to the parts of the plant.

leaf	petals	stem

Illustration © Baz Rowell/Beehive Illustration

■SCHOLASTIC

Assessment – 2

◼ How are these pictures different?
Draw (rings) around the things that are different.

PHOTOCOPIABLE

Assessment – 3

■SCHOLASTIC

UNIT 3 The environment

Lesson	Objectives	Main activity	Group activities	Plenary	Outcomes
Lesson 1 The school environment	• To learn that there are many features of the school environment, used for different purposes by different people, animals and plants. • To learn that we have to live together with other people, plants and animals.	Talk about the ways that the school grounds are used.	Talk about how other people, plants and animals use the school grounds. Make a list of rules for using the school grounds. Make pictures of a favourite activity in the school grounds.	Look at the rules in the code of behaviour together.	• Can recognise familiar places in their environment. • Begin to think about the needs of other people, other living things and the environment.
Lesson 2 Animals in our local environment	• To learn that many different kinds of animals live in, or visit, our school environment.	Talk about the places where you are likely to find animals in the school grounds.	Carry out an animal safari. Look closely at the animals found. Paint a picture of a chosen creature. Make a display of 'underground'.	Talk about the need to care for living things in the environment.	• Show concern for other living things. • Begin to consider the feelings of other living things. • Know that animals should be left in their natural environment.
Lesson 3 All kinds of plants	• To learn that there are many different kinds of green plants.	Find and list all the kinds of plants in the school grounds. Draw some.		Record the positions of the plants on a map of the area.	• Can identify a range of green plants • Are learning to care for plants in their natural environment. • Have begun to observe similarities and differences between plants. • Can record their findings in pictorial form.
Lesson 4 What makes plants grow?	• To learn that plants need to be looked after. • To learn that plants need water to survive.	Plant and care for indoor plants.		Read *The Tiny Seed* by Eric Carle.	• Understand the need to water plants regularly. • Can care independently for a number of different plants.
Lesson 5 Getting wet	• To learn that when it rains, we can prevent ourselves from getting wet. • To learn that some materials are waterproof and so help to keep us dry, but others are not.	Look at puddles and demonstrate how certain clothes and objects keep us dry when it rains.	Investigate waterproof materials. Test containers for leakage. Make wax-resist pictures. Make a display of clothes for rainy days.	Talk about the items in the display and how they are used to help keep us dry.	• Know that when it rains, we can get wet unless we protect ourselves from the rain. • Know that rain is water that falls from the sky. • Can recognise which materials are waterproof and begin to say why.
Lesson 6 Weather watch!	• To talk about the weather in terms of whether it is sunny, raining, windy, cold or snowing.	Sing and talk about the different kinds of weather. Record the weather on a chart.		Count up the number of days on which it rained, was windy and so on. Total these on the chart.	• Know that there are many kinds of weather. • Begin to describe the features of different kinds of weather. • Begin to keep a simple record of the different kinds of weather.
Lesson 7 Clothes for all weather	• To consider the different clothes that we wear at different times of the year.	Match clothing items to different kinds of weather.	Sort clothes according to weather. Add to a song about the weather. Race to select clothes for weather types. Make pictures of clothing for certain weather types.	Perform the song about the weather with the additional verses. Discuss the choice of collage materials.	• Know that we wear different kinds of clothing for different types of weather. • Know that the clothing we wear in different weather is made from different materials. • Know that people in different countries wear clothes that go with the main type of weather.

Lesson	Objectives	Main activity	Group activities	Plenary	Outcomes
Lesson 8 Why is it worn?	• To learn that hats are worn for a variety of reasons, including protection from the weather.	Look at a variety of hats and talk about why they are worn.	Sort hats according to why they are worn. Note and explain the features of hats. Dress up in hats for role-play. Make a hat for a favourite toy. Make a picture book of people wearing hats.	Talk about all the people who wear hats and say why they do so.	• Know that there are a variety of hats that are worn for different purposes. • Recognise hats that are worn to protect us from the weather. • Can identify similarities and differences between hats.
Lesson 9: A windy day	• To consider the effects of the wind on our lives.	Read a windy day story. Use paper objects outdoors to explore the effects of the wind. Make a windy day frieze. Peg out washed dolls' clothes. Make windmills.		Look at windmills and talk about how they move in the wind.	• Know that the wind makes things move. • Know that the wind helps to dry washing. • Know that it is harder to run against the wind than with it.
Lesson 10 Sounds in the environment	• To know that a variety of sounds can be heard in the local environment.	Collect sounds from the local environment. Explore how and why they and other sounds are made. Draw pictures of things that use sound as a message.		Explore different sounds made with a drum.	• Know that a range of sounds can be heard in the local environment. • Develop a range of vocabulary to describe the sounds they hear. • Know that we use our ears to hear.
Lesson 11 Tidy and clean	• To learn to keep their immediate surroundings tidy.	Learn to keep the classroom tidy. Discuss litter and recycling.		Talk about rubbish in the environment and safe behaviour.	• Know how to tidy up in the classroom. • Know how to keep the parts of the school that they use clean. • Know that they should never collect other people's rubbish.

Assessment	Objectives	Main activity	Activities 2 and 3	Activities 4 and 5	Outcomes
Lesson 12	• To assess the children's knowledge about the places where animals and plants live. • To assess the children's ability to recognise different kinds of weather and clothes appropriate for them.	Say where various animals live.	Match animal pictures to the correct habitats. Match pictures of clothing to the correct weather types.	Dress a teddy for a windy, wet or sunny day. Make a list of rules about caring for the environment.	• Know that there are a variety of different weather types. • Know that different kinds of clothing are worn for different types of weather. • Know that different animals live in different habitats. • Know that some animals are found in more than one habitat.

CONTEXT Caring for our school grounds

The next four lessons are set within a topic on caring for our school grounds. Children's natural curiosity should be encouraged; however, it needs to be kept within some restrictions when they are dealing with living things. All four lessons emphasise this principle.

Lesson 1 ▪ The school environment

Objectives
● To learn that there are many features of the school environment , used for different purposes by different people, animals and plants.
● To learn that we have to live together with other people, plants and animals.

Vocabulary
environment, live, co-operate, care, keep safe

RESOURCES
Main activity: Enlarged digital photographs of different places in the school and its environment, such as the playground, field, hall, courtyard, car park and classroom; computer and interactive whiteboard (optional).
Group activities: 1 Close-up photographs of specific features in and around the school, such as a hedgerow, tree, bush, pond, flowerbed and flowerpot; paper; pencils; computer and interactive whiteboard (optional). **2** Large sheet of paper; marker pen. **3** Paper; paints; coloured pencils or crayons.

PREPARATION
Take photographs of a number of places in the school and its environment, if possible using a digital camera so that you can zoom in and out on a computer linked to an interactive whiteboard to emphasise specific features of an area.

STARTER
On an Interactive Whiteboard if you have one, show the children each photograph, in turn, of the general areas in and around the school. Talk about the things that the children do in these areas: eat dinner, play football, plant flowers, play with friends, sit and talk, and so on.

MAIN ACTIVITY
Show the area photographs again. Ask the children whether they think other people use these areas as well. Can they think of anything else that might live in or use these areas? Talk about the plants that can be seen in each picture, and ask the children what kinds of animal they think may be around somewhere. Emphasise that we are not the only people or the only animals that use these places, and that we have to think of others' needs as well as our own.

Differentiation

Support
To support children, concentrate on either the plants or the animals in each habitat and spread the activities over a number of days.

Extension
Extend the activity by giving children appropriately levelled reference books or a CD-ROM to research the habitats of some of the animals and plants they thought of in Group activity 1.

GROUP ACTIVITIES

1 Working with groups of six children, show them the close-up photographs (using a computer linked to an interactive whiteboard if possible) and talk about the other people, animals and plants that may also use this particular area of the school environment. Ask the children to draw pictures of all the animals and plants they can think of that might be found in the school environment.

2 Ask an adult helper to work with the children, making a list of rules for looking after the environment. The list should be written in positive terms. For example, instead of saying 'Do not pull the leaves off the trees,' say 'Leave the leaves to live on the trees.'

3 Ask the children to paint and draw pictures of their favourite activity in the school grounds. These pictures can be displayed with the rules drawn up in Group activity 2 and the pictures drawn in Group activity 1.

ASSESSMENT

There are several things to note from this activity, including the children's understanding of where creatures live in the environment and the need to take care of it. These assessments can be followed up informally every time the children go into the environment to play and work. At the simplest level, it is important for the children to recognise that plants and animals are different and that they share a habitat.

PLENARY

Read out the rules that have been listed in Group activity 2. Display them on the display board with the children's pictures from Group activity 1.

OUTCOMES

- All children *must* be able to recognise familiar places in their environment.
- Most of the children *should* be able to identify some living things that live in the local environment and begin to think about the needs of other people, other living things and the environment.
- Some *could* identify a range of plants and animals.
- A small number *could even* recognise that different living things are found in different places.

LINKS

ECM 2: Staying safe and **ECM 4:** making a positive contribution to the community.

Across the curriculum: this lesson links well with personal and social development, since the children are asked to consider and show care for other people, for other living things and for the environment. Early geography skills are developed when the location of each of the habitats is discussed.

Lesson 2 ▪ Animals in our local environment

Objective
- To learn that many different kinds of animals live in, or visit, our school environment.

RESOURCES

Main activity: Copy of the poem 'Hurt No Living Thing' by Christina Rossetti; books, posters and CD-ROMs with photographs of the animals you are likely to find.

Group activities: 1 and 2 Cardboard boxes; polythene sheeting; logs; grass cuttings; dead leaves; orange segments; sugar; paper; pencils; magnispectors. **3** Paper; paints. **4** Sponge; brown paint; green tissue paper; scissors; tights; newspaper.

ICT link: Internet access or CD-ROMs containing pictures of different animals.

PREPARATION

Carry out a survey of the school grounds to make sure that the children will be able to find many different kinds of animal. Look around the bases of trees, under hedges and leaf piles. A few days before the lesson, place logs, polythene sheeting, grass cuttings and leaf piles in a number of places in the school grounds. Leave a sugar trail and orange segments to attract ants; damp and dry wood to attract woodlice; and wet cardboard boxes to attract centipedes, slugs and snails. Make sure that you do not disturb any nesting birds. Organise an additional adult to accompany you. We recommend that you follow your school's policy for outdoor trips.

STARTER

Read out the poem 'Hurt No Living Thing'. Spend a few minutes talking about all the animals in the world, and how we need to treat them properly. Explain that the children are going to go outside to look for different kinds of animals that live and visit our school grounds.

MAIN ACTIVITY

Talk about the kinds of places in the local environment where you might find animals. Show the children photographs of suitable animals from the CD-ROMs, books and other sources; name the animals and briefly talk about their size, shape and colour. Direct the children's thinking towards the places where you have left items to attract the animals you want to find. Also talk about shrubs and bushes, where (depending on the time of the year) you might find caterpillars, butterflies, flies, greenflies and/or spiders. The school field will host a number of birds, and the trees surrounding the grounds (if you have them) may attract squirrels. Under the soil surface is the best place to find worms and centipedes.

Explain the rules about outdoor visits to the children, and make sure they know what to do when they see an animal: look, not touch; listen, not shout; tell an adult what they have found.

GROUP ACTIVITIES

1 Working with groups of six children, go into the environment to look at the different habitats. (An adult helper will be useful.) Explain that you have left certain items to attract the animals and that these are all environmentally friendly: they will not damage the places where the animals live (their 'habitats'). Make a list of all the animals that the children see. If possible, collect one animal of each type in a magnispector to take back into the classroom.

2 As the group returns, give each child in turn a magnispector containing a small animal. Let them examine the animals, under close adult supervision; then ask them to talk (to you and each other) about the animal. What do they notice about the colour, size, number of legs, how quickly it moves and so on? Pass the containers around carefully, so that the children can notice all of the things mentioned and possibly think of some more. Encourage the children to compare their specimens with the photographs used in the Main activity. *Do they look the same?* At the end of each session, take the animals back and return them carefully to the place where they were found. Emphasise that you are doing this because we must look after living things and the places where they live.

Differentiation
Support
Support children by talking about the names of the animals. Focus on their colour and size, repeating the objectives from Unit 2, Lessons 7 and 8.
Extension
Give the group an opportunity to make close observational drawings of the creatures they bring back to the classroom. Use these to discuss the animals' features and habitats in more detail (as in Unit 2, Lessons 7 and 8). Ask the children whether the same animals were seen in a number of places, and whether these places had things in common. Were the animals found alone or in groups?

3 Ask the children to choose one of the animals they have seen and paint a picture of it for a big display.

4 Make an 'underground' section for your display by sponge-painting in a variety of brown tones for mud and cutting out green triangle spears from tissue paper for the grass above it. Make worms and centipedes by stuffing tights with scrunched-up balls of newspaper and painting them with brown lines to show the segments, adding legs as appropriate.

ICT LINK
Explore the internet or appropriate CD-ROMs for detailed pictures of the creatures the children have found.

ASSESSMENT
Listen as the children talk about the different animals they see. Make a mental note of the children's knowledge before the lesson and again at the end, so that you can assess new learning and progress. Note those children who are able to match the animal being observed to a picture in a book, on a poster or in a CD-ROM. Keep the children's drawings as evidence of their observational skills, and jot down briefly how they approached the task of observing and drawing the animals.

PLENARY
Read the Christina Rossetti poem again, and talk about how the children cared for the animals they collected and observed. Ask one child (who you are sure will be able) to talk about how the animals were returned to the places where they were found, and the care that was taken to keep them safe.

OUTCOMES
● All children *must* be able to show concern for other living things and to learn that animals should be left in their natural environment.
● Most of the children *should* be able to identify some living things that live in the local environment and begin to consider their feelings and needs.
● Some *could* identify a range of plants and animals.
● A small number *could even* recognise that different living things are found in different places.

LINKS
ECM 4: Making a positive contribution to the community.
Between units: Unit 2, Lessons 7 and 8 on observing insects and spiders.
Across the curriculum: this lesson links to personal and social development by raising the children's awareness of environmental issues.

Lesson 3 ▪ All kinds of plants

Objective
● To learn that there are many different kinds of green plants.

RESOURCES
Paper; pencils; scissors; wax crayons; large map of the local area or school grounds; adhesive; local environment (which could be the school grounds or local garden centre) suitable for exploring a wide range and considerable number of green plants.

Find a suitable place and make a list of all the green plants you can see. Make sure that it will be safe to look in this place. Check that none of your children has an allergy, especially hay fever or asthma. Organise additional adult help with the walk. Follow your school's policy for outdoor visits, and any Local Authority policies on which plants to avoid.

Differentiation
Support
Put children who need support with an adult helper who can check whether they are able to identify the range of plants in the local environment. If necessary, the helper should tell the children the names of four flowers, then encourage them to draw these and write their names for future reference.
Extension
Talk to children about the different species of flowers and trees. On returning to the classroom, ask them to make a chart showing the different kinds of flowers, trees and plants they have found.

MAIN ACTIVITY

Explain to the children that they are going out to look for all the plants they can find. Talk about the places where plants might be found: gardens, shops, parks, the school field, alongside footpaths and so on. Talk briefly about what the children will see. (Depending on the time of year, they may see leaves and blossom on the trees; there may be daisies and dandelions In the ground.) Explain that they will have to look very closely, and that there may be an opportunity to find out what some of the plants feel like. They should, however, ask first to make sure that touching the plant is safe both for them and for the plant. Emphasise that it is never safe to taste a wild plant, and that this is forbidden.

Take the children out and make a note of all the plants you find. Include grasses, trees, hedgerows, mosses, flowers, vegetables, shrubs, fruits and their cases, seeds, pot plants and wild flowers. You may need to get down on your hands and knees to look in the grass for some mosses. Other plants can be found around and under hedgerows. Ask the children to draw pictures of some of the plants they see. Cut these out if you have time. The children can make wax crayon rubbings of the different tree trunks, and compare the patterns at a later date.

ASSESSMENT

Listen to the children's conversations during the Main activity and use focused questions to assess their knowledge and understanding of plants. Use the children's recordings to gain further assessment information. Note those children who can recognise a plant – some may not be able to at the start of the lesson.

PLENARY

Record the children's findings on a large map of the local area, showing where they found the different plants. Allow the children to stick their pictures to the right places on the map.Talk about the colour, size and texture of some of the plants the children have found.

OUTCOMES

- All children **must** learn to care for plants in their natural environment.
- Most of the children **should** be able to observe similarities and differences between different plants.
- Some **could** record their findings in pictorial form.
- A small number **could even** identify and recognise a range of green plants and know that different plants are found in different places.

Lesson 4 ▸ What makes plants grow?

Objectives
- To learn that plants need to be looked after.
- To learn that plants need water to survive.

RESOURCES ◉

Bulb fibre; seed compost; bulbs (one for each child); large plastic tub (such as a two-litre ice cream tub); 'Bulb' diagram available on CD-ROM; collection of indoor and outdoor plants; packet of birdseed, water, black sugar paper; dark place; sand tray; paper; pencils; *The Tiny Seed* by Eric Carle (Puffin). Gather a range of plants to keep in the classroom, or identify some that need regular watering outside. These could be the sunflowers planted previously, other flowers and shrubs in your garden area, or plants in window-boxes and hanging baskets.

MAIN ACTIVITY

Organise a number of Group activities with adult help:
1 Show the children the indoor plants in your collection, find a place for them to live and organise a rota for watering them on a regular basis (this

Differentiation 🔘

Support
Repeat Group activity 3 with children a few weeks later to reinforce the learning.
Extension
Challenge children to talk about whether compost is needed for the bulbs to grow. Display the 'Bulb' diagram from the CD-ROM on the whiteboard to show children how to plant one bulb in a special container (see diagram) that allows the roots to reach water, and compare the growth of this bulb with the others. Allow the children to plant some bulbs outside and record when they start to grow. Talk about why the bulbs grow much faster inside than outside (because there is more light and warmth), and relate the discussion to the conditions of growth (plants need light, warmth and water to grow).

will depend on the kinds of plants you have). Show the children the outdoor plants you have, and explain that these will need watering when there has been no rain for a number of days.

2 Together, plant the birdseed in a tray on a bed of seed compost. Water the seeds and put them on a windowsill to germinate. Check the compost daily to make sure that it does not dry out; water it appropriately.

3 Ask groups of six children to mix the bulb fibre with water until it feels damp. Allow every child to feel the damp mixture. The children should plant the bulbs in a large plastic tub (October is the best time for this) and cover them with black sugar paper before placing the tub in a dark place. They should check the bulb fibre every week and make sure that it is still damp. Ask an adult helper to work with each group when the planting is finished, encouraging them to record in pictures or words what they did.

4 Allow the children to explore the texture of seed compost and bulb fibre in the sand tray. Check first that the fibre is safe: free from small creatures and sharp pieces.

ASSESSMENT
Note those children who remember to water the plants and bulbs.

PLENARY
Read *The Tiny Seed* by Eric Carle

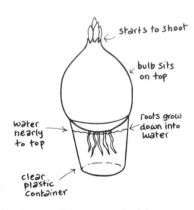

OUTCOMES
● All children *must* be able to learn to care for plants in their immediate environment.
● Most of the children *should* be able to understand the need to water plants regularly.
● Some *could* care independently for a number of different plants.
● A small number *could even* describe the basic conditions needed for plants to live.

CONTEXT

The weather

The next five lessons give the children the opportunity to consider the impact that the weather has on their lives, and the need to protect themselves from elements such as sunlight, rain, cold and wind. The lessons focus on how appropriate clothing changes with the seasons in order to protect us from the weather.

Lesson 5 ◗ Getting wet

RESOURCES

Main activity: Wellington boots; raincoat; umbrella; large sheet of plastic; empty bowl; watering can; water; metal tray.
Group activities: 1 Range of materials (some waterproof, some not); teddy bear; adhesive tape; adhesive sticks; scissors. **2** Water tray; range of containers (some waterproof, some not). **3** Wax crayons; paper; colourwash (thinly mixed paint). **4** Old raincoat; rain hat; cagoule; umbrella and pair of Wellington boots; books about rainy weather.
ICT link: Digital microscope; range of materials (see Group activity 1).

PREPARATION

Mix several pots of colourwash in a range of colours. You may choose to do this activity on a rainy day, when the children are able to go outside and splash in puddles; or following a dance lesson, when the children pretend to splash, stamp and jump in and out of puddles. Cover the floor with plastic sheeting.

STARTER

Show the children the Wellington boots and ask them when they would wear these. Invite one of the children to say why the boots are worn on rainy days. Next, show the children the raincoat. Pass it around, so that they can feel the material from which it is made. Ask them to describe the material, encouraging them to use words such as 'waterproof'.

MAIN ACTIVITY

Gather the children around you in a circle. Place the metal tray in the centre of the circle on the plastic sheeting. Sprinkle water from the watering can, held at a height so that when the water hits the metal tray it makes a pitter-patter sound. Talk about the sound the water makes and compare it to rain. Point out how a puddle forms on the tray. Empty the tray into a bowl. Ask the children whether they can think of a way to stop the tray from getting wet. After you have listened to their suggestions, invite a child to stand on the tray, and pretend to pour water over his or her head. When the squeals have died down, ask the children how you can keep the volunteer (victim) dry. Put the umbrella up at this point, and pour water from the watering can over the umbrella so that it runs down and onto the plastic sheeting. (Don't pour too much water!) Explain that the umbrella is made from a special material that stops the water going through it and prevents people getting wet. The material is 'waterproof'.

GROUP ACTIVITIES

1 Work with groups of four children to investigate a range of waterproof and non-waterproof materials and sort them into two sets. Use the materials to make a suitable raincoat for a teddy bear.
2 Allow a group of children to work unaided with a water tray, using a range

Differentiation

Support

Talk to children who need support as they play in the water about the containers that leak and the ones that do not. Once they have understood this basic idea, lead them to the concept of waterproof and non-waterproof materials. Set up a challenge for them to move the water from one tray to another without getting wet. Ask them if they chose a container made from waterproof materials.

Extension

Look at the shapes of umbrellas and rain hats and talk about their design. Point out how they spread out over the top of a person to take the water away from the body.

of containers: some that are waterproof, some that are not. Challenge the children to find the containers that leak or do not hold water.

3 Ask an adult helper to work with groups of four children, drawing pictures with wax crayons. As the children finish, the helper should help them to paint over the pictures with a thin colourwash and talk about how the wax comes through because it resists the water. He or she should explain that wax is waterproof: it resists water and doesn't get wet.

4 Together, make a display of clothing that is worn on rainy days.

ICT LINK

Use a digital microscope to examine each material to see whether the children can see small holes and gaps between the fibres. Shine a bright light through each material to see whether it leaves a dark or light shadow.

ASSESSMENT

Note which children are able to sort the materials into 'waterproof' and 'non-waterproof' and which can make a waterproof coat for a teddy bear, choosing from a range of materials. Note which children are able to select materials that are waterproof, thus showing an understanding of this property.

PLENARY

Talk about the display you have made of clothing that is worn on wet days. Emphasise that these items are made from waterproof materials, and that we wear them to keep ourselves warm and dry. Invite the children to bring items into school to add to the display.

OUTCOMES

● All children *must* be able to know that rain is water that falls from the sky and that when it rains, we can get wet unless we protect ourselves from the rain.
● Most of the children *should* be able to ask questions about why things happen.
● Some *could* observe which materials are waterproof by whether they let through water.
● A small number *could even* recognise which materials are waterproof and begin to say why.

LINKS

ECM 1: Keeping healthy.
Between units: this lesson links with Unit 4, Lesson 4 on 'bubbles'.

Lesson 6 ▫ Weather watch!

Objectives

● To talk about the weather in terms of whether it is sunny, raining, windy, cold or snowing.

RESOURCES ◉

Pictures of different kinds of weather; labels with the names of types of weather; chart on which to glue pictures (see illustration); 'The Weather Song' from *Spring Tinderbox* (A&C Black). You may wish to use children's pictures from an earlier lesson, or those from photocopiable page 104 (also 'Weather watch!' (red) available on CD-ROM). Interactive whiteboard or computer; graphing tool on the CD-ROM.

MAIN ACTIVITY

Sing 'The Weather Song', or a similar song. Talk to the children about the weather you have had recently. Encourage them to talk about whether the weather is sunny, frosty, foggy, rainy/wet, snowy, windy or cloudy. Describe the features of each type of weather – for example, on foggy days it is

Differentiation

Support
Ask children to draw a picture of their favourite type of weather, giving reasons for their choice. An adult helper can record their reasons for them.

Extension
Talk to children about shadows, and how these are clearer on sunny days. Challenge them to find shadows of objects and themselves when they go out to play. Analyse the weather statistics with this group of children at the end of the month, and transfer the information to a block graph using the graphing tool on the CD-ROM.

difficult to see, it is wet and cold; on rainy days we need to wear special clothes or carry umbrellas to help us keep dry.

Every day, talk about the kind of weather we are having and stick a suitable picture and label onto the space on the chart. Depending on your group and the time of year, you may wish to keep a weekly or monthly chart to discuss at the end of each week or month. You may also wish to record the weather two or three times during the day, if it is changeable enough to make this worthwhile. This in itself is an important learning outcome, as the children need to realise that the weather can change quickly.

ICT LINK

If you record this information on a computer linked to an interactive whiteboard, you can display and add to the chart each day.

Use the graphing tool on the CD-ROM to convert the data collected into a bar or pie chart.

ASSESSMENT

After a few weeks (depending on the children's ability), give each child a blank chart and ask them to record the different kinds of weather throughout the next week. They should work individually. Keep the records as evidence of the children's attainment.

	morning	afternoon
Monday	sunny	cloudy
Tuesday	cloudy	rainy
Wednesday	snowy	foggy
Thursday	cloudy	overcast
Friday	sunny	sunny

PLENARY

At the end of each week or month, count the number of sunny days, foggy days, rainy days and so on. Write each total at the end of the row or column for that kind of weather.

OUTCOMES

- All children **must** know that there are many kinds of weather.
- Most of the children **should** be able to begin to describe the features of different kinds of weather.
- Some **could** keep a simple record of the different kinds of weather.
- A small number **could even** think of their own ideas for collecting and recording weather information.

Lesson 7 ▪ Clothes for all weather

Objective

- To consider the different clothes that we wear at different times of the year.

RESOURCES

Main activity: Range of clothes for all types of weather; 'The Weather Song' from *Spring Tinderbox* (A&C Black).

Group activities: 1 Paper; pencils. **2** Dressing-up clothes for all types of weather. **3** Large sheets of paper; crayons; range of collage materials. You will need picture reference books for the extension activity.

Vocabulary
hot, sunny, wet, frosty, snowy, hail, cold, foggy, damp

STARTER
Sing 'The Weather Song' and talk about sunny, windy and rainy weather. Remind the children of other kinds of weather discussed in Lesson 6.

MAIN ACTIVITY
Invite the children to choose one of the types of weather and to find items of clothing that we are likely to wear in this weather. Talk about the type of material, its thickness, its texture and so on. Repeat the activity for other types of weather.

GROUP ACTIVITIES
1 Work with a group of six children, sorting the clothes into sets to wear on rainy, snowy, frosty, warm or sunny days. Ask the children to say which items of clothing can be worn for more than one type of weather (for example, a woolly hat for snowy and frosty weather). They can record their ideas by drawing pictures of the items, with the type of weather as a title.
2 Ask an adult helper to work with a group of children, making up additional verses for 'The Weather Song'. These could include verses on frost, snow and hail. The children could add body percussion to each verse.
3 Organise a dressing-up race for six children. Give each child a type of weather. When you say 'Go', the children have to get dressed appropriately. The first child to be dressed in the correct set of clothes is the winner.
4 Draw around three children. Together, use these to make large collage pictures of children wearing suitable clothes for wet, cold and sunny weather.

ASSESSMENT
Watch the children during Group activity 3, and note those who are able to choose the correct clothing for their designated weather type.

PLENARY
Ask the groups composing additional verses to the song to perform their compositions dressed in appropriate clothing. Talk about the clothes that the children in the large pictures are dressed in. Ask the children what kind of collage materials they chose for each item (for example, wool for a jumper, plastic for a raincoat).

OUTCOMES
● All children *must* know that we wear different kinds of clothing for different types of weather.
● Most of the children *should* be able to decide whether to wear a coat when playing outside.
● Some *could* know that the clothing we wear in different weather is made from different materials.
● A small number *could even* know that people in different countries wear clothes that go with the main type of weather (for example, to keep cool).

LINKS
ECM 2: Keeping healthy.
Across the curriculum: many stories and poems about the weather can be used as texts for literacy lessons and as starting points for writing and drama. There are also opportunities to talk about different kinds of cultural dress in order to develop the children's awareness and acceptance of other cultures.

Differentiation
Support
For support, take children outside every day and talk about whether they need a coat, a raincoat or a sunhat. Discuss why this is, and relate it to the weather on that day.
Extension
Challenge children to use books to research the clothes worn in other countries, for example a very hot or a very cold country. Talk about the differences and similarities between the clothes for these two extremes of weather.

Lesson 8 ▪ Why is it worn?

Objective
● To learn that hats are worn for a variety of reasons, including protection from the weather.

Vocabulary
hat, helmet, weather, protect, hard, waterproof

RESOURCES
Main activity: Range of (real and/or toy) hats such as a sun hat, police officer's helmet, crash helmet, builder's helmet, horse-rider's hat, bobble hat and rain hat; 'My Hat It Has Three Corners' from *Okki-Tokki-Unga* edited by Beatrice Harrop (A&C Black).
Group activities: 1 Photocopiable page 105 (also 'Why is it worn?' (red) available on CD-ROM); scissors; sorting rings; paper; glue. **2** Paper; pen. **3** Several clothing items and hats for the children to dress up in; digital camera. **4** Materials for making small toy hats (such as paper, plastic sheeting, tin foil, card and empty yoghurt pots). **5** Magazines with pictures of people who wear hats; scissors; adhesive; paper; pencils.
ICT link: Computer; printer; photographs of people wearing different hats; word processing-program.

PREPARATION
Ask the children's parents or carers whether they have any hats at home that you could borrow for this lesson. Make copies of photocopiable page 105 on to card and cut out the pictures.

STARTER
Sing the song 'My Hat It Has Three Corners'. Show the children one of the hats in your collection and make up other verses about this hat: it has no corners, it has a feather, it has a brim and so on.

MAIN ACTIVITY
Pass a toy police helmet (if you have one) around the group and ask the children each to say one thing about it. Prompt them to say whether it is hard or soft; big or small; square, round or flat. Can they tell you why this helmet is hard, tall and round? Explain that it is made to protect the police officer's head. Find all the other hats that are used to protect people's heads from injury, and put them to one side. Look at the other hats left in your collection. Ask the children to describe the features and properties of this group of hats. When they have finished, put these hats together and ask the children to say what they are all used for. If necessary, tell them that all the hats in this group are used to protect us from the weather. Explain that they are going to explore these hats during the Group activities.

GROUP ACTIVITIES
1 Work with a group of six children to sort the pictures of hats from a copy of photocopiable page 105 into sets, according to whether they are worn to protect us from the weather or from other things. Glue the pictures into the appropriate sets on paper as a simple record of the children's decisions.
2 Ask an adult helper to work with groups of four children at a time to explore the features of each type of hat. They should talk about specific features (the peak on a sun cap, the brim on a sombrero, the hardness of a crash helmet and so on), trying to explain them. Ask the helper to note down the children's ideas.
3 Put a variety of hats and dressing-up clothes in an area of the classroom and allow the children to dress up and act as various characters. Use a digital camera to record them.
4 Give the children a variety of materials and ask them to make a sun hat for their favourite doll or teddy, or a helmet for their Action Man.
5 Give the children magazines and ask them to cut out all the pictures of people who are wearing hats, stick them on to paper and add a sentence about each one before making the pages into a book.

ICT LINK

Instead of using magazine pictures in Group activity 5, insert pictures of photographs you have taken of people wearing different hats into a word-processing program. Add a sentence about each one before printing off and making a book.

ASSESSMENT

Use Group activity 1 to assess the children's understanding of why we wear certain hats. Question them about the materials from which each hat is made and the hat's suitability for its purpose.

PLENARY

Ask the group who cut pictures from magazines to talk about what they found and the types of hats the people were wearing. Reinforce the idea that we sometimes wear hats to protect us from the weather.

OUTCOMES

- All children *must* recognise hats that are worn to protect us from the weather.
- Most of the children *should* know that there are a variety of hats that are worn for different purposes, and identify similarities and differences between hats, according to their materials and features.
- Some *could* describe the features and materials in terms of their properties.
- A small number *could even* describe the similarities and differences between materials and use this information to sort the hats into groups.

LINKS

ECM 1: Staying safe and **EMC 2:** keeping healthy.
Between units: this lesson relates to work in Unit 4 on materials and their properties.
Across the curriculum: this lesson can be taught within a topic about 'People who help us', and can be related to work on any people who wear uniforms. It also provides a good context for the development of imaginative play.

Differentiation

Support
Give children 'Why is it worn?' (green) from the CD-ROM, which features a selection of more common hats which children will be familiar with, for them to sort into different sets as in Group activity 1.
Extension
Provide the children with 'Why is it worn? (blue) from the CD-ROM for the children to sort into sets. This includes a wider selection of hats, some of which the children may not recognise. Can they name all the hats shown?

Lesson 9 ▸ A windy day

Objective
- To consider the effects of the wind on our lives.

RESOURCES

A 'windy day' story, such as *A Windy Day* by Patrolman Pete (AA Publishing) or *Mrs Mopple's Washing Line* by Anita Hewett (Red Fox); strips of paper (one per child) 10cm wide and 1m long; fan (optional); sheets of A1 card; paper and art materials for making a frieze; set of doll's clothes, pegs, string; thin card or plastic sheeting; dowelling; pins; beads; scissors; adhesive; 'Windmill' diagram available on CD-ROM; kites; materials to make sailboats; 'Sailboat' diagram available on CD-ROM; water tray; interactive whiteboard.

MAIN ACTIVITY

If possible, take the children outside on a windy day. Read your chosen story to the children and talk about the effects of the wind.

Give each child a strip of paper. Ask the children to hold it out in one hand and see what the paper does. *Does it move or does it stay still?* Repeat the activity outside on a windy day, or use a fan to create a wind. Watch the shapes made by the paper. *Does the paper hang down or does it move about?* On returning to the classroom, talk about the movement of the paper and ask the children to make simple drawings of what happened.

Organise a number of Group activities with adult help:

Differentiation
Support
Support children by playing outside with kites on windy days (first make sure that there are no overhead cables). Encourage them to observe the effects of the wind on the kites' movement, and talk about the way the kites move.
Extension
Explore the push of the wind with the children. Display the 'Sailboat' diagram on the interactive whiteboard to show them how to make light sailboats to blow along in the water tray (see diagram).

1 Go outside on a windy day with sheets of A1 card and try to run against the wind.
2 Make a 'windy day frieze' in the classroom and add words to describe movement.
3 Wash a doll's clothes and peg them on a string 'washing line' outdoors.
4 Display the Windmill diagram from the CD-ROM on the interactive whiteboard to show children how to make windmills from thin card or plastic sheeting (see diagram). As the sails spin in the wind (or as the children blow them), talk about the way they move.

ASSESSMENT
Note those children who are able to talk about the effects of the wind as they contribute to the frieze. Note those who are unable to make suggestions; take them out on other windy days to observe effects such as leaves moving and hair blowing in their eyes.

PLENARY
Ask the group who made the windmills to talk about how these move when blown by the wind. Watch as they spin faster when someone blows harder. Leave them outside, stuck firmly in the ground, on a windy day and watch them as they spin.

OUTCOMES
● All children *must* know that it is more difficult to run against the wind than with it.
● Most of the children *should* be able to ask and answer questions about why the paper moves.
● Some *could* describe how the paper moves because of the force of the wind.
● A small number *could even* compare the movement of the paper's speed and direction with the strength and direction of the wind.

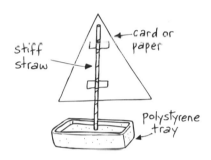

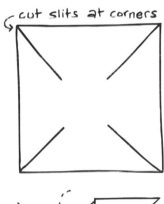

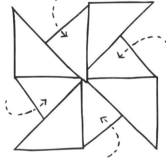

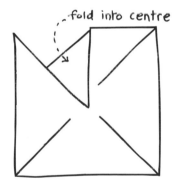

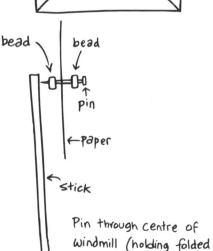

Lesson 10 ◾ Sounds in the environment

Objective
● To know that a variety of sounds can be heard in the local environment.

RESOURCES
Portable (battery-operated) cassette recorder or Dictaphone; paper, pencils; drum, objects for making sounds on a drum (see below); commercial audio tape or CD of everyday sounds (available from early learning centres).

MAIN ACTIVITY
Take the children out a few days before on a 'sound walk' and listen to the sounds all around. Make a recording of these using the portable tape recorder.

Remind the children of all the sounds they heard on the sound walk. Ask whether anyone knows which part of the body we use to hear with. (Our ears.) Play the tape from the walk, stopping it after each sound and asking the children what they think is making the sound. Talk about the types of sound the items make: a squeaking sound, a loud sound, a quiet, soft, whistling, grating sound and so on.

Organise a number of Group activities with adult help:

1 Work with an adult helper to draw pictures of things that make high, loud, quiet, whistling, whispering and/or squeaking sounds.

2 Explore the different sounds that can be produced on a drum, using a variety of objects such as a nailbrush, rice and erasers as well as a range of beaters.

3 Draw pictures of things that make a sound as a message, such as a doorbell, a telephone or an ambulance siren.

4 Small groups can play the 'recognising sounds' game (as above) with a commercially bought tape of sounds.

ICT LINK
Encourage the children to operate the tape recorder or CD player independently in order to develop their early ICT skills.

ASSESSMENT
Play the sound-walk tape to the children again, asking them to draw pictures of the things they can hear. To make this easier for some children, provide worksheets containing suitable pictures for them to colour and tell them which colour to use for each sound (so that you can keep track of their responses).

PLENARY
Ask the children exploring the drum to explain the range of sounds they can make. If you wish, find a suitable poem and use drum sounds to accompany it (depicting the sounds of rain, thunder and so on).

OUTCOMES
● All children *must* be able to notice sounds.
● Most of the children *should* know that we use our ears to hear and that a range of sounds can be heard in the local environment.
● Some *could* know that sound comes from a variety of sources, and can name what some of these are.
● A small number *could even* use a range of vocabulary to describe the sounds they can hear.

Differentiation
Support
Help children who need support to explore the sounds made by everyday objects such as a squeaky door, hammering wooden blocks and a doorbell. After they have listened to each sound, ask them to point to the object that makes the squeaking, ringing or banging sound. This will also help them to develop the vocabulary needed to describe a range of sounds heard in the environment.

Extension
Extend children's thinking by investigating how far away the sounds made by a range of everyday objects (such as a ticking clock, a dripping tap and a telephone) can be heard.

Lesson 11 ◨ Tidy and clean

RESOURCES
Digital camera; friendly cleaner; large sheets of paper; marker pen, paints; examples of objects that can be recycled.

MAIN ACTIVITY
Organise a particularly messy activity, such as cutting and pasting, and give the children very little time to tidy up! Take a photograph of the classroom at the end of the day, and another (with his or her permission) of the cleaner tidying up. Show the children the photograph and ask them whether they know where this photograph was taken. Do they know who cleaned the mess up? Show them the photograph of the cleaner.

Talk to the children about all the classroom activities they do that leave a mess. Make a list of these activities. Separate out the ones that involve leaving litter for others to clear up, such as spilling sand, water or paint. Ask the children how they could make the cleaner's job easier. What can they do to keep their classroom tidy? Together, make a list of rules for keeping the classroom tidy. Make the rules positive, and include directions on how to follow the rules. Include rules such as: 'Put all the rubbish in the bin'; 'Tidy your own place'; 'Hang your coat on your peg, don't leave it on the floor'. Ask the children to make 'Keep Our School Litter-Free' posters, and to design litter bins that would be fun to use. They can paint big pictures of these designs for display with the posters.

Make a collection of objects that can be recycled, and find out where the nearest recycling centre is. Many are adjacent to supermarkets. Write to parents and carers, asking them to point these out to the children on their next visit (perhaps taking newspapers, glass bottles or cans to be recycled).

After a busy day cutting and sticking, challenge the children to pick up all the litter. Explain that it is safe to do so because it is *their* rubbish and they know how it was made! Do a litter patrol when the children have finished, and count the bits of litter still left on the floor. Emphasise that the children should never pick up other people's litter: only adults should do this task, as the litter may be dangerous.

ASSESSMENT
This is a good opportunity to find out what types of litter the children are already aware of, including unsocial and unwelcome items. It is important that they know what to do if they find things that they think they should not touch because of health risks: tell an adult immediately.

PLENARY
Emphasise the idea that there are signs of people everywhere around us: some things that are nice and others that are not so nice. Reinforce the message that the children should never touch or pick up litter themselves, but that it is important that they (as individuals) use a litter bin or take their own litter home.

OUTCOMES
● All children *must* know how to tidy up in the classroom.
● Most of the children *should* be able to keep the parts of the school that they use clean.
● Some *could* know that they should never collect other people's rubbish.
● A small number *could even* sort their rubbish into recyclable and not recyclable bins.

Lesson 12 ▪ Assessment

Objectives
● To assess the children's knowledge about the places where animals and plants live.
● To assess the children's ability to recognise different kinds of weather and clothes appropriate for them.

RESOURCES ◉
Main assessment activity: Set of models or pictures of various animals, including some that live in water, on land and underground; blue, green and brown sheets of paper.
Assessment activities: 2 photocopiable page 106 (also 'Assessment – 1' (red) available on CD-ROM) and photocopiable page 107 (also 'Assessment – 2' (red) available on CD-ROM); scissors; adhesive sticks; **3** photocopiable page 108 (also 'Assessment – 3' (red) available on CD-ROM); pencils. **4** Teddy bear; sets of small clothes (for the bear) for wet, cold and sunny weather. **5** Paper, pencils.
ICT link: 'Animals' interactive on CD-ROM.

PREPARATION
Make enlarged copies of photocopiable pages 106 and 107. Make enough copies of photocopiable page 108 for one for each child.

STARTER
Show the children the models or pictures of animals in your collection. Ask them to identify and name each one.

MAIN ASSESSMENT ACTIVITY
Talk about the animals in your collection and ask the children where they live. *Do they live on land, in water or under the ground?* Ask the children, one at a time, to choose a model or picture of an animal and place it on a sheet of coloured paper to show where the animal lives for most of the time: green for on land, blue for in water or brown for underground. An adult helper will be useful to record the children's discussions during this activity as they make decisions about animals such as frogs, birds and worms. When you have set the others off with their activity, you may wish to extend the activity and work with the children sorting the animals into further groups, such as those who live in a hedgerow, in the desert, in the sea, in a pond or on a farm.

ASSESSMENT ACTIVITY 2
Ask the children to cut out the animal pictures on photocopiable page 106 and place them in the appropriate habitat on photocopiable page 107. Check their decisions, then stick the pictures in place. (If necessary, explain that the word 'habitat' means where an animal lives in the environment.)

ICT LINK ◉
Invite the children to play 'Animals' interactive on the CD-ROM. Children are shown a selection of animals which they must drag and drop into the correct habitat.

ASSESSMENT ACTIVITY 3
Ask the children to match each item of clothing to the correct weather picture on photocopiable page 108 by drawing lines.

ICT LINK ◉
Display 'Assessment – 3' from the CD-ROM on the interactive whiteboard. Use the line or drawing tool to match each item of clothing to the correct weather on screen.

ASSESSMENT ACTIVITY 4
Ask the children to select items from a range of clothing in order to dress the teddy bear for a windy, wet or sunny day.

ASSESSMENT ACTIVITY 5
Ask an adult helper to work with the children, making a list of rules for caring for the environment.

PLENARY
Talk about the dressed teddies, asking the children to say what kind of weather each one is dressed for. Ask: *How do you know?* Link their answers to the pictures on photocopiable page 99, which you may wish to complete with the children at the same time.

ASSESSMENT OUTCOMES
On completion of these Assessment activities, you should know which children have attained the following objectives linked to knowledge and understanding of the world:
● All children *must* know that there are a variety of different weather types.
● Most of the children *should* know that different kinds of clothing are worn for different types of weather.
● Some *could* know that different animals live in different habitats.
● A small number *could even* know that some animals are found in more than one habitat.

Weather watch!

■SCHOLASTIC

Why is it worn?

Illustration © Colin Shelbourn © Baz Rowell/Beehive Illustration

Assessment – 1

Illustration © Colin Shelbourn

◀SCHOLASTIC

Assessment – 2

Illustration © Colin Shelbourn

Assessment – 3

Illustration © Colin Shelbourn

■SCHOLASTIC

Lesson	Objectives	Main activity	Group activities	Plenary	Outcomes
Lesson 1 Exploring textures	• To develop the vocabulary, particularly of texture, associated with a range of objects made from a variety of materials.	Play 'texture dominoes' with objects.	Sort items with different textures. Make wax rubbings of wallpaper. Display textures of a given type. Role-play a hardware store.	Talk about the textures recorded by the wax rubbings.	• Can use pictures to record what they have done. • Can use simple language to describe texture. • Can use their sense of touch to explore items found in the home.
Lesson 2 What is it made of?	• To use the senses to explore, sort and identify the materials from which various objects are made.	Sort and match materials by appearance, texture and magnetic properties. Make texture collages. Role-play in the 'hardware store'. Make a metal-eating robot.		Make a wall of different textures for the children to explore.	• Know that there are many different materials. • Know that different materials have different textures and look different. • Can sort familiar materials by name.
Lesson 3 Recognising materials	• To recognise common materials and learn their names: wood, paper, fabric, metal.	Compare different kinds of paper. Make a display of paper items.	Make displays of fabrics, metal and wood. Play an 'Odd material out' game. Make paper decorations, fans and wrappers. Sort objects by material.	Add items to the displays according to the material from which they are made.	• Can recognise paper, fabric, metal and wood. • Can sort materials into named groups. • Can begin to describe the properties of wood, metal, fabric and paper.
Lesson 4 Blowing bubbles	• To learn that soap and water mixed together make bubbles.	Make bubble mixture and blow bubbles.	Make bubbles from different soapy materials. Make bubble sculptures. Draw bubbles. Make bubble paint patterns.	Look at the bubble patterns together and talk about what you can see.	• Know that soap mixes with water. • Know that mixing soap and water together makes bubbles. • Are able to co-operate, share and take turns.
Lesson 5 Oil and water	• To investigate what happens when we try to mix oil and water. • To learn that not all liquids mix with water.	Make oil pattern pictures. Explore how different types of oil behave in water.		Talk about the effects of oil on clothes and birds' feathers.	• Know that oil and water do not mix. • Know that oils can have different colours, and some oils are thicker than others. • Know that oil floats on water.
Lesson 6 Stir it up!	• To learn that the thicker a mixture is, the harder it is to stir. • To learn that the more water is added, the runnier a mixture becomes.	Explore how the thickness of a cornflour mixture affects how easy it is to stir and pour.	Order mixtures by how easy they are to stir. Make cornflour finger paintings. Stir and blend a range of liquids. Make dripping paint pictures.	Make a collection of liquids. Talk about what a liquid is.	• Know that a mixture can be thin (runny) or thick (stiff). • Can compare the thickness of two mixtures, and order mixtures by how thick or thin they are. • Recognise some of the physical properties of liquids.
Lesson 7 Sticking together	• To learn that sand, when mixed with the right amount of water, will stick together. • To learn that dry sand does not stick together. • To learn that damp or wet sand is made by mixing dry sand with water.	Make damp sand. Build sandcastles to explore the properties of damp sand.		Talk about the different sandcastles made by the children.	• Know that damp sand sticks together. • Know that you mix dry sand and water to make damp sand. • Know the similarities and differences between dry and damp sand. • Can describe what damp sand feels like.

Lesson	Objectives	Main activity	Group activities	Plenary	Outcomes
Lesson 8 Recipes	• To learn that the shape of a mixture can be changed by rolling.	Make dough for biscuits or pastry.	Make biscuits or pastry in groups. Flatten and roll out play dough. Role-play a baker's shop.	Enjoy the products and review the process.	• Know that squashing and rolling-out change the shape of dough. • Know that dry ingredients will mix together. • Know that dry ingredients will stick together when mixed with a liquid.
Lesson 9 Pizza base recipes	• To learn that the shape of materials can be changed by squashing, pulling and bending.	Make pizza bases. Prepare toppings. Make coils with play dough.		Put toppings onto pizza bases and cook.	• Know that the shape of dough can be changed by squashing, rolling and coiling round.
Lesson 10 Runny mix	• To learn that some dry ingredients will mix with water and that when you add more water, the mixture becomes runnier.	Make batches of cakes. Make and colour icing. Ice the cakes.		Sort dry ingredients into those that will and will not mix with water.	• Know that icing sugar will mix with water. • Know that when water mixes with a dry ingredient, the mixture is wet. • Know that a cake mixture changes when cooked. • Know that the colour of icing changes when food colouring is added.
Lesson 11 Oats	• To learn that the texture of a mixture can be changed by cooking.	Make porridge. Talk about the changes caused by mixing and cooking.	Taste toppings on the porridge. Make oat biscuits. Lay the table for the three bears. Order the steps in the process of making porridge. List foods that change when cooked.	Make a chart of the children's favourite toppings.	• Know that the way porridge looks changes when it is cooked. • Know that porridge has a different texture when cooked. • Know that heat is used to cook things. • Know that they should never touch hot things, as they can burn.

Assessment	Objectives	Main activity	Activities 2 and 3	Activities 4 and 5	Outcomes
Lesson 12	• To find out what the children know about changing the shape of materials.	Explain what is happening as the teacher makes a teapot from clay.	Make coil pots with clay. Explain the changes. Make a spiky clay hedgehog. Explain the changes.	Make thumb pots. Explain the changes. Make a clay model from free choice. Paint it. Explain the changes.	• Explain how the shape of clay changes when it is rolled, squashed, pulled and flattened. • Explain how they changed the colour of an object by painting it.

CONTEXT

The hardware store

The hardware store, haberdashery or DIY store is a great context through which to teach the variety and uses of materials. The next three lessons involve learning about texture, fabrics and the identification and recognition of common materials that the children are likely to come across in everyday life. The children are given opportunities to learn through investigative play, with a number of activities being set within the role-play area.

Lesson 1 ⬛ Exploring textures

Objective
● To develop the vocabulary, particularly of texture, associated with a range of objects made from a variety of materials.

Vocabulary
heavy, light, soft, hard, bristles, handle, bristly, rough, smooth, big, small, cold, warm, sticky, tickly, sharp, pointed, curved, bendy

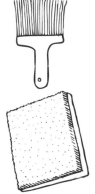

RESOURCES
Main activity: 1m² panel of soft wood; screws; nails; hammer; screwdriver.
Group activities: 1-4 Selection of materials (see Preparation). **1** Paper; pencils. **2** Embossed wallpaper; wax crayons.

PREPARATION
Set up the 'hardware store' role-play area in a section of your classroom. Include items such as tools, screws, nails, kitchen accessories, wallpaper, ceramic tiles, carpet and cushioned flooring tiles, curtains, cushions, shelving, shower curtain, taps, paintbrushes and a rubber mat. Start some nail and screw holes in a 1m² panel of soft wood.

STARTER
Talk to the children about the rules for playing in the hardware store. Explain the importance of taking great care when handling tools such as a hammer, a screwdriver, nails and screws. Explain which tools they can use under supervision only. You may prefer to use plastic toy versions of the tools for the children to use unsupervised.

   Show the children a nail and a screw. Ask them to tell you how these are alike and how they are different. Suggest that they are both sharp because they have points, but the nail is smooth while the screw has a thread. Ask the children whether they know what nails and screws are used for. Show them how to use the hammer and the screwdriver safely. Let one or two children hammer and screw some nails and screws into the wood, talking about how it feels.

MAIN ACTIVITY
Pass a paintbrush around the circle of children and encourage them to feel the handle and bristles. Show them what you mean by 'bristles'. Tell them that the bristles are 'rough' and 'bristly'. Do any of the children think the bristles are 'tickly' or 'itchy'? Tell them that the handle is 'smooth'. Invite a child to find something else in your collection that is smooth. Put this next to the paintbrush handle. Ask another child to find something that is 'rough' or 'tickly'. Place this item next to the bristles. Find other things from your collection that are partly smooth and partly rough, and put them together in a line (as in a matching dominoes game). An example is illustrated on the left.

GROUP ACTIVITIES
1 Ask an adult helper to sort the items with groups of four children. The children should choose items that are smooth or rough from the collection and sort them into two groups. Introduce other describing words to the children by using them to sort items in the collection – for example, soft and

Differentiation

Support

Support the activity by asking children to find items that match one describing word for each day.

Extension

To extend, play 'material dominoes' with the children. Choose an item whose texture can be described in two ways (for example, a brick is rough and hard) and place it on a table. Invite each child in turn to find an item that can match one property (such as a nail, which is hard and smooth) to continue a line of textures, and to name the material from which the item is made.

hard, cold and warm, heavy and light, stiff and bendy.

2 Ask the children to make wax crayon rubbings of embossed wallpaper.

3 Choose a texture-describing word (see Vocabulary) and make a daily display of items that have this texture.

4 Allow a group of children to play in the 'hardware store' role-play area.

ASSESSMENT

Ask the children to choose an item from the 'hardware store', draw it and write a list of words to describe it (either independently or with an adult acting as scribe).

PLENARY

Ask the group who made the wax rubbings to talk about what they did. Pass the wallpaper around for the children to feel the texture. Ask them how they can tell that this is a good surface to make a rubbing of. Make a list of other materials and objects that would be good to make rubbings of, such as tree bark and a stone wall.

OUTCOMES

● All children **must** be able to explore and find out more about a range of materials.
● Most of the children **should** be able to use their sense of touch to explore items found in the home.
● Some **could** use pictures to record what they have done.
● A small number **could even** use simple language to describe texture.

LINKS

ECM 2: Staying safe.

Across the curriculum: this lesson links (through sorting and making lists) with work on gathering information in ICT. The children are also developing their language and literacy skills by extending their vocabulary.

Lesson 2 ▸ What is it made of?

Objective

● To use the senses to explore, sort and identify the materials from which various objects are made.

RESOURCES 💿

Collection of objects from around the classroom made from paper, wood, plastic and metal (include a paintbrush, hammer, cushion, screwdriver, tap and curtain); offcuts of woodchip wallpaper; ordinary paper; fabric; cardboard (including tubes), plastic and foil; gravel; scissors; adhesive; photocopiable page 127 (also 'What is it made of? (red) available on the CD-ROM); pencils; magnets and magnetic materials.

MAIN ACTIVITY

Show the children the collection of objects. Choose one that is made from paper and ask the children to find others made from the same material. Together, arrange offcuts of paper and cardboard to make a pattern. Sort the items in your collection according to their colour, transparency or shininess. Can the children think of other ways in which the materials look the same or different? Invite the children to explore the materials and use photocopiable page 127 as a survey sheet to record their findings.

Set up Group play activities with adult supervision:

1 Let the children make individual collage pictures using gravel and offcuts of paper, cardboard (including tubes), fabric, metal foil, woodchip and plastic. Encourage them to write, or scribe for them, words to describe how the materials in their pictures feel.

2 Allow a group to play in the 'hardware store' role-play area.

3 Let a group make a large picture or model of a metal-eating robot. Give

Differentiation
Support
Work with small groups, sorting the objects into sets of the same material, using 'What is it made of?' (green) from the CD-ROM. Look at one material at a time, and do not move on to another group until you are sure the children are able to complete the task.
Extension
ask the children to make a survey of your collection and identify the materials from which the objects are made. They can use 'What is it made of?' (blue) from the CD-ROM, entering a tick for each material they can identify as part of each item. Make one copy and add any pictures of items in your collection not included on the sheet before handing out enough for the group.

them a selection of objects, some magnetic and some not. Give them a magnet and ask them to feed their robot, explaining that he only eats some metal items. (Do not include any aluminium cans in the collection, as they will not be attracted by the magnet.)

ASSESSMENT
As you work with the different groups, note those children who do not contribute to the discussions and target them for smaller groups in the next lesson. Keep the survey sheets as evidence of children's ability to identify familiar materials.

PLENARY
Make a 'feeling wall' from the children's pictures and describing words. Talk about the different materials in each 'brick', and the creative ways in which the children have arranged their materials.

OUTCOMES
● All children **must** know that there are many different materials.
● Most of the children **should** know that different materials have different textures and look different
● Some **could** talk about the different textures of materials they explore in terms of their properties.
● A small number **could even** sort familiar materials into named groups.

Lesson 3 ▪ Recognising materials

Objective
● To recognise common materials and learn their names: wood, paper, fabric, metal.

Vocabulary
metal, fabric, paper, cardboard, wood, wooden

RESOURCES
Main activity: Wallpaper; sugar paper; staple-gun; display board; table; collection of cardboard boxes, paper-wrapped items, books and magazines.
Group activities: 1-3 Collection of items made from wood, fabric and metal; display board and table for each material; kitchen foil; curtain material; scissors; adhesive; magazines with pictures of wooden and metal objects; labels; felt-tipped pen. **4** Coloured paper; scissors; adhesive; display board. **5** Four large sheets of paper; magazines with pictures of objects made from wood, metal, fabric or paper; adhesive.

PREPARATION
Collect items, and magazine pictures of items, made from wood, fabric, metal and paper.

STARTER
Tell the children that you are going to display different materials, putting all the items made from the same material together.

MAIN ACTIVITY
Select some wallpaper from the 'hardware store' and ask the children what material it is made from. If they do not know, tell them that it is made from paper. Staple the wallpaper to the display board and cover a table with sheets of sugar paper. Ask the children to look around the room for different kinds of paper. Talk about the thickness and texture of the papers before stapling them to the display board. Display a range of cardboard boxes, paper-wrapped objects, books and magazines on the table, and invite the children to add to this display at a later date.

GROUP ACTIVITIES
Repeat the Main activity in small groups for wood, fabric and metal, allowing each group to choose a material.

1 Take some curtain material or other fabric item from the store, spread it over a display table and staple some to a board. Ask the children what this material is. Some may say that it is 'material'. Explain that the name of this material is 'fabric'. Ask the children to find other fabric items from the 'hardware store' and around the classroom (such as cushions, soft toys, rugs, bean bags and towels). Ask them arrange them across the table, stapling some to the display board.

2 Use kitchen foil to cover the display board and table before arranging metal and wooden items on it. Ask the children to cut pictures of items made from wood and metal from magazines and add them to the display. They should write labels for each collection that describe the properties of all the items in it: 'shiny', 'smooth', 'I can see my face in it' and so on.

3 Ask an adult helper to play a 'Find the odd one out' game with groups of four children. The helper puts out two items made from the same material and one made from a different one, then asks the children to point to the odd material out.

4 Ask the children to make paper decorations to hang from a display board, make paper fans and wrap gifts. Talk with them about how the paper will fold, curl, bend and spread out.

5 Organise four large sheets of paper for the children to stick pictures of items made from wood, metal, fabric or paper. Ask an adult helper to work with this group to make sure each picture is stuck to the correct sheet.

ASSESSMENT
During the Group activities, ask the children in turn to find an object made from metal, wood, paper or fabric, and make a note of those who are successful. This will allow you to organise additional activities to reinforce the knowledge and understanding for those who are not always able to recognise a particular material.

PLENARY
Make a collection of items from each of the materials in the displays. Hold up each one in turn and ask the children which display it belongs to. Invite the children to bring non-precious things from home to add to the displays.

OUTCOMES
● All children *must* know that paper, fabric, metal and wood are different materials.
● Most of the children *should* know that these materials have similar and different textures.
● Some *could* talk about the different textures of materials they explore in terms of their properties.
● A small number *could even* sort these materials by name.

LINKS
ECM 5: Working together co-operatively to create displays contributes to the children's future economic well-being.
Across the curriculum: this lesson contributes to their personal, social and emotional development.

CONTEXT The water tray

The water tray is used well in most Reception classes. The next three lessons are examples of how planned, focused practical activities can provide a good context through which to develop scientific skills, knowledge and understanding.

Lesson 4 ◗ Blowing bubbles

Objective
● To learn that soap and water mixed together make bubbles.

Vocabulary
bubbles, mix, water, soap, liquid, round, float, mixture

RESOURCES
Main activity: Bubble mixture; bubble blowers; 'no tears' bubble bath and shampoo; water tray and water; washing-up liquid.
Group activities: 1 Bowl or bucket; water; **2** Hand-held whisks. **3** Circle templates; paper; pencils; paints. **4** Soap flakes. **5** Paint pots; straws; 'no tears' bubble bath; water; blank paper. Provide other bubble sources (such as washing-up liquid) for children to experiment with.

PREPARATION
Practise mixing bubble bath mixture, making sure that it is the correct consistency to blow bubbles. You may wish to let the children play with the bubble mixture for several days before doing these activities, as there is usually a great deal of excitement.

STARTER
Sit the children in a circle so that they can all see the bubbles. Blow a few bubbles from a bottle of bubble mixture and let the children catch them as they float to the ground.

MAIN ACTIVITY
While the children are watching, use 'no tears' bubble bath and water to make a bubble mixture. Explain that when a 'soapy' material is mixed with water, bubbles can be made. Invite one or two children to blow bubbles with the new mixture. Show the children the 'no tears' shampoo and washing-up liquid. Tell them that they are going to work in groups, mixing each of the 'soapy' things with water to make bubbles.

GROUP ACTIVITIES
1 Work with pairs or groups of three. Place a bowl or bucket, half-filled with warm water, in the centre of a table. Add the bubble bath or shampoo to the container, and let the children take turns to make bubbles by agitating the water. Challenge the groups to see who can make the bubbles 'grow' over the top of the bowl or bucket, using fresh water each time and alternating the two 'soapy' materials.
2 Allow a group of children to make bubble sculptures with the mixture in the water tray, using their hands or hand-held whisks to agitate the mixture.
3 Ask the children to use circle templates to draw pictures of bubbles. Display these on a board with the title 'Soap and water make bubbles'.
4 Ask an adult helper to show the children how to mix soap flakes and water while washing their hands, and how to blow bubbles from the frothy mix through their fingers and thumb.
5 Let the children make bubble patterns, using a mixture of paint and 'no tears' bubble bath in a paint pot. They should blow through a straw until the bubbles rise above the pot, then quickly make a print of the bubble pattern by placing a piece of paper on top of the pot before the bubbles all go 'pop'.

Differentiation

Support

Support children by allowing them time to play with the mixtures, then ask questions such as: *What is happening? What can you see? What are you doing to make the bubbles grow?* to develop their understanding and thinking skills. Tell them that the soap mixed with the water is making the bubbles.

Extension

Extend children's thinking by investigating different soap mixtures. If you add more bubble bath to the mixture, do you get bigger bubbles? Do you get the same results if you mix washing-up liquid with water? Is the cheaper brand as good as the more expensive brand? Take care that the children do not get the mixture in their eyes.

ASSESSMENT

Encourage the children to talk about what they are doing, and listen to their conversations. This is an activity where incidental chat will tell you a great deal about the children's understanding. A few simple questions will direct their thinking.

PLENARY

Ask the group who made the bubble patterns with paint to talk about what they did. Cut around a few prints that are dry and add them to your display. Ask: *Can you see where a bubble popped on the paper? How can you tell?*

OUTCOMES

● All children *must* know that soap mixes with water and that together the two can make bubbles.
● Most of the children *should* be able to ask questions about why things happen.
● Some *could* describe what is happening and possibly how.
● A small number *could even* find out with help which solution makes the best bubbles.

LINKS

ECM 1: Keeping healthy and **ECM 5:** contributing to their future economic well-being.

Across the curriculum: this lesson is good for developing social skills, as the children are encouraged to work together and take turns through a series of activities. They are also given lots of opportunities to talk about what they are doing and to ask questions. Discussion of soap and detergents can also be linked to hygiene and health.

Lesson 5 ▪ Oil and water

Objectives
● To investigate what happens when we try to mix oil and water.
● To learn that not all liquids mix with water.

Vocabulary
bubbles, mix, water, soap, liquid, round, float, mixture

RESOURCES

Cooking oil; water-based food colouring; A4-sized water tray; sheet of absorbent A4 paper (such as blotting paper); lidded jars of cold water; different kinds of oil (such as motor oil, olive oil and coloured bath oils).

MAIN ACTIVITY

Try out the demonstration first to gauge how much food colouring and oil you need to use.

Tell the children that you are going to find out what happens when you try to mix oil and water. Pour some water into the tray. Show them the cooking oil and explain that you are going to pour the oil on to the water. Do this, then ask the children what they can see. *Is the oil floating or sinking? Is it staying on top of the water or going to the bottom, or is it mixing with the water?* Mix some food colouring into the mixture so that the children

Differentiation
Support
Talk with children who need support to help them explain what the oil does. For example: *Does it mix with the water, sink to the bottom, float in the middle or float on top?* Point to the top, middle and bottom of the jar as you ask these questions to show the children what you mean by 'sink' and 'float'.
Extension
Half-fill some jars with warm water and add drops of oil. Challenge children to talk about whether the oil reacts differently with warm water. *Does it still float to the top?*

can see the result more clearly (only the water will take up the colour). Invite a child to give the mixture a good stir, making sure that he or she does not get oil on his or her clothes. Carefully place a sheet of absorbent A4 paper onto the top of the tray to soak up the oil. *What has happened? Where has the oil gone? Has it disappeared?* Look at the pattern on the paper.

Repeat the activity with groups of four children. Let each child make his or her own oil pattern.

Half-fill some jars with cold water. Look at different oils and talk about their colours and relative thickness. Add drops of different kinds of oil to each jar, then replace the lids. Carefully give each jar a shake and watch what happens to the oil. Look for colours spreading in the water.

ASSESSMENT
Observe the children as they watch the oil in the jar and NOTE those who understand that the oil and water do not mix.

PLENARY
Talk about the need to be careful when using oil. *What would happen if the oil got on to our clothes? If oil and water do not mix, how can we get oil out of our clothes?* Some children may be able to talk about oil slicks and the effects these have on birds. *How can we remove the oil from a bird's feathers?* Explain that soap and detergent mix with oil and with water, and so make it possible to wash away oil.

OUTCOMES
- All children *must* know what happens when oil is put into water.
- Most of the children *should* be able to ask questions about what is happening.
- Some *could* know that oil and water do not mix.
- A small number *could even* know that oils can have different colours, and some oils are thicker than others and that oil floats on water.

Lesson 6 ▸ Stir it up!

Objectives
- To learn that the thicker a mixture is, the harder it is to stir.
- To learn that the more water is added, the runnier a mixture becomes.

Vocabulary
thick, thicker, thickest, thin, thinner, thinnest, runny, runnier, runniest, consistency, hard to stir, easy to stir, harder, hardest, easier, easiest

RESOURCES
Main activity: Cornflour; water; mixing bowl; wooden spoon; tray.
Group activities: 1 Four bowls with different mixtures (see Preparation); hand-held whisk; rotary whisk; metal spoon; wooden spoon; stick. **2** Paper; cornflour mixture. **3** Different liquid foods (such as syrup and jam); metal and wooden spoons. **4** Paints; whisks; paper; squeezy bottles or straws.

PREPARATION
Mix cornflour, food colouring and water to make four bowls with different consistencies of mixture. Only use one of each colour, so that the children will have a colour to refer to when discussing the mixtures. Do not make any mixture too thick, or it will harden and not stir.

STARTER
Settle the children around a table on which you have a bowl, water, cornflour and a wooden spoon. Pour about half a litre of water into the bowl and slowly mix in the cornflour to a smooth consistency, adding one spoonful at a time. Add food colouring if you wish. As you mix the cornflour and water, talk about the thickness of the mixture, whether it runs off the spoon and how it becomes thicker and less runny as you add more cornflour.

Differentiation

Support

Work with pairs of children who need support, so that they have an opportunity to explore and talk about the mixtures on a one-to-one basis. Provide some paint and let them use their fingers to spread the paint across a table (with a wipe-clean surface) to make pictures.

Extension

Challenge the group to say which of the mixtures has the most cornflour just by their thickness. Let them make its own mixtures of water and cornflour; encourage them to make a runnier or thicker mixture than the ones you have made.

MAIN ACTIVITY

Pass the bowl around and allow the children to stir the mixture. Discuss what it feels like when stirring the mixture. *Is it stiff or runny? Is it hard or easy to stir?* Collect a spoonful of the mixture and let it dribble onto a tray, making a pattern. Talk about the movement of the mixture. *Does it drip in blobs, or does it stick together in a line? How could we make the mixture thicker? How could we make it runnier?*

GROUP ACTIVITIES

1 Work with four children at a time, stirring the mixtures with a selection of spoons, whisks and sticks, and talking about their texture and consistency. Work out together which colour mixture is the easiest and the most difficult to stir, then put the mixtures in order. As the children stir the thinnest mixture, ask them questions such as: *Is this mixture the easiest to stir? How easy is it to stir?* Repeat the questions with the other mixtures.

2 Ask an adult helper to do cornflour finger painting with the children, encouraging them to feel the mixture running through their fingers and to talk about its consistency.

3 Set up a table of different liquid foods (such as syrup, jam and water) for the children to explore by stirring or blending with various objects and machines, then letting the mixture run back into the container.

4 Ask the children to make pictures by dripping paint on paper and making curled streaks of paint. They can either use 'squeezy bottles' (such as empty washing-up liquid bottles) or dip a straw into the paint and then let the paint fall out.

ASSESSMENT

Assess the children's use of language, and particularly their comparisons. Do they understand the difference between 'thick' and 'thin' mixtures? Note those children who understand that to make a mixture thinner, you need to add more liquid.

PLENARY

Make a collection of liquids to reinforce the children's understanding of what a liquid is.

OUTCOMES

● All of the children *must* be able to explore and talk about how mixtures feel.

● Most of the children *should* know that a mixture can be thin (runny) or thick (stiff).

● Some *could* recognise some of the physical properties of liquids.

● A small number *could even* compare the thickness of two mixtures, and order mixtures by how thin or thick they are.

LINKS

Between units: this lesson links with Lesson 9 in Unit 7, involving making different colours of icing for biscuits.

CONTEXT

The sand tray

The sand tray, like the water tray, lends itself well to work in the early years. The next lesson shows how this resource can be used for focused, planned development of early skills in scientific investigation.

Lesson 7 ▸ Sticking together

Objectives
● To learn that sand, when mixed with the right amount of water, will stick together.
● To learn that dry sand does not stick together.
● To learn that damp or wet sand is made by mixing dry sand with water.

RESOURCES
Buckets; spades; moulds (including one that is transparent); dry sand in a sand tray; damp sand in a shallow tray. Make sure the sand has the right consistency for making good sandcastles.

MAIN ACTIVITY
Put some dry sand in a shallow tray and pass it around for the children to feel its texture. Encourage them to use phrases such as 'dry', 'runs through the fingers', 'gritty' and 'rough'. Mix some water with the sand to make it damp. Pass the tray around again and ask the children how the texture has changed. Encourage them to use words such as 'damp', 'wet', 'cold' and 'sticks together'. *How has it stayed the same?* (It is still gritty and rough.) Ask them to grab a handful of the sand and to squeeze it tightly so that the sand sticks together. Talk about what has happened.

Fill the transparent container with damp sand, talking to the children all the time about how the sand is filling the container so that there is no space left inside. When the container is full, press the sand in tightly so that it is well stuck together. Turn the container over, and ask the children what they think will happen when you remove the container. They may suggest that there will be a sandcastle left in the same shape as the container. Demonstrate this.

Organise Group activities with adult support:
1 Ask an adult helper to work with four children at a time, mixing dry sand and water to make the right consistency to make perfect sandcastles.
2 Look at some sand mixed with too much water. Challenge the children to build a sandcastle with this mixture. Can they explain why they did not succeed?
3 Allow the children to play with a range of buckets and moulds (including a transparent mould) to make sandcastles. Ask them to predict the shape of

Differentiation
Support
Some children may not have the strength and physical dexterity to do this activity unaided, and may need the support of an adult.
Extension
Give children some dry sand and talk to them about the differences and similarities between the two textures. Do they understand that they cannot make sandcastles with dry sand because it does not stick together, but flows like a liquid? Can they mix the right amount of water with the sand to make a good material for building sandcastles?

each sandcastle before they remove the bucket or mould. Can they match each finished castle to the correct container?

ASSESSMENT
Note those children who understand that the damp sand sticks together, and so remains in the shape of the container that it has filled.

PLENARY
Talk about which children managed to make a sandcastle. *Who made the biggest sandcastle?* Ask the child in question to fetch the container from which it was made. *Did anyone build one sandcastle on top of another?* Demonstrate this to the children by making a tower of sandcastles.

OUTCOMES
- All children *must* know that damp sand sticks together and dry sand does not.
- Most of the children *should* know that you mix dry sand and water to make damp sand and the similarities and differences between them.
- Some *could* describe what damp sand feels like.
- A small number *could even* use their learning to mix their own sand.

CONTEXT The baker's shop

The next four lessons are set in the context of a baker's shop and focus on making bread, biscuits, cakes and pies. Although I have used specific items for these lessons, the food items made can be changed to fit each school's circumstances. For example, the children could make sweets of other cultures instead of cakes or biscuits.

Lesson 8 ▪ Recipes

Objectives
- To learn that the shape of a mixture can be changed by rolling.

Vocabulary
rolling, flat, flatter, spread out, shape, change, mixture

RESOURCES ◉
Main activity: The traditional story 'The Gingerbread Man'; mixing bowl; wooden spoon; rolling pin; pastry board; pastry cutters; oven; baking trays; flour; margarine; milk. You will need various biscuit and cake ingredients for the follow-up lessons.
Group activities: 1, 2 and 4 Cooking utensils and ingredients as for Main activity; photocopiable page 128 (also 'Recipes' (red) available on CD-ROM); paper; pencils. **3** Play dough, rolling pins.
ICT link: Digital camera and computer or printer.

PREPARATION
Make up a fresh lot of play dough.

STARTER
Read the story of 'The Gingerbread Man' to the children. Talk about the ingredients that were used to make the biscuit man. Do the children think the gingerbread biscuit was tasty? Why do they think this?

MAIN ACTIVITY
Working with groups of children, mix the ingredients to make dough at the right consistency to roll out. Show the children the ball of dough and talk about its shape and size. Ask them how you could make the ball of dough flat so that you could make flat biscuits. Flatten the dough with your hands, explaining that you are squashing the mixture flat. Use a rolling pin to roll

Differentiation 💿
Support
Support children when they
are making their pastry or
gingerbread biscuit recipe by
allowing them to use 'Recipe'
(green) from the CD-ROM,
which has a clearer step-by-
step approach for the children
to follow.
Extension
Extend children's skills by
asking them to follow simple
recipe cards (perhaps
following the format of
photocopiable page 128 to
make their biscuits and cakes
with little supervision.
Question them to find out why
they are rolling out their
mixture. Talk about the
changes that take place when
the mixture is baked or
heated. (Please note there is
no 'Recipes' (blue) on the CD-
ROM for this activity.)

out the mixture to the correct thickness (let the children say when this is),
explaining that you are now pushing the mixture out to make a different,
flatter shape. Ask the children to describe the size and shape of the mixture
now. Make sure they understand that there is the same amount of mixture
as before.

Repeat the activity over the next week. On day 1, you could make
gingerbread biscuits, on day 2, jam tarts, on day 3, chocolate biscuits, on day
4, mince pies, and on day 5, a peach flan. Talk each day about whether the
mixture is easy or difficult to stir, whether it sticks together when milk or
water is added, and whether it changes its shape when squashed or rolled
out.

GROUP ACTIVITIES
1 Ask an adult helper to work with groups of four children, making a biscuit
or pastry mix, using the recipes on photocopiable page 128. Prompt the
adult to talk about how the mixture is ready to be rolled out when it sticks
together.
2 When the mixture is ready, you should repeat the Main activity with small
groups of children.
3 Let groups of six children play with play dough, making biscuits, jam tarts
and other play food. Let them flatten the mixture with their hands as well as
using rolling pins.
4 Allow four children to play in the 'baker's shop' role-play area.

ICT LINK
Use a digital camera to take photographs at different stages of making the
biscuits and use them for the 'Assessment' ordering activity below.

ASSESSMENT
Ask the children to draw four pictures to show the ingredients being mixed,
the mixture sticking together, the mixture being rolled out to change its
shape and the finished biscuit or cake. Keep these pictures as evidence of
the children's understanding.

PLENARY
Let the children enjoy the biscuits with milk at snack time. Make a large
chart to show the four steps outlined in the Assessment section or talk
through the recipe sheet on photocopiable page 128 to remind the children
of how they made the biscuits.

OUTCOMES
● All children *must* be able to notice the changes that take place when
mixing and rolling dough.
● Most of the children *should* be able to change the shape of dough by
mixing and rolling.
● Some *could* say what happens when the dough is rolled and squashed.
● A small number *could even* describe ways the dough can be changed by
mixing, rolling, stretching and squashing; and note the changes caused by
baking (or heating).

LINKS
ECM 5: This activity contributes to the children's future economic well-
being.
Across the curriculum: this lesson develops physical dexterity skills
through stirring with a spoon and using a rolling pin to roll out the mixture.
The children should use their senses of smell and taste to evaluate the
quality of the finished biscuits and cakes.

Lesson 9 ▪ Pizza base recipes

Objective
● To learn that the shape of a material can be changed by squashing, pulling and bending.

RESOURCES
Photocopiable page 129 (also 'Pizza base recipes' (red) available on CD-ROM); flour; salt; water; yeast; olive oil; oven or microwave oven; jar of pizza topping; tin of tomatoes; cheese; cheese grater; cooked sausages; pineapple rings; knife; chopping board; ready-made pizza; play dough.

MAIN ACTIVITY
Check for food allergies and dietary requirements. Make enough dough (with the children's help if you wish to reinforce previous learning objectives) for each child to have a piece the size of a tennis ball.
Show the children a ready-made pizza and ask them what ingredients they can see. Make a list of all the things they say, then add any things that they have omitted. Explain that before you can put the topping on a pizza, you must first make the base.

Show the children photocopiable page 129 and ask them to follow the recipe steps and help you to make the pizza base dough.

Place the ball of dough on a board and talk about its size and shape. What does the finished shape need to look like? The children may say that you need to flatten the dough into a shape like a plate. Demonstrate how you could make the base of the pizza in this way. Now say that you have another way of making it. Slowly roll the dough into a long sausage shape, pulling it out from time to time. Ask the children how long they think the sausage needs to be. When the dough is about as thick as your thumb, stop rolling and look at the size and shape again. Pull the dough out into a straight line. Coil the sausage shape into a disc and press the edges together to make a pizza base. Place the base on a plate and cook in an oven for ten minutes.

Organise Group activities with adult support:
1 Follow the recipes on photocopiable page 129 to make pizza bases with groups of six children, reinforcing what they are doing to change the shape of the dough.
2 Ask a group to mix together tinned tomatoes and a jar of pizza topping. Use this to reinforce their learning about mixing substances together.
3 Ask an adult helper to supervise the children closely as they grate cheese for the topping. Make sure the adult does not let the children grate small pieces of cheese, in case their fingers get too close to the grater. If necessary, the adult should grate and the children should watch. The adult should talk with the children about what is happening to the cheese.
4 Ask a group to cut the pineapple rings and sausages into pieces to place on top of the pizza. Talk about the changing shapes of these food items.
5 The children could practise making coils with play dough.

ASSESSMENT
Note those children who can work independently and know how to roll and flatten the dough. As they work listen to the children's chat to hear the vocabulary they are using. Question the children to find out their level of understanding.

PLENARY
Together, put the toppings on the pizzas. With the children well back, cook the pizzas (in batches) until they are golden brown, then remove them and let them cool. Let the children enjoy the finished pizzas.

Differentiation 💿
Support
Support children by giving them 'Pizza base recipes' (green) from the CD-ROM to follow when they are making their pizza base. (Please note there is no 'Pizza base recipes' (blue) for this activity.)

OUTCOMES
● All children *must* notice the change in shape of the dough.
● Most of the children *should* be able to talk about what they are doing to make the dough change shape.

- Some *could* know that the shape of dough can be changed by squashing, rolling and coiling round.
- A small number *could even* describe how the shape of dough can be changed by squashing, rolling and coiling round.

Lesson 10 ▪ Runny mix

Objective
● To learn that some dry ingredients will mix with water and that when you add more water, the mixture becomes runnier.

RESOURCES
Ingredients for making batches of small cakes; microwave oven; icing sugar; icing bag; food colouring; chocolate; biscuits; dried pulses; flour; sugar; powder paint; salt; pots of water.

MAIN ACTIVITY
Make batches of cakes with groups of children, reinforcing learning objectives from the previous lessons in this unit. Add food colouring and chocolate to the mixtures, so that each group makes cakes of a different colour. Watch the changes that take place.

Ask groups of six to eight children to ice the cakes. Mix the icing together, and change the colour by adding food colouring or chocolate to each mixture. Allow the children to spread the icing on to the cakes with a knife. When it is dry, use an icing bag to squeeze blobs of different-coloured icing on to the centre of each cake. Ask the children which colour food colouring was added to the icing.

Let the children work with an adult helper to make faces on biscuits with icing sugar.

Put a range of dry materials (pulses, flour, sugar, powder paint, salt) out with pots of water, and let the children investigate whether each dry material will mix with water.

ASSESSMENT
Listen to the children as they ice the cakes. How many ask questions and comment on how the mixture feels? Do they use words such as 'spread', 'mixture', 'runny' and 'thin' to describe the mixture? Ask: *What makes the mixture spread easily?* Does anyone see a relationship between the thickness of the mixture and the ease with which it spreads?

Differentiation
Support
Children who need support should have the experience of icing their cakes in order to feel how the icing squeezes out of the bag, sticks to the cake and spreads across its surface. They may then be ready to talk about the consistency of the icing during the biscuit-decorating activity.
Extension
Introduce the word 'dissolve' with children to extend the activities. Ask them to sort the dry materials into sets according to whether they dissolve (that is, become invisible) in water. (Sugar and salt will dissolve, the others will not.)

PLENARY
Talk about the dry materials that do and do not mix with water. Sort them into two sets. Ask the children to find other things (under adult supervision) at home or in school that will mix with water.

OUTCOMES
● All children *must* know that icing sugar will mix with water.
● Most of the children *should* know that the colour of icing changes when food colouring is added and talk about the differences and similarities.
● Some *could* make a more general connection that when water mixes with a dry ingredient, the mixture is wet.
● A small number *could even* know that a cake mixture changes when cooked.

LINKS
Across the curriculum: this lesson develops physical dexterity skills through stirring with a spoon and spreading icing on the cakes with a knife. The children should use their senses of smell and taste to evaluate the quality of the finished cakes.

Lesson 11 ◼ Oats

Objective
● To learn that the texture of a mixture can be changed by cooking.

Vocabulary
dry, wet, heat, cook, liquid, microwave oven

RESOURCES ◉

Main activity: Copy of 'Goldilocks and the Three Bears'; instant porridge oats; milk; bowl; cup; spoon; microwave oven.
Group activities: 1 Sugar; salt; three bowls; several spoons. **2** Recipe and ingredients on photocopiable page 130 (also 'Oats – 1' (red) available on CD-ROM). **3** Photocopiable page 131 (also 'Oats – 2' (red) available on CD-ROM); scissors; adhesive sticks; paper; pencils. **4** Paper; pencils; paints. **5** Table with bowls and spoons in three sizes. **7** Various ingredients and cooking utensils.
ICT link: 'Oats' interactive from the CD-ROM; interactive whiteboard.
Plenary: Graphing tool from the CD-ROM.

PREPARATION

Move the microwave oven to the classroom and carry out a risk assessment.

STARTER

Read the story of 'Goldilocks and the Three Bears'. Say that porridge should never be touched when it is cooking on the stove, and should be left to cool down otherwise. Emphasise that the mouth is easily burned.

MAIN ACTIVITY

Pass the oats around in a bowl and invite the children to feel the texture. Next, pass milk around in a cup for the children to dip a finger into. Tell the children that you are going to mix a dry ingredient, the oats, with a liquid ingredient, the milk, to make porridge. Mix the oats and milk and show the children the runny mixture. Ask them whether the oats have mixed with the milk as the icing sugar did with the water. *How do the two mixtures look different?*

Put the porridge mixture in the microwave oven and cook it, giving it an occasional stir, until it has a smooth consistency. Show the mixture to the children, stirring it to show the new texture. When the mixture is cool, allow the children to stir it so that they can feel the difference in the texture. Ask them to explain what has happened to the mixture. *What has made it change?* Talk about how the heat from the microwave oven has changed the texture of the mixture: it has helped the dry oats and the liquid milk to mix together.

GROUP ACTIVITIES

1 Make porridge with groups of six children. When the porridge is cool enough, empty it into three bowls and add salt to one, sugar to another and nothing to the third. Invite the children to taste each one and say which is their favourite.
2 Ask an adult helper to make oat biscuits using the recipe on photocopiable page 130 with groups of six children for the class to enjoy at snack time.
3 Give the children a copy each of photocopiable page 131. Ask them to cut out the pictures and stick them down on another sheet of paper in the correct order (in two rows).
4 Ask the children to paint or draw pictures of the three bears eating their porridge.
5 Organise a table with three different-sized bowls and spoons piled up. Ask the children to lay the table for the three bears' breakfast.
6 Make a list of other foods that change when cooked, such as apples, potatoes, cakes or bread.
7 Make other snacks with the children to reinforce the learning objective, such as rice pudding, custard or pancakes.

ICT LINK
Let the children play 'Making porridge' interactive from the CD-ROM, where they must click on the ingredients in the right order to make a bowl of porridge.

ASSESSMENT
Use Group activity 3 to assess the children's understanding of the process of cooking porridge.

PLENARY
Talk about which porridge topping the children liked best and record their choices on a tick chart. Use the graphing tool on the CD-ROM to convert the information collected into a bar or pie chart. This can then be displayed on the interactive whiteboard.

OUTCOMES
● All children *must* know that they should never touch hot things, as they can burn.
● Most of the children *should* be able to notice the similarities and differences between uncooked and cooked porridge.
● Some *could* know that the way porridge looks changes when it is cooked.
● A small number *could even* know that porridge has a different texture when cooked and that heat is used to cook things.

LINKS
ECM 1: Keeping healthy **ECM 2:** Staying safe.
Across the curriculum: this lesson links to personal, social and emotional development through personal hygiene and washing of hands, taking care not to touch the hot porridge, and making a choice of a favourite porridge topping.

Differentiation ◉

Support
Ask the children to follow the oat biscuits recipe on 'Oats – 1' (green) from the CD-ROM, which features simple steps for the children to follow.

Extension
Extend the activity by inviting the children to read the text and sort the pictures on 'Oats – 2' (blue) from the CD-ROM, into the correct order to make a bowl of porridge.

Lesson 12 ▬ Assessment

Objective
● To find out what the children know about changing the shape of materials.

RESOURCES
Main assessment activity: Collection of ceramic ornaments and pots; cup; teapot; balls of clay; board or piece of non-stick flooring, pots of water.
Assessment activities 2-5 Rolling pin; paper and pencils; work area with easily washable flooring (these are messy activities – an outside area is best).

PREPARATION
Make a collection of ceramic items. Make enough balls of clay (about the size of a tennis ball) for each child to have one, and place them in an airtight container to keep them moist. If necessary, wrap each ball separately in cling film.

STARTER
Show the children some of the ceramic items in your collection. Ask them to think of words to describe these items. Ask questions such as: *How would you make the spout for the teapot? How do you think the handle was put on the cup?* Ask the children whether they think the teapot started out looking like this, or looked different in any way. When they have finished expressing their opinions, show them a ball of clay.

MAIN ASSESSMENT ACTIVITY

Ask the children whether they believe you when you say that the teapot probably started out looking like this ball of clay. Some will, but many will not. Remove three small pieces of clay from the ball. Show the children how to make a bowl shape by pushing into the clay with your thumbs. Talk about how the shape of the bowl is changing. Next, roll out a piece of clay and attach it for the handle. Roll out another piece for the spout, and finally flatten a piece of clay for the lid. Ask the children what you are doing, and what is happening to the shape of the clay, at each stage. This will provide you with information about the children's understanding of how the shape of the clay is being changed. Use words such as 'pull', 'roll', 'push' and 'flatten'. Ask the children how you could make the teapot look a different colour, and note their suggestions.

ASSESSMENT ACTIVITY 2

Make coil pots with the children. Ask them to explain what is happening to the clay as they roll it out to make a long sausage shape. As they coil the length into a pot shape, talk about how the shape of the clay is changing. At the end of the activity, ask the children to draw three pictures to show the different shapes of their clay.

ASSESSMENT ACTIVITY 3

Give the children a piece of clay and ask them to pull out bits to make the nose and spikes of a hedgehog. Ask them to describe what is happening to the clay as they pull out the spikes. Ask them to draw 'before' and 'after' pictures.

ASSESSMENT ACTIVITY 4

Show the children how to make thumb pots out of lumps of clay. Ask them to explain how the shape of the clay changes as they push into it with their thumbs.

ASSESSMENT ACTIVITY 5

Give the children a small ball of clay and ask them to make anything they like. When they have finished, ask them how they changed the shape of the clay to look like their finished article (name what each child has made). Let the children paint their finished models. Ask them to explain how they changed the colour of the items by painting. Encourage them to compare all the different models they have made.

PLENARY

Talk about the differences between a ball of clay and a finished model; compare the different models.

ASSESSMENT OUTCOMES

On completion of these Assessment activities, you should know which children have attained the following objectives to support the development of their knowledge and understanding of the world:
● All children *must* be able to use their senses to explore a natural material.
● Most of the children *should* talk about the differences between a ball of clay and a finished model in terms of shape, size and colour.
● Some children *could* explain how they changed the colour of an object by painting it.
● A small number *could even* explain how the shape of clay changes when it is rolled, squashed, pulled and flattened.

What is it made of?

✔ the material.

	wood	metal	plastic	fabric

Illustration © Colin Shelbourn

Recipes

Pastry recipe
230g plain flour
115g margarine
a pinch of salt
approximately 2 tablespoons
   cold water to mix

- Sieve the flour and salt into a mixing bowl.
- Rub the margarine into the flour with your fingertips.
- Add the water, a little at a time, and rub in.
- Gather the mixture into a ball.
- Roll out to the required thickness.

Ginger biscuit recipe
345g plain flour
2 level teaspoons ground ginger
115g butter
1 cup soft brown sugar
4 tablespoons golden syrup
1 egg

- Sift together the flour and ground ginger.
- Rub the butter into the mixture.
- Add the sugar and mix well.
- Beat the egg and warm the syrup slightly, then add both to the mixture.
- Stir the ingredients together to make a pliable dough.
- Roll out and use a cutter to make the shape of gingerbread people.

Illustration © Colin Shelbourn

Pizza base recipes

Pizza base (baking powder method)

3 cups self-raising flour
1 teaspoon baking powder
90g butter or margarine
milk and water to mix

- Sift the flour and baking powder together.
- Rub in the butter or margarine and mix to a firm dough with milk and water.
- Turn onto a floured board and knead.

Pizza base (yeast and oil method)

3 cups plain flour
a pinch of salt
1 tablespoon olive oil
1 teaspoon dried yeast
pint warm water

- Sieve the salt and flour into a basin.
- Make a hole in the centre and add the oil.
- Sprinkle the yeast into the water.
- Pour the yeast mixture over the oil.
- Sprinkle flour over the yeast mixture.
- Cover with a cloth and leave in a warm place for 15–20 minutes, until the yeast mixture starts to bubble.
- Blend all the ingredients together and knead until smooth.

Illustration © Colin Shelbourn

Oats – 1

Ingredients
230g oats
115g plain flour
115g sugar
115g margarine
milk for mixing
half teaspoon baking powder
a pinch of salt

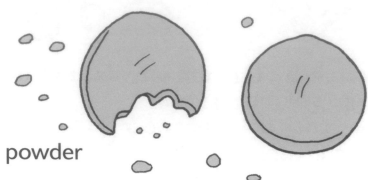

- Mix together the flour, oats, sugar, salt and baking powder.

- Rub in the margarine.

- Mix to a dry paste with the milk.

- Roll out to the required thickness.

- Cut into shapes.

- Bake for 30 minutes on medium heat.

◾SCHOLASTIC

Illustration © Colin Shelbourn

Oats – 2

UNIT 5 Electricity

Lesson	Objectives	Main activity	Group activities	Plenary	Outcomes
Lesson 1 Do not touch	• To learn that electricity is dangerous.	Identify electrical switches, plugs and sockets. Talk about the dangers of electricity.	Attach 'Do not touch' stickers to plugs and sockets. Make posters about the dangers of electricity. Role-play a hairdresser's and a home.	Create a set of class rules about what the children may touch and what they must not.	• Know that electricity is not safe: it is dangerous. • Know which electrical appliances they may touch and which they must never touch.
Lesson 2 On and off	• To learn that many electrical appliances have switches that need to be used safely. • To begin to ask questions about how things work.	Practice turning on a range of electrical items that your school policy allows. Reinforce the dangers of electricity.		Attach 'Yes' and 'No' stickers to appliances to show whether the children are allowed to touch them.	• Know that switches allow electricity through to make things work. • Know which switches are safe to touch and which should never be touched. • Can ask questions about how things work.
Lesson 3 Things that use electricity	• To learn that a range of household appliances use electricity.	Sort a range of household electrical appliances by the room they are used in.	Repeat the sorting activity. Make models of electrical items for a model house. Play with a doll's house and in the home role-play area. Paint pictures of household items.	Make a large wall display with the children's pictures. Ask the children to talk about their work.	• Know that certain household appliances work by electricity. • Can sort appliances according to the room they are usually found in. • Can identify some household appliances that do not work by electricity.
Lesson 4 What does it do?	• To learn that electrical items may produce heat, sound, light and/or movement.	Sort electrical appliances by whether they produce sound, heat, light or movement. Label and use 'play' appliances.		Talk about how the appliances with motors work.	• Know that electrical items can give out heat, light, sound and/or movement. • Can sort objects according to given criteria. • Can use drawings to record findings.
Lesson 5 How does it work?	• To learn that a battery is a portable supply of electricity. • To learn that some toys and other items are powered by batteries.	Talk about how the flash on a camera works. Talk about a range of items that use batteries.	Explore a range of items that work by battery. Identify things that work by battery and by mains electricity. Paint pictures of a favourite battery-operated toy. Find objects that work by battery. Play with battery-operated toys.	Talk about the paintings of battery-operated toys. Make a display of things that work by battery and things that do not.	• Can recognise batteries. • Know that batteries are a source of power and make things work. • Know that some things work by battery and others do not. • Know that batteries can be dangerous if not handled properly.
Lesson 6 Switch it off!	• To learn that many battery-operated items have a switch to turn them on and off.	Identify the switches on a variety of battery-operated items. Explore how these items are switched on and off.		Talk about a favourite battery-operated item. Invite the children to say how the switch makes it work.	• Can identify the switch on a battery-operated item. • Know that a switch may be needed to make something work. • Can record findings by making drawings. • Can begin to describe the movement of familiar objects.

Assessment	Objectives	Main activity	Activity 2	Activity 3	Outcomes
Lesson 7	• To assess the children's ability to identify and sort items by whether mains electricity or batteries power them. • To assess the children's understanding of the dangers of electricity.	Sort items according to whether they work by mains electricity or batteries. Talk about how electricity is dangerous.	Identify items powered by mains electricity or by battery.	Sort items according to whether they work by electricity, batteries or neither.	• Know that some things work by mains electricity, some work by battery and some use neither. • Identify whether familiar objects work by battery or mains electricity. • Know that electricity can be dangerous.

CONTEXT

My home

The lessons in this unit can be taught through a topic on 'My home'. Set up the role-play area as a 'home', containing a kitchen, lounge and bedroom area (if possible). Allow the children to rearrange the furniture from time to time.

Lesson 1 ▪ Do not touch

Objective
● To learn that electricity is dangerous.

Vocabulary
dangerous, danger, electricity, electrical, switch, lead, socket, plug

RESOURCES ◉
Main activity: Electrical items including a table lamp, hairdryer and CD or cassette player; stickers cut from photocopiable page 38; adhesive.
Group activities: 1 Photocopiable page 38 (also 'Do not touch – 1' (red) available on CD-ROM – see Unit 1 Lesson 6); scissors; adhesive. **2** Large sheets of paper; felt-tipped pens. **3** Dolls; combs; hairbrushes; shampoo; conditioner; hand towels; washbasin; hairdryer. **4** The 'home' role-play area; range of toy household electrical items.
ICT links: Photocopiable page 38 (also 'Do not touch – 1'(red) available on CD-ROM – see Unit 1, Lesson 6); digital camera; pictures of electrical items, plugs and sockets; interactive whiteboard.

PREPARATION
Colour and cut out two 'Do not touch' stickers from photocopiable page 129.

STARTER
Gather the children together so that they can see the lamp and a wall socket nearby. Ask them how you can make the light come on. Point out the plug, switch and lead on the lamp, then point out the wall socket as you plug in the lamp and switch it on. Tell the children that this is something they must not do. Explain that the lamp works by electricity, which travels from the socket through the plug and lead to the bulb, making it light up. Explain that although electricity makes the lamp work, it is very dangerous and must never be touched. Explain the dangers of electric shocks and the class rules about electricity.

MAIN ACTIVITY
Repeat the demonstration with the other electrical items. Point out the switch on the wall socket and the switch on the appliance that makes it work. Ask the children which part of the appliance they should never touch; after their response, attach 'Do not touch' stickers to the plug and the wall socket. Explain again that they should never touch these things because, once something is plugged in and switched on, electricity travels from the socket to make things work and this electricity is dangerous. It may be appropriate to tell the children that it is the electricity, not the appliance itself, that is dangerous; people have made the appliance safe by wrapping the wires in plastic and putting something called a fuse inside the plug. The concept of electricity is a difficult one, however, and children can easily become confused if explanations are too long.

GROUP ACTIVITIES
1 Ask an adult helper to work with six children to cut out stickers from copies of photocopiable page 38 and attach them to electrical plugs and wall sockets in the classroom.

Differentiation
Support
Repeat the activity with children who need support over a number of days until they fully understand that they should never touch plugs, switches or sockets.
Extension
To extend, talk to children about the path that the electricity takes. Point out the socket and its switch, then the plug, lead and switch on the appliance. Explain that when the switches are 'on', it allows electricity to flow from the socket through the plug and lead to make the appliance work.

2 Work with groups of six children to make large posters about the dangers of electricity. Display these prominently in the classroom.
3 Set up a 'hairdresser's shop' role-play area for the children to comb, shampoo and dry the dolls' hair.
4 Allow four children to play in the 'home' role-play area. Put out as many toy household electrical items as you can for them to use: cooker, iron, TV, heater, telephone, shower, lamp and so on. Emphasise that the children must not touch the real items.

ICT LINK ⊙
Set up the 'Do not touch' stickers and pictures of electrical items, plugs and sockets. Take photographs of them with a digital camera and insert these into the software on the interactive whiteboard. During the main activity, as you talk about each electrical item, plug and socket, drag this onto the screen and drag and drop the 'Do not touch' sticker onto them.

ASSESSMENT
Watch the children as they ask an adult to attach their stickers to things around the classroom. Note those who show awareness of the dangers of electricity by putting their stickers in appropriate places.

PLENARY
At the end of the activities, work with the whole class to write a set of class rules about what the children are and are not allowed to touch (with particular reference to plugs and switches).

OUTCOMES
● All children *must* know that electricity is not safe: it is dangerous.
● Most of the children *should* be able to know which electrical appliances they may touch and which they must not touch.
● Some children *could* say what happens when an electrical item is switched on and off.
● A small number *could even* know how different electrical devices work, for example produce light, sound, heat and/or movement.

LINKS
ECM 2: Staying safe.
Between units: this lesson links to Unit 1, Lesson 6 on hazardous substances and to Unit 8, Lesson 6 on awareness of the dangers of sunlight.
Across the curriculum: a link with personal, social and emotional development is made through the children's growing awareness of how to keep themselves and others safe.

Lesson 2 ▸ On and off

Objectives
● To learn that many electrical appliances have switches that need to be used safely.
● To begin to ask questions about how things work.

Vocabulary
dangerous, danger, electricity, electrical, switch, lead, socket, plug

RESOURCES
Computer, CD player and any other items (including light switches) in your classroom that you want the children to use independently; sticky labels; felt-tipped pen. Make sure that the items in your collection actually work!

MAIN ACTIVITY
With groups of four to six children, sit around the computer. Talk about the dangers of electricity, and reinforce the learning from the previous lesson. Explain to the children that they are going to learn how to turn the computer and monitor on by using the correct switches. If you want them to do this only under adult supervision at all times, explain this. Ask an adult helper to show other groups how to operate a CD player and other

appliances in the classroom. Talk about safety and explain that switches are for turning a machine on and off; allow the children to ask questions about how the items work.

With small groups of children, show them how to turn the items in the collection on and off safely. Be aware of your school's policy on which items the children are allowed to turn on and off independently. It may be that you want to reinforce the message that switches operate these items, but that the children should never touch any switch without an adult. In any case, the children must not operate the switch by a wall socket. Explain that the danger arises because the items work by using electricity, which is dangerous. Many schools allow children to turn lights on and off, so teach safety procedures for doing this if appropriate. Explain the necessary rules to the children: making sure their hands are dry, taking turns to touch a switch rather than reaching for it together, and so on.

ICT LINK
Incorporate the children's ideas from the assessment activity into a set of illustrated rules to display around the classroom.

ASSESSMENT
Assess the children's understanding by asking them to draw pictures showing the rules you have talked about. Ask them to write (either independently or with an adult as scribe) a short sentence explaining the rules for the use of switches and electrical items in the classroom.

PLENARY
Talk about the children's pictures and read some of their sentences to reinforce the message about not touching electrical appliances or to detail those appliances that the children are allowed to turn on and off independently. Add stickers with 'Yes' or 'No' (or a tick or a cross) to each appliance to show whether the children are allowed to touch it.

OUTCOMES
● All children *must* know which switches are safe to touch and which should never be touched.
● Most of the children *should* be able to ask questions about how things work.
● Some children *could* know that switches allow electricity through to make things work.
● A small number *could even* say whether the device produces light, sound, heat and/or movement.

Lesson 3 ▪ Things that use electricity

RESOURCES
Main activity: Soft toy; four large cardboard boxes; carpet squares; models of household furniture and electrical appliances found in different rooms (pictures cut from magazines and stuck to small cereal boxes are cheap alternatives).
Group activities: 1 Magazines and catalogues with pictures of electrical items, copies of photocopiable page 143 (also 'Things that use electricity – 1' (red) available on the CD-ROM) and photocopiable page 144 (also 'Things that use electricity – 2' (red) available on the CD-ROM); sorting rings to represent different rooms, or pictures of different rooms; labels. **2** Pictures from Group activity 1; scissors; adhesive sticks; small cardboard boxes (such as toothpaste and cereal boxes). **3** The 'home' role-play area. **4** Paper; paints.
ICT link: 'Things that use electricity' interactive available on CD-ROM.

PREPARATION

Make a doll's house with four rooms from cardboard boxes (all the same size) that the children will be able to reach into easily. Alternatively, create a model of four rooms with corrugated card strips, so that each room is approximately 50cm long, 50cm wide and 25cm high. Line the rooms with carpet squares or another suitable floor covering.

STARTER

Sit the children in a circle. Ask them to pass a soft toy around the circle. As each child takes the toy, he or she has to name an item in his or her home. (If the child does not wish to contribute, he or she can just pass the toy to the next person.) Ask questions such as: *Which item do you like best in your bedroom? Why do you like this one the best?* Talk about all the things the children have mentioned that work by electricity. Explain that these are things that work when plugged into a wall socket and switched on, or when given batteries and switched on. As the children mention the names of electrical items that are in your collection of models, place these in the centre of the circle so that all the children can see them. Say that all the things in this new collection have something in common. After allowing the children to guess what (there are several things that the items may have in common), explain that the one you want them to learn is that the items all work by using electricity.

MAIN ACTIVITY

Gather the children around your cardboard model of four rooms and tell them the names of the rooms that they represent. Choose one of the electrical items from the collection and invite the children to say in which room in the house it is found. Invite the children in turn to choose an item and place it in the room in which they think it belongs (for all or most of the time). Continue until all the items have been placed in the correct room. You may need to have more than one model of certain items, such as televisions and lamps.

GROUP ACTIVITIES

1 Work with groups of six children at a time to cut pictures of electrical items from magazines and catalogues and/or photocopiable pages 143 and 144, sorting them into sets according to the rooms in which the items are generally found. You may need more than one copy of some pictures (such as lamps and televisions).

2 Ask an adult helper to supervise the children while they stick the pictures from Group activity 1 on to small cardboard boxes and put them into the correct rooms in the model house.

3 Allow two children at a time to play with the doll's house, and four to play in the role-play area.

4 Ask the children to paint pictures of things in the house that work by electricity and things that do not. The latter could work by another power source (such as a gas fire) or not 'work' at all (such as a table).

ICT LINK

Invite the children to play 'Things that use electricity' interactive, where children drag different electrical items into the rooms of a house where they might be found. This is an open-ended activity, which means it can be used to stimulate class discussion.

ASSESSMENT

Talk to the children about their paintings to find out who has or does not have an understanding of which things work by electricity.

PLENARY

Use the children's paintings to make a large wall display, inviting the children to say which half of the display each item belongs in (see illustration below). Ask the group making the model items to show what they have made and to identify which items work by electricity.

OUTCOMES

● All children **must** know that certain household appliances work by electricity.
● Most of the children **should** be able to sort appliances according to the room they are usually found in.
● Some **could** identify some household items that do not work by electricity.
● A small number **could even** say whether the device produces light, sound, heat and/or movement.

LINKS

ECM 2: Staying safe.
Across the curriculum: this lesson links with other aspects of knowledge and understanding of the world through the development of design and technology skills associated with joining and assembling materials.

These things use electricity

These things do not

Lesson 4 ▶ What does it do?

RESOURCES ◎

Magazines and catalogues with pictures of electrical items including washing machines, lamps, radios, CD and DVD players, cookers, microwave ovens, heaters, fans, computers and TV sets; scissors; photocopiable page 145 (also 'What does it do?' (red) available on the CD-ROM) enlarged to A3 size; sorting rings; collection of portable electrical items; the 'home' role-play area; labels; felt-tipped pen; 'What does it do?' interactive available on the CD-ROM; computer

MAIN ACTIVITY

Show the children the pictures of electrical appliances in your collection. Talk about what each one is used for. Sort the pictures into rows according to whether each appliance gives heat, sound or light. Talk about the ones that also have a moving part, such as the drum in a washing machine or the blades on a fan.

Organise Group activities with adult support:

1 Work with groups of up to six children to cut out pictures of electrical items from magazines and catalogues, and/or from a copy of photocopiable page 145, and talk about them. As the children cut out each picture, ask them why and how the appliance is used. *Does it gives out light, sound or heat? Does it have a moving part?* You may wish to sort the pictures into sets according to these properties. You may need to have more than one picture of some items that fit into more than one set (for example, a television gives out light and sound). Some children may cope with the concept of overlapping sets.

2 Ask an adult helper to sort a collection of electrical appliances with groups of four children at a time. Use portable appliances such as a kettle, hairdryer, food mixer, lamp, portable CD player, cassette recorder, radio, iron and toaster.

3 Ask four children at a time to take it in turns to iron the doll's clothes, prepare a meal and listen to a taped story in the 'home' role-play area. Encourage them to think about how they are using electricity.

4 With a small group of children, label the play 'electric' items in the 'home' role-play area according to whether they give out light, sound, heat or none of these.

ICT LINK ◎

Play 'What does it do?' interactive from the CD-ROM. Children must sort the items into the correct groups, under the headings 'light', 'sound', 'heat' and 'moving parts'.

ASSESSMENT

Record the children's responses to your questions in Group activity 1, and note those who will need further support. How many children can find the appliances that have moving parts? Ask different ability groups to draw different numbers of items that give out heat, sound or light or make things move; keep the drawings as evidence of their understanding.

PLENARY

Ask the group to talk about the items in the collection that have motors, explaining that these items all work with electricity and pointing out the bits that move.

OUTCOMES

● All children *must* be able to notice what happens when an electrical item is turned on.

Differentiation

Support

In Group activity 1, give children 'What does it do?' (green) from the CD-ROM which features fewer items for them to sort into sets. Play 'Pick up a picture', challenging them to find a picture of something that provides light, heat or sound. As their understanding develops, ask them to find a picture of something that gives out light *and* heat, light *and* sound and so on.

Extension

Give the children 'What does it do?' (blue) from the CD-ROM, and encourage the children to sort items into sets depending on whether they have one, two, three or four uses.

- Most of the children *should* know that electrical items can give out heat, light, sound and/or movement.
- Some *could* make drawings to record what they have found out
- A small number *could even* describe the basis for their sorting.

CONTEXT

The toy shop

You may wish to keep this context as part of a topic on 'My home', but it fits equally well into a topic on 'Toys'. Set up a 'toy shop' in the role-play area and use its resources as a starting point for the next two lessons.

Lesson 5 ◻ How does it work?

Objectives
- To learn that a battery is a portable supply of electricity.
- To learn that some toys and other items are powered by batteries.

Vocabulary
not safe, move, work, battery

RESOURCES

Main activity: Collection of batteries of different types and sizes; digital camera; collection of toys and other items that work by battery, including a talking bear or doll, a watch, a pottery wheel, a baby's musical mobile, a torch, a moving toy car.

Group activities: 1 Paper; pencils. **2** Magazines or catalogues with pictures of battery-operated toys; scissors; photocopiable page 146 (also 'How does it work?' (red) available on CD-ROM); pencils. **3** Paper; paints. **4** Battery-operated classroom objects (such as a radio, torch, calculator, clock, stopwatch and personal stereo).

ICT link: 'How does it work?' (red) on the CD-ROM; interactive whiteboard; remote-control cars and other battery-operated toy vehicles.

PREPARATION
Test the things in your collection to make sure that they all work. Have spare batteries to hand.

STARTER
Organise the children so that they are sitting in a circle. Place the batteries in front of you. Ask the children if they know what these are called. Confirm that they are all 'batteries'. Ask the children whether they know what these are used for. Confirm that they are used to make things work. Explain that a battery contains a kind of electricity that is safe for us to use – but emphasise that batteries are not toys and should not be played with. We

Differentiation

Support
Support children in thinking about the differences between batteries and mains electricity by giving them 'How does it work?' (green) from the CD-ROM to fill in, which features more common household items to talk about.

Extension
Challenge children to say whether an item can use both batteries and mains electricity, using 'How does it work?' (blue) from the CD-ROM. For example, a portable radio could be plugged in or run by using batteries.

must take care with batteries in the same way that we take care with electricity. Explain that batteries usually contain a substance called 'acid' that is poisonous and can be very nasty when touched. It is safe to use battery-operated toys as long as we do not touch the battery. We must certainly never try to find out what is inside it. If we find a leaking battery, we must always tell an adult straight away.

MAIN ACTIVITY

Invite the children to smile at this point, and take photographs of them all. Did they notice the flash? Ask whether they know what made the camera flash. You will get lots of answers to this question: the button, the bulb, the flash and so on. Explain that you had to press the button for the camera to work and that the bulb was what lit up, but that a battery inside the camera is providing the power to make the bulb light up. Without the battery, the flash would not work.

Look at the other things in your collection and talk about how the battery causes each item to work. Discuss whether the battery makes the item produce a sound, a light or a movement.

GROUP ACTIVITIES

1 Work with groups of six children to explore the range of items in the collection. Look inside each item to find the battery or batteries, and point these out to the children. Ask them to choose one of the toys and draw it with the battery compartment open, showing where the batteries are.

2 Ask an adult helper to work with groups of four children, cutting out pictures of battery-operated toys from catalogues and magazines. Each group should then work together to complete photocopiable page 133 by sorting the pictures into things that are battery-operated and things that are not. Check that the children are familiar with Scalextric sets.

3 Set up a painting table and ask the children to take it in turns to paint a picture of their favourite battery-operated toy.

4 Ask the children to find all the things in the classroom that are operated by battery. Make sure you have left one or two objects around for them to find, but also remember to remove things that you do not want them to touch (such as the DVD remote control).

5 Support children by giving them the opportunity to play with a selection of battery-operated toys.

ICT LINK

Talk to the children as they play with remote control cars and other toy vehicles. Ask them to show you how they move the controls to make the car move forwards and backwards and how they make it turn. Challenge them make the car follow a designated pathway.

Display 'How does it work?' (red) from the CD-ROM on an interactive whiteboard. Use the drawing tool to complete the worksheet as a whole-class activity.

ASSESSMENT

Photocopiable page 146 asks the children to identify items that are operated by batteries and items that contain no batteries. If completed independently, the sheet can be retained as evidence of the children's understanding. Make a note of the amount of help given to those children who required it.

PLENARY

Talk about the children's paintings of toys. Together, make a display of things that work by battery and things that do not, similar to the display in Lesson 3 of this unit.

OUTCOMES

● All children **must** be able to recognise batteries and that they can be dangerous if not handled properly.
● Most of the children **should** be able to ask and answer questions about how things work.
● Some **could** know that batteries are a source of power and that they make things work.
● A small number **could even** compare how batteries make different items work.

LINKS

ECM 2: Staying safe.
Across the curriculum: a link with personal, social and emotional development is made through the children considering how to keep themselves and others safe.

Lesson 6 Switch it off!

RESOURCES

Range of battery-operated toys and other items. Make sure that all the items all work, and that you have spare batteries if necessary; paper; pencils.

MAIN ACTIVITY

Help the children to identify the switches on all the items in your collection. Organise Group activities with adult support:
1 Ask an adult helper to work with a group of four children at a time, investigating and exploring how a range of battery-operated toys and other items work. The children should try to find the on/off switch on each item.
2 Allow the children to play with the items, so that they are familiar with using the switches to make the items start and stop working.
3 Work with groups of six to eight children, drawing pictures of an individually chosen item and labelling the on/off switch.

ASSESSMENT

Keep the children's pictures of their chosen items and note on each one whether the task was completed independently or with support.

Differentiation

Support
For support, children should be allowed to play with the items for five minutes before being directed to do Group activities 1 and 3.
Extension
Extend children's skills by encouraging them to work independently on Group activity 2 before making their drawings. They have no need to complete Group activity 1.

PLENARY

Ask two or three children to talk about their favourite item and explain how they made it work by using the on/off switch. Talk about how the switch worked: *Did you push it or slide it?*

OUTCOMES

● All of the children *must* be able to identify the switch on a battery-operated item.
● Most of the children *should* be able to know that a switch may be needed to make something work.
● Some *could* record their findings by making drawings.
● A small number *could even* describe the movement of familiar objects.

Lesson 7 ▪ Assessment

Objectives
● To assess the children's ability to identify and sort items by whether mains electricity or batteries power them.
● To assess the children's understanding of the dangers of electricity.

RESOURCES ◉
Main assessment activity: Collection of small electrical items, both mains-operated and battery-operated.
Assessment activities: 2 photocopiable page 146 (also 'How does it work?' (red) available on the CD-ROM – see Lesson 5 in this unit); pencils. **3** Pictures of items that work by mains electricity, by battery and by neither (the latter items might work by springs, hand force, solar power); sorting rings.
ICT link: 2 'How does it work?' (red) on CD-ROM – see Lesson 5 in this unit.

PREPARATION
Make sure that the electrical items in the collection work. Make one copy for each child of photocopiable page 146.

MAIN ASSESSMENT ACTIVITY
Look at the things in your collection. Show the children how the mains-operated items work before letting them play with the battery-operated items. Spend a few minutes talking about how the items work before sorting them together into two sets: those operated by mains electricity and those operated by battery. Find out by questioning which children understand that electricity is dangerous.

ASSESSMENT ACTIVITY 2 ◉
Ask the children to complete photocopiable page 146, which asks them to identify items powered by mains electricity or by battery.

ICT LINK ◉
Display 'How does it work?' (red) from the CD-ROM on an interactive whiteboard. Use the drawing tool to complete the worksheet as a whole-class activity.

ASSESSMENT ACTIVITY 3
Work with groups of four children to sort a set of pictures (different from those on photocopiable page 146) into items that work by electricity, items that work by battery and items that use neither.

PLENARY
Look at the set of pictures used in Assessment activity 3, with a few additional ones, and sort these together into two sets: those appliances powered by mains electricity and those powered by battery.

ASSESSMENT OUTCOMES
On completion of these Assessment activities, you should know which children have attained the following objectives linked to knowledge and understanding of the world:
● All the children *must* know that electricity can be dangerous.
● Most of the children *should* identify whether a range of familiar objects work by battery or by mains electricity.
● Some *could* know that some things work by mains electricity, some work by battery and some use neither.
● A small number *could even* talk about what they have found and point out which devices the batteries make work.

Things that use electricity – 1

PHOTOCOPIABLE

Things that use electricity – 2

 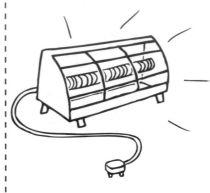 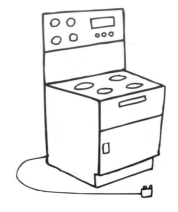

Illustration © Colin Shelbourn

■ SCHOLASTIC

What does it do?

How does it work?

■ In the box by each picture, write **b** if it works by battery and **m** if it works by mains electricity.

Illustration © Colin Shelbourn

◗SCHOLASTIC

Lesson	Objectives	Main activity	Group activities	Plenary	Outcomes
Lesson 1 Pulling and pushing	• To learn that string, rope, laces, cords and other non-rigid items must be pulled and not pushed.	Pull and push a skipping rope. Talk about things that use a cord or string. Make pulley systems. Explore the effects of pulling and pushing strings and laces.		Ask children to demonstrate and explain their pulleys and pull-along toys.	• Know some uses of rope, string and cord. • Know that rope, string and cord are pulled, not pushed, when they are used. • Know that it is sometimes easier to lift things with pulleys than by hand.
Lesson 2 Pull it on	• To discover that we need to pull (not push) most of our clothes on when we get dressed.	Explore how we pull items of clothing on and off.	Play the 'Dress the teddy' computer game and a 'Dress the bear' board game. Use dressing-up to explore how clothes are pulled on. Make a bed.	Invite an adult to put on a sari or turban.	• Know that most items of clothing are put on with a pull. • Can take photographs to record what they have found out. • Can identify simple things that certain items have in common.
Lesson 3 Moving around	• To learn that some toys move when pushed, some when pulled, and others when either pushed or pulled. • To begin to sort objects according to the way they are moved.	Explore and label a collection of toys that work with a push, with a pull or with either.	Sort the toys. Investigate the movement of a rocking horse. Ride tricycles and see-saws. Develop bat and ball skills. Role-play a toy shop.	Talk about how the children made the tricycles move. Sort the children's photographs.	• Know that some toys work by being pushed, some by being pulled, and some by being either pushed or pulled. • Can investigate the movement of familiar things. • Can record the results of an investigation. • Can talk about what they have found out.
Lesson 4 Prize vegetables!	• To explore how a range of familiar objects can be moved by pulling.	Talk about what things are pulled in the story 'The Enormous Turnip'. Make string patterns. Pull cards from envelopes. Play 'Dress the bear'.		Label items in the classroom that operate by a pull.	• Know that some things move when pulled. • Can draw pictures to record their findings.
Lesson 5 Wheel it along	• To explore a range of objects that move or work by being pushed.	Push a wheelbarrow and talk about its movement.	Explore finger painting. Ice cakes. Make symmetrical blob patterns. Blow paint through a straw. Push vehicles on a trail.	Talk about how the straw-blown paintings and symmetrical patterns were made.	• Explore and identify a range of things that move when pushed. • Can explain how they used their fingers and air to push paint around paper. • Can explain how they used their fingers to push icing out of a bag or tube.
Lesson 6 Bouncing balloons	• To learn that when air is pushed into a balloon, the balloon stretches and changes shape.	Learn vocabulary to describe how a balloon changes size and shape as it is inflated.	Watch balloon models being made. Inflate balloons. Keep a balloon in the air. Investigate how designs on balloons change as they are inflated.	Demonstrate and talk about how balloon models are made.	• Understand that when air is pushed into it, a balloon gets bigger and changes shape. • Can record changes by drawing 'Before' and 'After' pictures. • Can recognise familiar objects that can be made bigger by pushing air into them.
Lesson 7 Make a stick puppet	• To learn that when a push is applied to an object, it may move.	Demonstrate how to make a stick puppet. Talk about how it works.	Make stick puppets. Create a puppet play. Order pictures to record the process of making the puppets.	Perform puppet plays. Discuss how the puppets work.	• Know that a push can make something move. • Have begun to understand that a pushing force is opposite to a pulling force. • Can show what they did by putting pictures into a sequence.

Lesson	Objectives	Main activity	Group activities	Plenary	Outcomes
Lesson 8 Pipe-cleaner puppets	• To learn that pushing can change the position and shape of some objects.	Perform bending actions to a rhyme. Make pipe-cleaner sculptures, pipe-cleaner puppets and wire sculptures. Explore a range of 'bendy' materials.		Demonstrate how their puppets can be bent into new shapes and positions.	• Know that some materials will bend when pushed. • Know that some things can change shape and position. • Can select from a range of materials to make models and sculptures.
Lesson 9 Moving cards	• To investigate how pushing or pulling a stick can make something move.	Look at books that have moveable parts. Make cards and a display with parts that move. Make puppet theatres.		Talk about the things they have made, explaining how the parts that move work.	• Know that sticks can make things move. • Know that a push or a pull can make something move. • Can persevere to produce a model with moving parts.

Assessment	Objectives	Main activity	Activities 2 and 3	Activity 4	Outcomes
Lesson 10	• To assess the children's ability to identify whether items need a push, a pull, either or both to make them work.	Sort a collection of fasteners by how they work.	Sort various other items in a similar way. Identify objects that need a pull, a push or either to work.	Find objects in the classroom that need a pull, a push or either to work.	• Can say whether familiar objects require a pull, a push or either to make them work. • Know that the fasteners on our clothes need to be pushed, pulled or pushed and pulled to open and close them. • Can sort familiar objects into three sets according to given criteria.

CONTEXT  The toy shop/rhymes

This lesson can be set in the context of a toy shop (see Lessons 3–9) or a 'Stories and rhymes' topic. For example, it could follow up a literacy activity looking at rhyming words.

Lesson 1 ▪ Pulling and pushing

Objective
● To learn that string, rope, laces, cords and other non-rigid items must be pulled and not pushed.

RESOURCES

Skipping rope; length of string, curtain cord or blind cord; the classroom window-blind; collection of pull-along toys; short pieces of string; old shoe and shoelace; model car with a trailer attached loosely by a shoelace; buckets of sand. Make a display of 'Hickory Dickory Dock' and 'Little Miss Muffet', with text, pictures and models of a spider and a mouse.

MAIN ACTIVITY

Have a ten-minute skipping session with the children, talking about how the skipping rope bends and curls. *Can you keep it straight?* Tell them that they can only keep it straight by pulling it out tight.

Sit the children in a circle and arrange the skipping rope as a smaller circle in front of them. Challenge them to push the rope away from them. Repeat the activity with a length of string or cord. Talk about how items such as string and rope cannot easily be pushed somewhere, because they are bendy and not stiff or rigid.

Show the children how the blind in the classroom works. Encourage them to think of other things that work by a length of cord or string being pulled, such as pulleys, 'up and over' garage doors and curtains.

Organise Group activities with adult support:

1 Ask an adult helper to work with groups of up to eight children, making a pulley system to help the mouse go up the clock and the spider fall next to Miss Muffet. Emphasise that in the latter case, the cord is used to pull the spider up to the top. Each time the cord is pulled, the mouse and spider both go up. Extend children's thinking by asking them to explain this as they make the pull.

2 Make a pulley system outside for groups of four children to use – for example, to pull buckets of sand to the top of a table from the ground. Invite the children to explain what they are doing.

3 Allow a group of six children to play with a range of pull-along toys. Challenge them to push the toys using only the string.

4 Attach string to some of the toys in the classroom for groups of up to six children to pull along.

5 Work with groups of six children on lacing a shoe; talk about threading and pulling. Discuss the reason why the end of the lace has a hard bit. Challenge the children to push the lace all the way through the holes until it is tight. Does anyone manage it? If anyone says they can, ask them to show you!

ASSESSMENT

Note those children who have a good understanding of what a pull is. Note those who can describe how a rope can be pulled to make it straight, but cannot be pushed. Ask the children to name other things around the classroom that can be pulled but not pushed, and note those do.

PLENARY

Ask the children who have been playing with the pull-along toys to demonstrate how they have to pull these toys to make them move. Ask a

Differentiation
Support
Organise children into pairs, with one rope between them. Ask them to pull the rope straight. Explore what you mean by 'tight', 'rigid' and 'straight'. Now challenge them to push the rope. Explore what you mean by 'slack' and 'bendy'.
Extension
Introduce the term 'towing' and investigate situations where ropes are used for pulling – for example, to lead animals. Ask them to record all the situations they can think of. Talk about why a rope is not used for towing a caravan. Use a model to demonstrate that when the car stops, a trailer on a rope will crash into it.

group who raised buckets of sand to explain how they got them to the top of the table without straining their backs. Point out that the string in the pulley was used to pull, not push.

OUTCOMES
● All children *must* explore how rope, string and cord are pulled not pushed.
● Most of the children *should* start to ask and answer questions about how things work.
● Some *could* be able to say that rope, string and cord are pulled, not pushed, when they are used.
● A small number *could even* find out that it is sometimes easier to lift things with pulleys than to lift them by hand.

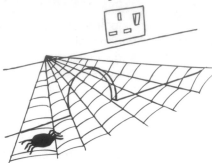

CONTEXT Taking care of myself

Teaching the children to take care of themselves is a good topic to base the following lesson in. The lesson focuses on the children's dressing and undressing skills.

Lesson 2 ▶ Pull it on

Objective
● To discover that we need to pull (not push) most of our clothes on when we get dressed.

Vocabulary
pull, socks, boots, hat, mittens, jumper, trousers, sunglasses, sari, turban

RESOURCES 💿
Main activity: the song 'I Jump out of Bed in the Morning' from *Okki-tokki-unga* edited by Beatrice Harrop (A&C Black); paper; pencils; the children in shoes and socks; digital camera.
Group activities: 1 photocopiable page 163 (also 'Pull it on' (red) available on the CD-ROM); coloured pencils. **2** Socks, Wellington boots, hat, mittens, jumper, trousers and sunglasses to fit four teddy bears or dolls; spinner and board (see Preparation). **3** Dressing-up clothes; four PE hoops. **4** Dressing-up clothes. **5** Toy bed with bedclothes.
ICT link: The *My World* 'Dress the teddy' program; 'Pull it on' interactive on the CD-ROM.

Plenary: An adult visitor dressed in a sari or a turban.

PREPARATION
Make a board with a spinner and pictures of the types of dressing-up clothes in your collection (see illustration, facing page). Send a letter to parents and carers, asking for clothes to fit the teddy bears or dolls.

STARTER
Sing the song 'I Jump Out of Bed in the Morning', adding verses for getting dressed such as

'I pull on my socks in the morning'. Take photographs of all the items that the children suggest they have to pull on when they get dressed.

MAIN ACTIVITY

Ask the children to pull off their shoes. Now ask them to pull off their socks. Organise them into pairs and challenge them to push each other's socks back onto their feet. *Who can do this?* If anyone says they can, ask them to show everyone so that you can all copy! Explain that we always pull our socks off, and we have to pull them on also. You may need to tell them that the only thing pushing is their feet, not the socks and shoes. Link this to Lesson 1 if you wish. Ask the children to think of other items of clothing that always have to be pulled on and off. Add these to your collection of photographs.

GROUP ACTIVITIES

1 Show the children photocopiable page 163 and talk about all the items that the teddy has to pull on as he gets dressed. Ask the children to colour each item that needs to be pulled on and off.
2 Play a 'Dress the bear' board game with four children at a time. They should take turns to spin the arrow: when it stops on an item of clothing, the child whose turn it is can find that item and put it on his or her teddy bear. If the bear is already wearing the item, the child has to wait for his or her next turn. The clothes cannot be put on in the wrong order (for example, boots before socks or boots before trousers). The first child to dress his or her bear completely is the winner.
3 Set up a dressing-up race outside (or indoors if it is cold): the children have to run through a sequence of four hoops, each containing a type of clothing, and put on one of each item. The first child to become fully dressed is the winner. Afterwards, ask the children to photograph all the clothes they pulled on.
4 Play with the dressing-up clothes in an area of the classroom, occasionally asking the children which items of clothing they put on by pulling, asking them to photograph these and adding them to the collection of pictures.
5 Set up a toy bed in one corner of the classroom. (You could relate this to the story of the Three Bears, reminding the children that Goldilocks took Baby Bear's bed as well as his porridge.) Ask the children to work in pairs to make the bed by pulling on the pillowcases, pulling the sheets over the mattress and pulling the duvet or blankets straight. Make a display of 'Making a bed', writing instructions for the children to follow with the word 'pull' underlined.

ICT LINK

Ask an adult helper to play the computer game 'Dress the teddy' with pairs of children.

Invite the children to play the 'Pull it on' interactive from the CD-ROM.

ASSESSMENT

Use the photographs taken by the children in the Main activity and Group activities 3 and 4, as evidence of knowledge and understanding of clothes that are put on by pulling. Note which children are able to think of additional clothes to the ones used in the lesson.

PLENARY

Ask an adult to show the children how a sari or a turban is put on. Both items require lots of pulling around the body, and are fascinating to watch.

OUTCOMES

- All children **must** find out more about how we get dressed.
- Most of the children **should** know that most items of clothing are put on with a pull.
- Some **could** record what they have found out in photographs.
- A small number **could even** compare items of clothing and identify what certain items have in common.

LINKS

Across the curriculum: this lesson also develops physical skills, personal skills of dressing and social skills of taking turns and playing fairly.

CONTEXT   The toy shop

The context of the next seven lessons is the toy shop. For this, you can use a range of toys already in the classroom and any that you have used to set up the role-play area. These resources can be used in all of the lessons to investigate pushing and pulling. Choose some toys from the outset that only need a push to work, some that only need a pull, and some that need either a pull or a push (see Lesson 3 below).

Lesson 3 Moving around

Objectives
- To learn that some toys move when pushed, some when pulled, and others when either pushed or pulled.
- To begin to sort objects according to the way they are moved.

Vocabulary
pull, push, open, close, in, out, forwards, backwards, to and fro

RESOURCES

Main activity: Collection of things found in a toy shop that can be pulled and/or pushed, including a toy piano, a talking toy with a pull cord, a talking book with buttons to operate its sound effects, a variety of push and pull toys, Lego bricks and other construction kits; labels marked 'Push', 'Pull' and 'Push and pull'.
Group activities: 1 Digital camera and printer. **2** Rocking horse. **3** Tricycle; pram; pushchair; 'sit and ride' toy; see-saw. **4** Bats and balls. **5** The 'toy shop' role-play area.
Plenary: Large sheet of paper; felt-tipped pen.

PREPARATION

Set up a tricycle track outside. Organise an adult helper to direct the learning of the group playing with the bats and balls, while you supervise the other groups.

Differentiation
Support
Allow children to push cars around a play mat. Talk about what they are doing, without relating the push to the movement of the car. Give them pull-along toys to play with, and tell them that they are pulling the toy along. It is appropriate for them to learn only what is meant by a push and a pull; if they are ready, go on to relate this to the movement of the toy. Use this activity as an assessment with this group.
Extension
Set up a skittle game for children to play. Talk about how the ball pushes the skittles over. Which children are able to say that they are pushing the ball, which is pushing the skittles over?

STARTER
Allow the children some time to play with the toys in the collection, either at the beginning of the lesson or during a previous play activity. This will ensure that they are able to talk about them from first-hand experience of their movements, knowing whether they need a push, a pull or both to be operated.

MAIN ACTIVITY
Play a tune that the children will recognise on a toy piano. Ask the children what you are doing to make the piano work. Explain that you are *pushing* the keys down, and this makes the piano play the notes. Now pick up the talking book and show the children how the sound effects are operated when you push the buttons. Emphasise that these two toys work when something is *pushed*. Put them together to one side.

Pick up a toy that talks and pull its cord. Listen as it talks, and watch the cord returning to its starting place. Invite one of the children to say what you did to make the toy talk. He or she should say that you pulled the cord. Select another toy from the collection that requires a pull to make it work. Put these two toys together in another place.

Repeat the activity with two toys that need either a pull or a push to operate them, such as building bricks or a pram. Put these into a third place together. Label the three groups.

GROUP ACTIVITIES
1 Ask an adult helper to supervise groups of six children as they talk about the three groups in turn, adding other toys from the collection and recording by photographing and printing out pictures of their decisions.
2 Work with a group of four children, investigating the movement of a rocking horse. Let each child have a turn at riding the horse while the others watch. Afterwards, talk about how the horse was made to rock forwards and backwards. Show the children how it works by using your hand and possibly feet to rock the horse: first pushing on the front of the horse to make it go forwards, then pushing on its back to make it go backwards. Explain what is happening as you do so. Reinforce the children's understanding that they push forwards and then backwards to make the horse rock by letting each child have another turn, feeling the different pushes as the horse rocks.
3 Set up a tricycle track outside and allow the children to ride around it. Use any other wheeled toys you have for the children to play with, including prams, pushchairs and 'sit and ride' toys. You may also have a see-saw for the children to explore. All of these require a push to move, and the children should be able to feel this as they push with their legs.
4 Ask an adult helper to work with groups of six to eight children, playing outside with bats and balls. As they throw, catch and hit the balls, the helper should talk about how they are pushing a ball through the air with their hands or a bat, making the ball go forwards and/or upwards.
5 Allow a group of four children to buy and sell toys in the 'toy shop' role-play area.

ASSESSMENT
Keep one or two additional toys to one side. At the end of Group activity 1, ask the children to say whether each of these items needs a push, a pull or either to work.

PLENARY
Ask a group who were riding tricycles and playing with wheeled toys to talk about what they were doing. Ask a child to explain how he or she made the tricycle move. Many will tell you that they 'pedalled' or 'rode' it, but some may say that they 'pushed the pedals round'. Emphasise or provide this explanation of how the tricycle works. Together, make three sets of

photographs: toys that need a push to work, toys that need a pull and toys that need either.

OUTCOMES
● All children *must* explore toys and notice how they move when pushed and pulled.
● Most of the children *should* be able to investigate the movements of familiar things.
● Some *could* know that some toys work by being pushed, some by being pulled, and some by being either pushed or pulled.
● A small number *could even* start to use scientific language to talk about and record what they have found out.

LINKS
Between units: this lesson links with Unit 4, Lesson 8, where the pushing force of rolling out dough to make biscuits is discussed.
Across the curriculum: this lesson provides opportunities to develop speaking skills by talking about what they are doing, and to develop gross motor and hand-eye co-ordination skills while using the various toys.

Lesson 4 ▸ Prize vegetables!

Objective
● To explore how a range of familiar objects can be moved by pulling.

RESOURCES
Version of 'The Enormous Turnip' (*Ladybird Tales* series, Ladybird Books); collection of vegetables (including carrot, parsnip, potato, onion, cauliflower and cabbage); paper; pencils; string; paint in a variety of colours; cards (some of which say 'You have won a prize. Well done!') in envelopes; sheet of pictorial stickers; digital camera; interactive whiteboard; 'Dress the bear' board game with appropriate resources from Lesson 2 of this unit; Post-it Notes.

MAIN ACTIVITY
Read 'The Enormous Turnip', a traditional tale, and talk about all the people who had to pull up the turnip. Talk about the other vegetables that are pulled out of the ground. You may wish to say at this point that weeds can be pulled up, but wild flowers should never be. Show your collection of vegetables and ask the children to paint a pictorial list of all the things that are pulled up. Refer back to Lessons 2 and 3 in this unit to talk about pulling and pushing different objects.
Organise Group activities with adult support:
1 Make string patterns with the children and talk about how they are pulling the string to make a pattern.
2 The children pull a card from an envelope to find out whether they have won a prize. The prizes are stickers that require pulling from a sheet.
3 Play the 'Dress the bear' board game from Lesson 2 of this unit again.

ICT LINK
Take photographs of real vegetables from the story and insert them into the interactive whiteboard for the children to drag and drop into a pictorial list.

ASSESSMENT
Ask the children to draw pictures of all the things that they pulled during the Group activities. Note those children who include things that they

pushed, and repeat some activities to reinforce their understanding of pushes and pulls.

PLENARY

Ask the children to identify all the things in the classroom that need to be pulled. Invite some children to label these, using Post-it Notes with the word 'Pull' written on.

OUTCOMES

- All children *must* know that some things move when pulled.
- Most of the children *should* start to ask and answer questions about how things work.
- Some *could* talk about how they change the movement of objects when they pull them.
- A small number *could even* start to compare the change in direction of objects when pulled.

Lesson 5 ▪ Wheel it along

Objective
- To explore a range of objects that move or work by being pushed.

Vocabulary
topple, balance, squeeze, push out

RESOURCES

Main activity: Wheelbarrow.
Group activities: 1 Tubes of thick paint; paper. **2** Icing in an icing bag; cakes. **3** Thick paint; paper. **4** Straws; paints in a range of colours; paper. **5** Collection of wheeled toys.

MAIN ACTIVITY

Look at a wheelbarrow together and discuss how to make it work. Talk about the wheel and how important it is to keep the wheelbarrow balanced, as it can easily topple over. Ask: *Do you pull or push the wheelbarrow? Can you do both?* Explain that it is possible to do both, but we usually push the barrow because we can steer it better and can watch to make sure that it stays balanced. Demonstrate this to the children.

GROUP ACTIVITIES

1 Work with groups of four children to explore finger painting. Let the children push thick paint from a tube or plastic bottle by squeezing, then swirl the paint around by pushing it with their fingers into recognisable shapes, letters and numbers, or into imaginative drawings and patterns. Finally, while the painting is still wet, they should make a print of it.
2 Ask an adult helper to work with groups of four children, using icing bags to ice cakes. This requires the children to push the icing out with their hands and fingers. They can use different-patterned nozzles to create different shapes and patterns.
3 Let the children work independently to make symmetrical patterns by blobbing paint into the centre of a sheet of paper, then folding the sheet and pushing the paint outwards and around between the sides.
4 Let the children make pictures and patterns in several colours by blowing air on to paint with straws, so the paint moves across the paper. Make sure that they don't get paint in the straws.
5 Set up a trail outside for the children to push toy wheelbarrows, prams, pushchairs and shopping trolleys around.

ASSESSMENT

Ask the children to draw a picture of their favourite activity and to label the pushing action in the correct place. Note those children who are able to do this unaided. (Also see Plenary).

Differentiation

Support
For support, give children plenty of opportunities to play with a range of toys and objects that need a push. Make sure that they receive adult intervention to challenge their thinking, and that they talk about the pushes they are exerting on the objects to make something move.

Extension
Extend the activity by asking children to go on a 'pushing safari' and label all the things they can find that require a push to make them move or work: a light switch, a door handle, a doorbell, a computer keyboard and so on.

PLENARY
Ask the children to talk about how they made their straw-blowing and symmetrical pictures and patterns. This will allow you to check on the success of these activities and to assess the children's understanding of how they pushed the paint by blowing or using their fingers.

OUTCOMES
- All children *must* show how they used their fingers to push paint around the paper.
- Most of the children *should* start to say how they used their fingers and hands to push icing or paint out of the bag or tube.
- Some *could* identify how they moved the paint and icing by pushing them.
- A small number *could even* start to compare the change in direction of objects when pushed.

LINKS
Across the curriculum: some of the activities in this lesson can be used to develop the children's creativity by giving them the freedom to create their own pictures and patterns. The control they need to exercise when icing the cakes supports the development of their fine motor co-ordination skills.

Lesson 6 ▪ Bouncing balloons

Objective
- To learn that when air is pushed into a balloon, the balloon stretches and changes shape.

Vocabulary
grow, bigger, air, blow up, inflate, round, long, stretch, bounce, float, thinner, change shape

RESOURCES
Main activity: Balloons; balloon pump.
Group activities: 1 Thin balloons that can be 'sculpted' into models (modelling balloons can be bought specifically for this purpose).
2–5 Balloons in different shapes and sizes, including some with pictures, words and numbers printed on them. **4** Paper; pencils. **5** Felt-tipped pens; labels.

PREPARATION
Find an adult helper who can make animals and other models from thin balloons.

STARTER
Blow up a balloon until it is quite big, then release it for the children to watch what happens. As the balloon darts about the room, prepare another and release it. Talk about the pathways taken by the balloons.

MAIN ACTIVITY

As you inflate a balloon, talk to the children about how the pump is pushing air into it. Emphasise the *pull* and *push* of the balloon pump. Ask one or two children to say what is happening to the balloon as the air is pushed in. Use words such as 'expanding', 'growing', 'stretching' and 'getting bigger'. Ask: *Is the balloon getting thinner? How do you know? Is the balloon changing shape? What will happen if air keeps on being pushed into the balloon?* Compare an inflated balloon with one that has no air.

GROUP ACTIVITIES

1 Ask an adult helper to come into the classroom and make balloon animals and other models. Ask him or her to talk about how the balloon is stretching and changing shape.
2 Ask the same adult to help individual children inflate a balloon using the balloon pump and add it to a balloon display. This could be a frame for a birthday graph or a display about a recent celebration.
3 Play a game in PE in which the children must keep a balloon in the air. Talk about how they need to push the balloon with their hands or feet to keep it up off the ground.
4 Work with a group of six children, observing what happens to printed numbers, pictures and words as a balloon is inflated. The children should draw 'Before' and 'After' pictures and write words to describe what the balloon looks like before and after it is inflated. Reinforce the vocabulary that describes how the balloon changes: *It stretches, expands, grows, gets bigger and changes shape as it is inflated.*
5 Ask the children to draw faces or write numbers on inflated balloons with felt-tipped pens. Remind the children not to bear down too hard on the balloon. Display the faces above labels with the children's names, or display the numbers in a line.

ASSESSMENT

Use the 'Before' and 'After' pictures to assess whether children understand that a balloon gets bigger and changes shape when air is pushed into it. Ask older children to write about, or draw pictures of, other things that get bigger and change shape when air is pushed into them.

PLENARY

Ask the adult helper to make balloon animals and models while the whole class watches. Talk about how the shape of the balloon is changing as it is twisted and turned, and how the air inside is pushing the rubber wall in different directions.

OUTCOMES

● All children *must* show an awareness that balloons are made bigger by pushing air into them.
● Most of the children *should* recognise that balloons can be made bigger by pushing air into them.
● Some of the children *could* record changes by drawing 'Before' and 'After' pictures.
● A small number *could even* understand that when air is pushed into it, a balloon gets bigger and changes shape.

LINKS

Between units: this lesson links with Unit 4, and can be used as a context to talk about materials changing shape. To extend, children can explore the properties of elastic materials under careful adult supervision.

Differentiation
Support
Make sure that children who need support take part in Group activities 2 and 4. Give them further opportunities to inflate a balloon, talking about how it changes in size.
Extension
Talk with children to extend their knowledge about other things that can be inflated, such as balls, bouncy castles and space hoppers. Talk about the materials from which these things are made and their properties. Inflate a ball and space hopper and invite the children to explain what is happening as each one is inflated. Can they apply this to explain what is happening when a bouncy castle is inflated?

CONTEXT　Puppet show

The next three lessons are still set in the context of a toy shop, but they can also be taught as part of a topic on puppets.

Lesson 7 ▸ Make a stick puppet

Objective
● To learn that when a push is applied to an object, it may move.

Vocabulary
pop up, push, move

RESOURCES
Main activity: Pop-up scarecrow puppet.
Group activities: 1 Photocopiable page 164 (also 'Make a stick puppet – 1' (red) available on the CD-ROM); materials to make each puppet, such as a plastic or card cup, a square of fabric approximately 20cm × 20cm, a length of dowelling approximately 20cm long, a circle of paper, a table-tennis or polystyrene ball, a strip of card 2cm wide and the same length as the diameter of the top of the cup; felt-tipped pens; adhesive tape; PVA glue; scissors; paper; pencils. **3** Dowelling; paper. **4** Photocopiable page 165 (also 'Make a stick puppet – 2' (red) available on the CD-ROM); scissors; glue; paper.
ICT link: 'Make a stick puppet' interactive (available on the CD-ROM); interacative whiteboard or computer.

PREPARATION
Make a large prototype scarecrow puppet (see instructions on photocopiable page 164).

STARTER
Sit in a circle and show the children the puppet. At the appropriate time, make the puppet pop out of the cup and watch the children's reaction.

MAIN ACTIVITY
Show the children your puppet and talk about the things you used to make it. Demonstrate how you made the puppet, using the Blue Peter method (*Here's one I made earlier...*). Make a list of the items used in the order that you used them, giving each one a number. Talk about how the puppet works. Show and tell the children that as you push the stick, the puppet appears out of the cup. Say: *The push makes the puppet move.*

GROUP ACTIVITIES
1 Working with groups of four children, give each child the necessary materials to make their own puppet and a copy of the instruction sheet (photocopiable page 164). All the children should complete this activity. When they have finished, talk to them about how the puppet works. Ask them to draw their puppet and label it to show how it works.
2 Ask the groups, as they finish their pop-up puppets, to work with an adult helper, making up a short puppet play to show the other children in the class.
3 Allow children who are sufficiently able to work independently in groups of six, making their own stick puppets from dowelling and paper.
4 Give the children photocopiable page 165 and ask them to cut out the pictures and arrange them in the correct order, then stick them in place.

ICT LINK
Show the children 'Make a stick puppet' interactive from the CD-ROM, on a computer or interactive whiteboard. Ask the children to drag and drop the pictures into the correct sequence, to show how to make a stick puppet.

Differentiation

Support
Support children by giving them 'Make a stick puppet – 2' (green) from the CD-ROM and encourage them to cut out the pictures and stick them into the correct order.

Extension
Extend children's thinking skills by giving them 'Making a stick puppet – 2' (blue) from the CD-ROM, which features pictures in more detail for the children to cut out and sort. Ask them what they should do to make the puppet go back into the cup. Note the ones who say that you can either pull it back down using the stick (especially if they say that they need to pull it back in because they pushed it out, thus showing awareness that a pulling force is the opposite of a pushing force) or push it back in from above.

ASSESSMENT
Use the children's labelled drawings to assess their understanding of how the puppet works. Use their work with photocopiable page 165 or the interactive game on the CD-ROM to assess their understanding of how the puppet is put together.

PLENARY
Ask the children to perform their puppet plays for each other. At the end, talk about how they made their puppets work.

OUTCOMES
● All children *must* notice and talk about how to make the puppet work.
● Most of the children *should* know that a push can make something move.
● Some *could* begin to understand that a pushing force is opposite to a pulling force.
● A small number *could even* start to talk about how their pushes and pulls affect the speed and direction of the puppets.

LINKS
Across the curriculum: this activity links well with literacy work, as the children can be asked to develop their plays over a number of days. The plays can be used as a context for text-level work and/or guided writing. The children's speaking and listening skills and experience of instructional texts will also be developed by this work.

Lesson 8 ▪ Pipe-cleaner puppets

Objective
● To learn that pushing can change the position and shape of some objects.

RESOURCES
Plastic-coated garden wire; pipe-cleaners; simple coat or tunic (to dress a puppet); adhesive tape; paper; felt-tipped pens; sharp scissors; digital camera; range of bendy materials such as paper, plastic straws, strips of cardboard and so on. Making a puppet beforehand will give you more confidence during the lesson, and will give you the opportunity to identify any likely pitfalls for the children.

MAIN ACTIVITY
Play a game, using a rhyme to the tune of 'Here We Go Round the Mulberry Bush'. Sing: *This is the way I bend my...* (bending a part of the body). Invite the children to stand up and do the actions.

Give each child a pipe-cleaner. Let the children play with these for a while before asking them to make an interesting shape or model. Give them another pipe-cleaner and ask them to attach it to the first. Let pairs look at each other's sculptures. Show the children how to twist the ends of pipe-cleaners together to make a join. Explain that pipe-cleaners are made from a material that can be pushed to bend it into different shapes. Look at some garden wire and repeat the activity.

Organise Group activities with adult support:
1 Work with a group of six children to make a puppet. Use the pipe-cleaners and wire to make a body shape. Twist the pipe-cleaners into a circle to make the feet, and use five smaller pieces to make fingers. Dress the puppet in a simple tunic made from two squares of fabric. Draw features on a paper circle to make a face; attach it with tape. Ask the children to draw a picture of their puppet and use arrows to show the places where a human body would bend (elbows, waist, knees and neck).
2 Let the children explore a range of 'bendy' materials that can be pushed into different shapes: paper and plastic straws, sheets of paper, strips of

Differentiation
Support
Support children by giving them lots of time to explore and talk about how they are bending and twisting the materials to change their position and shape. Encourage them to use the appropriate vocabulary.
Extension
To extend the activity, work with children sorting the range of materials into groups: 'Will fold', 'Will not fold'; 'Will twist', 'Will not twist'; 'Will bend', 'Will not bend'. Include some materials that will do none of these things, such as wood.

cardboard. Let them select their own material to make sculptures. Provide adhesive tape for them to join their structures with.

ICT LINK
Ask an adult helper to supervise the children as they explore plastic-coated wire to make simple three-dimensional sculptures. Help the children to use a digital camera to photograph these.

ASSESSMENT
Ask an adult to take photographs of the children as they bend the selected body part during the song and note those who correctly bend the right part. Play the game again with those who do not and extend the selected body parts with those who do.

PLENARY
Ask the children to show their puppets to the class and demonstrate how they bend and change position. Reinforce the learning objective: the puppets are being pushed into new positions and shapes.

OUTCOMES
● All children *must* comment on how their pipe-cleaners are bending to change shape.
● Most of the children *should* be able to select from a range of materials to make models and sculptures.
● Some *could* know that some materials will bend when pushed.
● A small number *could even* know that some things can change shape and position when a push or pull is applied.

Lesson 9 ▸ Moving cards

Objective
● To investigate how pushing or pulling a stick can make something move.

RESOURCES
Some of the Spot books by Eric Hill (Puffin); large display area; lollipop sticks; paper circles; adhesive; variety of paper, fabric, card and sticks; cardboard boxes; scissors; paint; brushes. Cover the display board with paper and cut-out card in wavy shapes.

MAIN ACTIVITY
Look at some books that use cardboard strips to make things move on the page and paper flaps to hide things, such as the Spot books by Eric Hill. Talk about how the things in the book move. Look closely at how a picture can be moved when it is stuck to the end of a cardboard strip or lollipop stick. Give each child a lollipop stick and a card circle or sticker to play with, and show how these can be moved about.
   Organise Group activities with adult support:
1 Let the children make cards showing the nursery rhyme 'Hey Diddle Diddle', making the cow jump over the Moon by attaching a picture to the end of a lollipop stick.
2 Let the children make cards decorated with flowers, with a slit across the middle at the bottom that starts and finishes about 2cm from either edge so that an animal can 'run' across the front of the card.
3 Together, sponge-paint wave shapes and staple them at each end to the top of the display board. Design, paint and cut out fish shapes, attach them to strips of card and thread them through the waves, so that the children can make the fish move across the display.
4 Help the children to make puppet theatres from cardboard boxes with slits cut in the back, top and sides. They should stick drawings of characters to

lollipop sticks or card strips, thread these through the slits in the box and make them move. Let them perform their own puppet shows.

ASSESSMENT
In the Plenary session, listen to check whether the children can describe how their model works.

PLENARY
Let the children show the things that they have made. Ask them to say how each one works. How do they make the things move? Do they push or pull the sticks?

OUTCOMES
- All children *must* know how to make their models move.
- Most of the children *should* be able to ask and answer questions about how things work.
- Some *could* be able to explain how their model works by relating their actions to its movements.
- A small number *could even* compare the way their model moves with a friend's and note the similarities and differences.

Lesson 10 ◾ Assessment

RESOURCES
Main assessment activity: Selection of clothes with zips, buttons, hook-and-eye and press-stud fastenings; selection of shoes with Velcro fasteners, buckles and laces; three sorting rings labelled 'Push', 'Pull' and 'Push and pull'.
Assessment activities: 2 Collection of objects used in Lessons 1–5 of this unit. **3** Collection of objects used in Lessons 1–5 of this unit; three cards labelled 'Push', 'Pull' and 'Push and pull'; sorting rings from Main assessment activity 1. **4** More sets of labelled cards (one card per child).
ICT link: 2 Digital camera; interactive whiteboard.
Plenary: A3 paper; pencils.

STARTER
Show the children the items of footwear and clothing, and focus on all the different fasteners. Ask each child, in turn, to show the others how one fastener works.

MAIN ACTIVITY
Talk to the children about the zip fastener. *Is the zip pulled or pushed to make it move up and down, or does it need to be pushed one way and pulled the other way?* Tell them that a zip is always pulled to open and close it. Put the zip into the sorting ring labelled 'Pull'. Note (or ask an adult helper to note) the children's responses. Now talk about the Velcro and ask the same question. If necessary, say that the Velcro is pulled to undo it but is pushed to fasten it. Put the Velcro into the sorting ring labelled 'Push and pull'. Repeat the activity with the other items in your collection. Talk about the sorted items.

ASSESSMENT ACTIVITY 2
Repeat the Main assessment activity with a different set of objects (including those used in Lessons 1–5 of this unit), working with groups of four children. Repeat the assessment a few days later with those children who did not quite understand the first time. With children who need support, repeat the Main assessment activity in groups of two, three or four.

ICT LINK
You may wish to take photographs of the objects in your collection, and set up the pictures on the interactive whiteboard for the children to sort the items into the appropriate groups. Do this for a number of days after the activity.

ASSESSMENT ACTIVITY 3
Place the collection of items in the centre of a group of eight children. Shuffle the label cards and hold up the one on top. Invite one child to find an item that matches the label exactly (for example, if 'Pull' is held up then the child should find an object that requires only a pull to work). Ask the child to explain his or her choice, and invite the rest of the group to say whether the child is correct. If correct, the child may keep the object. When the game is finished, count up the number of objects each child has. Place the three sorting rings in the centre of the group and label them 'Pull', 'Push' and 'Push and pull' (tell the children what the labels say). Ask the children to put their objects into the correct sorting rings.

This game can be differentiated in many ways. To extend the activity, make sure that children are left with more challenging and less obvious items to distinguish, including some that they have not explored before. Support children by asking them to select from objects included in previous lessons in the unit.

ASSESSMENT ACTIVITY 4
Give each child a 'Push', 'Pull' or 'Push and pull' label. Ask the children to find an object in the classroom that works in that way. When they have done so, ask them to say why they chose the object they did. Tick the names of the children who are able to complete this activity.

PLENARY
Together, make three lists of all the items identified in Assessment activity 4: one list of items that require a push, another list of items that require a pull, and a third list of items that work by either a push or a pull (or by both).

ASSESSMENT OUTCOMES
On completion of these Assessment activities, you should know which children have attained the following objectives linked to knowledge and understanding of the world:
- All children *must* explore and make a range of familiar objects work.
- Most of the children *should* know that the fasteners on our clothes need to be pushed, pulled or pushed and pulled to open and close them.
- Some *could* say whether familiar objects require a pull, a push or either to make them work.
- A small number *could even* sort familiar objects into three sets according to given criteria.

Pull it on

■ Colour all the things that we **pull** on and **pull** off.

PHOTOCOPIABLE

Make a stick puppet –1

1.

2.

3.

4.

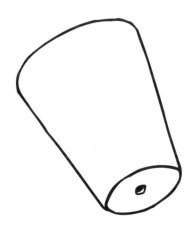

5.

6.

Illustration © Colin Shelbourn

◖SCHOLASTIC

Make a stick puppet – 2

■ Cut out and stick in the correct order.

Illustration © Colin Shelbourn

UNIT 7 Light and sound

Lesson	Objectives	Main activity	Group activities	Plenary	Outcomes
Lesson 1 Colour recognition	• To learn that there are lots of different colours in the world. • To learn and recognise the names of familiar colours. • To sort objects into sets of the same colour.	Make lists of objects that have familiar colours.	Make colour displays. Sort objects and shapes by colour, considering shades. Paint pictures of coloured objects. Make coloured, textured patterns from paper and fabric.	Sort the children's paintings by colour and add them to the display.	• Can recognise and identify familiar colours in the environment. • Understand that there is a range of colours in the local environment. • Can make simple recordings of their observations. • Are developing early observation skills.
Lesson 2 Light sources	• To learn that some things produce and give out light, and that these are called 'light sources'.	Explore light sources. Talk about things that give out light. Draw and find pictures of light sources. Play 'torch tag'.		Make a book of the children's pictures. Turn on the displayed light sources.	• Know that certain objects produce and give out light. • Can make simple recordings of their findings. • Are developing early observation skills.
Lesson 3 Colour mixing	• To discover what happens when two colours are mixed together. • To learn that colours change shade when mixed with white or black.	Make patterns by mixing different amounts of red and yellow paint.	Make patterns by mixing different amounts of two primary-coloured paints, and by mixing white or black paint with a primary colour.	Talk about the shades and colours the children have made, reinforcing vocabulary.	• Can explore what happens when two colours are mixed together. • Can explore what happens when white or black paint is mixed with a colour. • Understand the terms 'darker', 'lighter' and 'shade'. • Develop early observation and communication skills.
Lesson 4 Colour changes	• To discover that things seem to change colour when looked at through coloured cellophane.	Look at familiar objects through red, green and blue cellophane paper. Explore the effects of looking through this paper. Look at kaleidoscopes		Talk about the colour of the same object when seen through different-coloured 'windows'.	• Can observe how various colours look when seen through red, blue and green cellophane. • Can communicate their findings by talking about what they can see. • Can develop their exploration skills by finding other objects to investigate.
Lesson 5 Dull and shiny	• To learn that some things are dull and others are shiny. • To learn that when things are shiny, they reflect light.	Look for a self-image in a range of materials. Sort them into two groups and identify the materials that reflect as 'shiny'.	Make a mirror. Find shiny and dull objects. Look for a self-image in a range of metals. Blow bubbles and look for reflections.	Talk about what they have found out when exploring metal objects and foils.	• Carry out an investigation with support. • Can record, by speaking and drawing, what they have found out. • Are developing observation skills. • Can select materials suitable for a given task. • Know what is meant by 'shiny' and 'dull'.
Lesson 6 Light and dark	• To identify light and dark places. • To learn how to make a dark place.	Find and make dark places. Talk and write about darkness.		Talk about their feelings when they visited the dark place, and what they could see.	• Can use their sense of sight to explore dark places. • Know that darkness is the absence of light. • Can investigate how blocking light forms a shadow.

Lesson	Objectives	Main activity	Group activities	Plenary	Outcomes
Lesson 7 Hunt the thimble	• To learn that it is more difficult to find an object in the dark than in the light.	Play 'Hunt the thimble' in the dark place. Talk about how the thimble was found.	Play the game again in the dark, with a torch and in full light.	Talk about whether it was easier to find the thimble in the dark or with a torch.	• Know that it is only possible to see when there is light. • Know that we use our eyes to see.
Lesson 8 Colours in the dark	• To learn that colours look different when it is nearly dark.	Explore the colours and shades of objects in bright light and in dim light.		Record which objects looked a darker colour and which looked the same.	• Know that light is needed to see. • Know that colours can look different in near dark and in bright light. • Can say what happened in an investigation.
Lesson 9 Colours of the world	• To know that there is a variety of colours in the world. • To sort objects by their colour. • To change colours by mixing materials. • To identify objects that are dull and shiny.	Make coloured biscuits.	Make coloured icing. Ice the biscuits. Make jellies and talk about how they look. Make and label sandwiches with coloured fillings. Make drinks and fruit salad.	Enjoy the 'colour party'.	• Recognise and name familiar colours. • Identify things that are dull and things that are shiny. • Identify things that reflect light. • Predict the outcome of mixing two colours.
Lesson 10 Can you hear?	• To learn that we use our ears to hear.	Explore the sounds of a range of musical instruments. Make different sounds with drums and beaters. Make shakers.		Demonstrate their shakers and talk about the sounds they make.	• Can make different sounds with the same instrument. • Know that we hear with our ears. • Can use the sense of hearing to compare different sounds.
Lesson 11 High and low	• To learn that different materials make different kinds of sounds. • To explore different ways of producing high and low sounds.	Explore different wind chimes. Order them by how high or low a sound they make.	Sort instruments by whether they make a high or a low sound. Make wind chimes from a range of materials. Order the sounds made with musical triangles of different sizes.	Listen to the children's wind chimes. Link the findings with wind chimes to those with triangles.	• Can explore different sounds made with instruments. • Know that longer tubes make lower notes. • Can observe similarities and differences between different objects, including the sounds made with them.
Lesson 12 The weather	• To learn that sounds can be loud or quiet. • To investigate how to make loud and quiet sounds using a range of materials.	Make sound effects to accompany one verse of a poem about the weather.	Make sound effects for all the verses. Paint pictures of the types of weather in the poem. Listen to a CD of the weather and identify the sounds. Listen to the sound effects on a computer story.	Perform the poem with the added sound effects.	• Can explore and change the sounds made with instruments. • Understand what we mean by 'quiet' and 'loud' sounds. • Can listen carefully to each other and work together. • Know that we use our ears to hear.

Assessment	Objectives	Assessment activity 1	Assessment activities 2 and 3
Lesson 13	• To assess the children's understanding of the different sounds made by musical instruments. • To assess the children's ability to explore a range of sounds made by a variety of materials, and to identify objects from their sounds. • To assess the children's understanding that sounds can be changed. • To assess the children's ability to identify objects from their sounds.	Listen to and identify sounds all around. Say whether they are loud, quiet, high or low.	Make sound effects to accompany a poem. Make different kinds of sound using a range of musical instruments. Make a musical instrument from a range of materials. Draw it and name the type of sound it makes. Match unseen instruments to pictures.

CONTEXT Colours around us

The first nine lessons in this unit are all set within a colour theme. Although they are concerned with changing and comparing colours in paint, food and light, they first of all provide a context for developing enquiry skills. The first lesson can be developed over a number of days or weeks. The book *The Rainbow Fish* by Marcus Pfister (North-South Books) could be read with the children to introduce the topic.

Lesson 1 ▪ Colour recognition

Objectives
● To learn that there are lots of different colours in the world.
● To learn and recognise the names of familiar colours.
● To sort objects into sets of the same colour.

Vocabulary
sort; the names of the colours in your collection(s)

RESOURCES 💿
Main activity: Large display board (or more than one) and surface(s); backing paper and drapes in a range of colours, including those of the rainbow; several cardboard boxes in different shapes and sizes; few shapes in different colours; sheets of A3 paper; marker pen.
Group activities: 1 Paper; coloured pencils or crayons. **2** Sets of coloured shapes and other coloured classroom objects; sorting rings. **3** Paper; paintbrushes; paints in a range of colours. **4** Scraps of paper and fabric in a range of colours, including the colours of the rainbow, silver and gold; adhesive; collage materials.
ICT link: Simple paint program; computer; graphing tool from the CD-ROM
Assessment: Photocopiable page 186 (also 'Colour recognition' (red) available on the CD-ROM).

PREPARATION
Cover the display board(s) with your chosen backing material. Arrange several cardboard boxes of different shapes and sizes along the top of the display surface, and cover them with matching fabric or paper.

STARTER
Tell the children that they are going outside to look for all the different colours that can be found in our world. Take them outside for a short session and ask them to look for different colours around them. Ask an adult helper to note down the children's observations for use in the Group activities and for the finished display. Ask the children which colours they can see most of outside. The answers will depend on your particular setting and the time of year, but they are likely to include a range of colours.

MAIN ACTIVITY
Gather the children around the display board(s) and talk about the colours that they have seen outside. Try to recall an example of an object for each colour in your intended display. For example, you could include bricks, doors, television aerials, trees and leaves. Show the children one of the coloured shapes in your collection. Ask them whether they can think of something they saw outside that had the same colour. Make a note of their suggestions by drawing pictures on a large sheet of paper. Repeat this for a few other coloured shapes. Stop when you feel that the children understand the activity.

GROUP ACTIVITIES
1 Ask an adult helper to work with six children, continuing with the Main activity but asking the children to record their observations independently. They could do this by drawing pictures in the same colour on separate paper.

Differentiation
Support
Be sensitive to any children who are colour-blind, and only ask them to contribute to a colour display that they are able to discriminate.

To support children, work with one colour at a time over several days or weeks. Reinforce the names and shades of the colours with this group, sticking to the more familiar colours: green, red, blue, orange and yellow.
Extension
Challenge the children to think of things outside school that they did not see directly on the visit. For example, they could think about road signs and perhaps suggest why certain colours have been used. (For example, warning signs and signs telling you to do something usually have a red border because this makes them easy to notice.) You may wish to move on to discussing simple logos on shop or restaurant signs.

The children's individual pictures can be stapled to the correct colour display at a later date.

2 Work with groups of six children in turn to sort shapes and other interesting colourful objects into sets according to their colour. Talk about what other things have these colours. Can the children think of examples of things outside school that have the same colour? Discuss the different shades in the collection – for example, talk about the similarities and differences between the colours in the 'red' set. The children can place the sets in the cardboard boxes of the same colour.

3 Set up a painting table and invite the children to paint pictures of some of the things they saw outside.

4 Set up colour tables (one table for each colour) and ask groups of children to use scraps of fabric and paper to make textured patterns to add to the display.

ICT LINK
Use a simple paint program to create paintings and patterns using shades of one colour. Use the 'line' tool to draw a wiggly pattern and 'fill colour' tool to fill in with shades of the line colour.

Alternatively, use the graphing tool on the CD-ROM to create a bar or pie chart to show the children's favourite colour.

ASSESSMENT
During the sorting activity, note those children who recognise certain colours reliably. Use a simple recording chart for this, such as the one on photocopiable page 169, which includes familiar and not so familiar colours. Keep some of the children's work from Group activity 1 to show their knowledge of the range of colours found in the local environment.

PLENARY
Look at some of the children's paintings and talk about why particular things were chosen. Ask the children to which colour board each picture should be attached. Explain that you will leave the shapes and sorting rings out, so that the children can re-sort any shapes that accidentally get muddled.

OUTCOMES
● All children *must* know that there is a range of colours in the local environment.
● Most of the children *should* be able to recognise and identify familiar colours in the environment.
● Some *could* make simple recordings of their observations.
● A small number *could even* begin to notice that some colours are used for a particular purpose, for example can be seen easily or give people a message.

LINKS
Between units: this lesson links with Unit 8, Lessons 2 and 4.
Across the curriculum: links are made with mathematical development through the sorting activity and the use of shapes. The textured colour sheets could be used to develop the children's sense of touch by encouraging them to explore different-feeling surfaces. Development of the colour theme into creative work is also possible. Over the next few weeks, add real items from the environment to the display; encourage the children to explore these using their senses.

Lesson 2 ◼ Light sources

Objective
● To learn that some things produce and give out light, and that these are called 'light sources'.

RESOURCES

Collection of objects that produce and give out light, including an electric lamp, candle, oil lamp, torch and overhead projector; picture of the Sun; magazines with pictures of light sources; several torches of different types; spare batteries; paper and pencils; paint and paintbrushes. Set up a surface to display the collection of objects.

MAIN ACTIVITY

It is very easy to confuse young children if you go too deeply into explanations on what gives out light and what reflects light. For example, the Moon does not give out light directly but reflects light from the Sun. Young children, however, will not understand this principle, since we cannot see the Sun at night but we see better when the Moon is full. If children suggest the Moon as a light source, simply say that it does not give out light but reflects the light of the Sun. Stars *do* give out light: our Sun is a star. I suggest that you refer only to objects that can easily be identified as giving out light: items that can be turned on and off (such as lamps and torches) and items that can be extinguished (such as candles). Should the children suggest objects that appear to give out light but technically do not, simply state that these are not light sources without trying to explain why.

Show the torch and ask the children to tell you what its purpose is. Pass the torch around the group and ask the children whether they can make it give out light. Spend a few moments switching the torch on and off. Repeat the activity with the other objects in your collection. Look at the picture of the Sun. Ask the children how we can turn the Sun on and off. This question will allow you to assess the children's conceptual level of understanding regarding day and night. Some children may know that the Sun cannot be switched off and does not disappear: it is giving light to another part of the world.

Organise Group activities with adult support:

1 Ask the children to draw and paint pictures of things that give out light (are light sources).

2 Ask the children to find pictures in magazines of objects which produce light.

3 Let a group set up a shop in the role-play area, selling different kinds of torches.

4 Play 'torch tag' with a group in a darkened room. Give each child a torch; they have to chase and 'tag' each other's light on the ceiling and walls.

ASSESSMENT

In Group activity 1, encourage the children to draw or collect pictures of all the light sources they can think of. Use these pictures as a record of their understanding. There will, inevitably, still be children who draw the Moon when you have explained that it is not a light source.

PLENARY

Talk about the children's pictures and the objects they have drawn. Use these to reinforce the learning objective and to iron out any misconceptions. Stick the pictures into a book to record what the children have done, and display this next to the collection of light sources for the children to look at. At some point in the day, make a special point of turning on all the light sources. Remember to turn them off when you leave the room.

OUTCOMES

● All children *must* develop early skills in observation.
● Most of the children *should* know that certain objects produce and give out light.

Differentiation
Support
In Group activity 1, ask children who need support to draw pictures of things in the 'light source' collection only.
Extension
Work with children to extend their ability to identify which part of the object actually gives out light, and which part is the energy source (for example, the bulb and battery respectively in a torch). Ask them to draw a picture of one item and to label the part that gives out the light.

● Some *could* recognise that light comes from a variety of sources and be able to name some of these.
● A small number *could even* start to compare the brightness or colour of different lights.

Lesson 3 ▸ Colour mixing

RESOURCES
Main activity: Red and yellow paint; large sheet of paper; large paintbrush; water; mixing plate.
Group activities: 1 and 2 Large sheets of paper; large paintbrushes; water; mixing plates; several adult helpers (or organise the activities over several days); black, white, yellow, blue and red paint; small pots.
ICT link: Simple paint program; computer.

PREPARATION
Put the paint into little pots for the children to use. Either powder paint or ready-mixed paint will be suitable.

STARTER
Show the children the red and yellow paint. Explain that you are going to make a pattern on the paper by mixing these two colours together. Go through the procedures for mixing paint – for example, the need to wash the brush before putting it into a different colour (although, if you have lots of small pots of different paints, it will not cause too much of a disaster if the children forget in their excitement).

MAIN ACTIVITY
Use red paint to make a shape somewhere on the large sheet of paper. Show the children how to wash the brush out thoroughly before using yellow to paint a yellow shape. Now take a little red paint and mix some yellow with this to make a different colour. Paint a shape with your new colour. Repeat this, adding different amounts of red and yellow paint to make many shades of red, yellow and orange, until the sheet is almost covered. You don't need to worry about running one colour into another because this should make a new shade of orange. If you wish, when you are sure that the children understand the process, you could invite a small group to help you paint the shapes.

GROUP ACTIVITIES
1 Set up six tables with paint in different colours. Three tables should have two colours (such as blue and yellow) and three should have one colour with white and black (for example, red, white and black). This will cover all the possible combinations. Talk to the children about whether they have made a darker or lighter shade as they mix the colours. Allow them to walk around and see the colours being made by the other groups.
2 Repeat the activity over a number of days, so that the children have the opportunity to mix different colours. Unless they have had first-hand experience of mixing a range of colours, their understanding of colour mixing cannot be assured.

ICT LINK
Use a paint program to make paintings in shades of two colours.

ASSESSMENT
Question the children during the activity, asking them to predict the colours they will make when they mix each pair of colours. Ask them whether they

will make a darker or lighter shade if they mix black with their chosen colour. Note those children who are able to answer or those who are not, whichever group is the smaller.

PLENARY

Talk about all the shades of colour the children have made. Create a colour-mixing poster to show which pairs of colours make orange, purple and green. Add the sheets to the colour displays created during Lesson 1 of this unit. Reinforce the vocabulary 'shade', 'lighter' and 'darker' by finding out exactly what happened when white and black paint was mixed with each colour. How many new colours were the children able to make by mixing pairs of colours?

OUTCOMES

● All children *must* explore what happens when two colours are mixed together.
● Most of the children *should* understand the terms 'darker', 'lighter' and 'shade'.
● Some *could* start to talk about similarities and differences in terms of the shades and tints created.
● A small number *could even* explain how they are changing one colour into another by mixing paints.

LINKS

ECM 3: enjoying and achieving.
Across the curriculum: this lesson links to creative development. The colour-mixing theme can be developed through other topics. The story *White Rabbit's Colour Book* by Alan Baker (Kingfisher), in which a white rabbit jumps into a series of paint pots, is a useful stimulus.

Lesson 4 ▪ Colour changes

RESOURCES

Red, green and blue cellophane; collection of bright green, blue and red objects; three mesh bins; black sugar paper; cardboard tubes; pipe-cleaners; paper clips; adhesive; adhesive tape; kaleidoscopes. Cut some of the cellophane into squares approximately 15cm × 15cm.

MAIN ACTIVITY

The primary colours of light are red, blue and green, and the children will need to know this in Key Stage 2. Using only these colours at this stage will help to prevent later confusion. It is not necessary to explain why you have restricted the choice to these three colours.

Give each child a piece of red cellophane to look through. Ask the children to say what they can see. Repeat with the blue and green squares. Respond to any questions and remarks such as, *Look, it's changed colour* constructively, perhaps by asking another question such as *Look again without the cellophane. Has it really changed colour, or did it just look that way through the cellophane?* Explain that when we look through coloured glass or paper, things may seem to be a different colour.

Organise Group activities with adult support:
1 Cover three quarters of a window with green, blue and red cellophane, leaving one quarter plain glass, and invite the children to look at objects outside. Take suitable objects outside for them to look at through the window; they can also look at trees, cars and so on. What do they notice about the way that green, blue and red objects look through each of the colours? The red and yellow 'Crazy Coupe' range of wheeled toy cars is good

for this, as they show very different colours when seen through each of the coloured windows.

2 Cover three mesh bins with red, green and blue cellophane. Take three objects of the same colour and place one inside each upturned bin in the morning. Ask the children to guess the 'true' colour of the objects. Allow them to notice any changes that appear to take place when the objects are removed from underneath the bins at the end of the day. Each day, change the set of objects for a set with a different colour.

3 Let the children make stained-glass windows by sticking coloured cellophane over holes cut in black sugar paper, then look through these and note apparent changes.

4 Let the children make model telescopes from cardboard tubes, and spectacles from pipe-cleaners, with coloured cellophane for the lenses.

5 Leave several kaleidoscopes around for the children to explore.

ASSESSMENT

Note those children who are able to describe the difference between the colours of objects when looked at through different-coloured pieces of cellophane.

PLENARY

Ask those children who are able to describe what they saw when they looked through the coloured windows. *What colour does the tree look when seen through the red, blue and green windows? What colour does it look when seen through the plain window? How many of you agree? Who thinks something different?*

OUTCOMES

● All children *must* observe how various colours look when seen through red, blue and green cellophane.
● Most of the children *should* be able to talk about what they can see and start to ask questions about why the colours seem to change.
● Some *could* find other objects to investigate.
● A small number *could even* start to draw conclusions about what they have found out.

Differentiation

Support
Use one colour only, developing the activity over a number of days or weeks. Choose objects that look darker and lighter when placed behind the chosen cellophane. It may be appropriate for the children to make comments while wearing glasses with coloured lenses throughout the day. Note any children who are colour-blind, and allow for this during the activity.

Extension
Ask children to explore a range of objects that, when looked at through coloured cellophane, look a different colour. Ask them to decide which colour looked the most different through each type of cellophane. Some may be able to predict the changes (for example, it will look darker, greener and so on) before testing their prediction with the cellophane – but be prepared for them not wanting to risk being wrong. The skill of prediction is about maturity as well as ability. Encourage the children to use the language developed in the previous lesson.

Lesson 5 ▸ Dull and shiny

Objectives
● To learn that some things are dull and others are shiny.
● To learn that when things are shiny, they reflect light.

Vocabulary
image, reflection, bent, upside down, mirror, dull, shiny

RESOURCES

Main activity: The story of 'Snow White and the Seven Dwarves'; mirror; collection of polished and dull wood; various metal and plastic objects.
Group activities: 1 Various sheets of metal foil (see Preparation); plastic sheeting; hardboard; cardboard; adhesive. **2** Sorting rings; selection of dull and shiny objects around the classroom. **3** Large polished metal spoons; metal objects; mirrors; paper; pencils. **4** Silver and coloured foils (see Preparation). **5** Bubble mixture and blowers.

PREPARATION

Provide mirror-sized pieces of various good-quality foils (at least 20cm × 20cm) for the children to stick on to pliable hardboard, thick cardboard or plastic sheeting. Make sure the foil has no creases. A good reflective covering, of the type used for car windows, will be effective for this activity (but this may be expensive).

STARTER

Read the story of 'Snow White and the Seven Dwarves', showing the children a mirror at the appropriate point in the story. At the end of the story, ask the children whether they can see their 'reflection' in the mirror. Explain that this is also called an 'image'.

MAIN ACTIVITY

Show the children your collection of dull and polished metals, wood and plastics. Pass the things around for the children to handle, and invite them to say whether they can see their image in the materials. Together, sort the materials into two piles: those that reflect an image and those that do not. Tell the children that the ones that show an image are 'polished' or 'shiny', and those that do not are 'not shiny' or 'dull'.

Compare the shiny things with the mirror. *Which is best for seeing your own image?* Elicit the response that the mirror is best. Now tell the children that Snow White's wicked stepmother has lost her mirror. *What can she do?* Tell the children that you want them to make a new mirror for the stepmother.

GROUP ACTIVITIES

1 Ask an adult helper to work with a group, each child making a new mirror for Snow White's stepmother from the materials in your collection. Provide a range of foils and different backing materials: plastic sheeting, hardboard and cardboard. Make sure that some of the materials are shiny and others are not. The children will need to select the best material.
2 Ask a parent or carer to help groups of up to ten children to find shiny and dull things for a display from around the classroom. He or she should reinforce the vocabulary 'shiny' and 'dull'. You may wish to provide sorting rings for the groups to use when they sort the objects. Leave the sorted collection on a display surface for the children to add items to during the week.
3 Work with groups of six children, investigating how their image looks in a selection of metal objects – some with a flat surface and some with concave or convex surfaces. Include the pliable mirrors the children have made, as well as large spoons and ordinary mirrors. Explain that the reflecting material in a mirror is a thin layer of metal. Encourage the children to talk about how their image looks in the different objects. Ask them to draw a picture of the image they see in each of the things they look into.
4 Leave the coloured foils on a table and invite groups of six children to explore their image in these foils. Ask them to find out whether one colour is better than another, and whether any colour reflects a clearer image than the silver foil.
5 Leave bubble mixture and a range of blowers for the children to explore. Ask them to look for reflections in the bubbles.

ASSESSMENT

Note those children who choose the most reflective material to make their mirrors. To ascertain their conceptual level, invite children to explain why their image is upside down in some items.

PLENARY

Ask the groups exploring the collection of metals and the coloured foils to talk about what they have found out.

OUTCOMES

● All children *must* know what is meant by 'shiny' and 'dull'.
● Most of the children *should* be able to select materials suitable for a given task.
● Some *could* record, by speaking and drawing, what they have found out.

● A small number *could even* start to notice that shiny things give the best reflection.

LINKS
Across the curriculum: this lesson links with the design and technology aspect of knowledge and understanding of the world. The story of Snow White can be used as a starting point for language and literacy lessons, and for work on investigating the number 7 in maths.

Lesson 6 ▪ Light and dark

Objectives
● To identify light and dark places.
● To learn how to make a dark place.

RESOURCES
Several thick curtains or blankets; tent or large cardboard box (that two children can sit inside comfortably); fixing equipment such as pegs and masking tape; torches; paper; pencils. Make sure that the 'dark places' you intend to visit are safe.

MAIN ACTIVITY
Take the children on a walk around the school, looking for dark places. There is usually at least one cupboard that can be explored. On return to the classroom, ask the children to say which places were dark and to give reasons why they think this was. Explain that these places were dark because there was no light: all the light had been blocked out. Tell the children that you are going to make a dark place for them to explore. Use a large cardboard box, curtains and blankets to make a tent-like construction. (You may wish to use an actual tent with extra covers over the top.)

Invite the children to use torches to explore the inside of the 'tent'. Limit the time for this activity, to give everyone a chance. An adult helper (or yourself) should sit inside the tent with the children, both to talk about the darkness and to supervise behaviour. Another adult should help the other children to record (in pictures) how they made the dark place. They should then write a simple sentence to say what darkness is: *Darkness is when all the light has been blocked out.*

ASSESSMENT
Note those children who understand that darkness is the absence of light. This will become apparent following their comments as they enter and leave the tent. The Plenary session will give you an opportunity to target those children to whom you've not had the opportunity to talk during the lesson.

Differentiation
Support
Children who need support should be allowed to explore the dark place both with and without a torch. Work with these children in small groups to make their own dark place (as in the Main activity).
Extension
Set up a play activity and challenge the children to investigate shadows by creating hand puppets and simple stick puppets, using a projector and a white screen. Encourage them to create a shadow play.

PLENARY
Gather the children together when they have all visited the 'tent'. Talk about how they felt when they first went into the 'dark place'. *Was anyone frightened? Can you say why you were frightened?* Ask some of the children to say what they could see when the torch was turned off and when it was turned on. Record some of the children's responses if you wish.

OUTCOMES
● All children *must* use their sense of sight to explore dark places.
● Most of the children *should* be able to notice that when light is removed, the place becomes dark.
● Some *could* know that darkness is the absence of light.
● A small number *could even* investigate, with help, how blocking light forms a shadow.

Lesson 7 ▪ Hunt the thimble

Vocabulary
dark, light, shiny, reflect

RESOURCES
Main activity: Dark place from Lesson 6 in this unit; metal thimble (or similar object).
Group activities: 2 Torch; paper; pencils.
ICT link: Computer with internet access.

PREPARATION
Test your dark place to make sure that the thimble cannot be seen without a light.

STARTER
Play 'Hunt the thimble' with the children, so that they understand the game: you hide the thimble, they try to find it!

MAIN ACTIVITY
Explain to the children that they are going to play the 'Hunt the thimble' game while inside the 'dark place'. Hide the thimble inside the dark place. Pick two children on whom you can rely to explain well and accurately what they have done. Invite them to go inside the dark place, making sure that very little light enters, and to try to find the thimble. Tell them that they are going to do this without a torch. When they have found the thimble and rejoined the class, ask them to explain how they found the thimble. *Which sense did you use? Did you use your sense of sight only, or did you use another sense to find it?*

GROUP ACTIVITIES
1 Ask the children to go inside the dark place one at a time and find the thimble, so that they all experience looking for something in the dark.
2 Accompany the children into the dark place two at a time. Ask them to look for the thimble again, but this time using only their eyes. They must not move about. After a very short time, turn on the torch and time how quickly the children are able to see the thimble. You may wish the children to record by drawing what they could see inside the tent when it was dark and when the torch was turned on.
3 Allow groups of four children to play the game again in a (light) classroom.

ICT LINK
Using the internet, ask the children to search for pictures of nocturnal animals. Talk about the size of their eyes and how they manage to see so well in the dark.

ASSESSMENT
During the Plenary session, note (or ask an adult helper to note) those children who realised that the light enables us to see, and those who have no understanding of this. It may also be useful to note those who claim that they could see the thimble in the dark. This again is a question of maturity as well as ability: the child may understand that we cannot see in the dark, but may not want to appear 'wrong'.

PLENARY
When all the children have had a turn at looking for the thimble, talk about whether it was easier to find the thimble in the dark or when the torch was turned on.

OUTCOMES
● All of the children *must* explore looking at a range of coloured objects in the dark.

Differentiation
Support
Ask an adult helper to accompany those children who may be frightened or who will not be able to report accurately how they found the thimble.
Extension
Extend the activity by asking children to think about why they can see the thimble better when the torch is turned on. (Because there is more light available to be reflected from the thimble.)

- Most of the children *should* know that we use our eyes to see.
- Some *could* say what changes are happening when light is introduced.
- A small number *could even* know that it is only possible to see when there is light.

LINKS
Between units: this lesson links to Unit 8, Lesson 4 on day and night.

Lesson 8 ▸ Colours in the dark

Objective
- To learn that colours look different when it is nearly dark.

Differentiation
Support
Be sensitive to any children who are colour-blind; omit the use of the particular colours they are unable to discriminate.

Children who need support should repeat the activity from Lesson 7: help them to find the coloured shapes with and without a light. This will reinforce the learning objective that light is needed in order for us to see.

Extension
To extend, relate the activity to the vocabulary used in Lesson 3 by asking the children to say whether the colours looked darker or lighter when it was dark and when it was light. Encourage them to decide which colour looked the darkest in the dark and which one looked the lightest – or did they all look the same shade?

RESOURCES
Red square; blue triangle; green circle; rectangle in any colour; torch; 'dark place' (see Lesson 6 of this unit); A3 paper and pen. Make sure that the dark place will have enough light for the children to see the shapes. You may need to carry out the activity with the torch switched on.

MAIN ACTIVITY
Talk to the children about light and dark. *How many of you like going out in the dark? Why not?* Explain that places look very different when it is nearly dark. For a start, everything looks gloomy. Talk about the colours that the children saw outside the school in Lesson 1. Look at some of the pictures that they drew. Ask them what they think these colours will look like when it is nearly dark. Many will say that they will look darker. Explain the following activity before starting it.

Work with groups of four children inside the 'dark place'. Turn on the torch if necessary, depending on the amount of light. Show the children the red square and ask them what colour it is. When they have all answered, shine the torch directly on to the shape and ask them again. Did they get the colour right? Ask: *Does it look exactly the same, or is it a different shade of red?* Encourage the children to say whether the shape looks darker, lighter, brighter or duller. Open the doorway to the dark place at this point, and ask the children whether the shape looks the same colour. *Has the shade of red changed?* Repeat the activity with the other shapes.

Ask an adult helper to play the same game with other groups of children in another dark place, if one is available.

ASSESSMENT
Listen to the children's responses during the activity to judge their level of understanding. How many children built on their learning in the previous lesson and understood that if it is nearly dark, they will not be able to see anything clearly?

PLENARY
Talk about what the children have discovered. *How did the colours look different? Did any colours look the same?* Record the children's findings on a large chart.

OUTCOMES
- All children *must* notice changes in the way colours look.
- Most of the children *should* know that colours can look different in near-dark and in bright light.
- Some *could* say what happened in an investigation.
- A small number *could even* know that light is needed to see.

CONTEXT Party time

The activities in this lesson draw together the learning objectives of the previous eight lessons. You can also use it as a context to assess the children's knowledge and understanding of mixing and how forces change the shape of materials. Invite the children to come to school dressed in one colour (for example, all blue or all green) on the day of the party. Please check for food allergies before the children eat any food. Carry out a risk assessment for Group activity 2 during the planning stage.

Lesson 9 ▪ Colours of the world

Objectives
● To know that there is a variety of colours in the world.
● To sort objects by their colour.
● To change colours by mixing materials.
● To identify objects that are dull and objects that are shiny.

Vocabulary
colour words; dull, shiny, transparent

RESOURCES
Main activity: Milk; food colourings; chocolate powder; biscuit mix; rolling pin; cutter; basins; clean paintbrushes; oven; paper plates.
Group activities: 1 Icing sugar; large bowl, spoon; droppers; disposable cups; round-bladed knives. **2** Red, green, yellow and orange jellies; bowls; water; spoons; cooker or microwave oven. **3** Bread; margarine; sandwich fillings in different colours (including cress, cheese, cucumber, tomato and pickle); paper plates; labels; pencils. **4** Fruits; sharp knife (adult use only); plate; large bowl; blue raspberry cordial; blackcurrant squash; water; transparent plastic cups; large table.
Plenary: Lots of bowls, plates, cups, spoons and paper napkins.

PREPARATION
Make enough biscuit mix for the children to have two biscuits each. You may wish to make a set of different shapes, animals or people.

STARTER
Tell the children that the day has come to celebrate all the work they have done on light and colour. Explain that you are going to make lots of things to eat for a party later in the day. At the same time, you are going to find out all the things they have learned about light and colour.

MAIN ACTIVITY
Roll out the biscuit dough and cut it into interesting shapes. Pour some milk into four different basins and mix in red, yellow, green and blue food colouring. Place a biscuit shape on a plate in front of you and ask the children what colour it is. Show them the different food colourings and chocolate powder and explain that they are going to use them to decorate the biscuits. Invite them to predict what colour the biscuit will turn if painted with the red, yellow, green or blue food colouring. Decorate your biscuit at this point and talk about whether their predictions were correct. Invite the children to decorate their biscuits. Place the biscuits in the oven to cook, then remove them before they turn brown. Give each child two biscuits.

GROUP ACTIVITIES
1 Work with groups of six children at a time to ice biscuits for the party. Mix a large bowl of icing sugar and place the food colourings on the table with a dropper in each bottle. Give the children three disposable cups each with small amounts of the icing sugar mix inside. Invite them to ice their biscuits using three colours. They can use the cups to mix small amounts of the colourings. Talk about the colours they could make, referring them to the

lesson when they mixed colours. Note those children who remember how to make orange, purple, pink, brown and green.

2 Ask an adult helper to make jellies with groups of six children, using a cooker or microwave oven. The helper should show the children the jelly before it is made, and ask them to say what colour it is and whether they think it will change colour when water is added. When the jellies are set and cool, the helper should turn them out and ask the children to think of words to describe the jellies, encouraging them to name the colour of each jelly and say whether it is dull or shiny. Can they see their reflection? Can they see through the jellies?

3 Make sandwiches with groups of children at the beginning of the afternoon. Invite the children in each group to choose a colour and to use sandwich fillings of that colour only. Ask them to label the plates of sandwiches by their colour.

4 Make a fruit salad for the children to enjoy. Mix some fruit-flavoured drinks. Talk about the colour of the water and the changes that happen when the cordial is added. Lay the table with the children, placing foods of the same colour together. Place the fruit salad and decorated biscuits in the centre. Before the party begins, talk about the things on the table that have been made by mixing colours. Ask the children to name all the things that are red, orange, yellow, dull, shiny and so on. Pour out drinks into transparent plastic cups, so the children can see the colour of each drink.

ASSESSMENT
Note those children in Group activity 1 who remember how to make orange, purple, pink, brown and green. Ask the helper in Group activity 2 to note the use of colour in their descriptions. Can the children in Group activity 4 point to anything that reflects light?

PLENARY
Enjoy the party food together!

OUTCOMES
- All children *must* identify things that are dull and things that are shiny
- Most of the children *should* recognise and name familiar colours.
- Some *could* identify things that give and reflect light.
- A small number *could even* predict the outcome of mixing two colours.

LINKS
Between units: this lesson follows up the biscuit-making experiences in Unit 4, Lesson 8

CONTEXT Music and dance

The last three lessons in this unit can be taught through the musical elements of the creative development area of early learning. You may wish to set up a music shop in the role-play area, so that the children can pretend to listen to and purchase CDs of various kinds of music and even buy musical instruments – it depends on how sturdy your nerves are! You may wish to develop some of the ideas through dance, both for creative development and for physical development. These lessons also develop the concepts taught in Unit 1, Lesson 9.

Lesson 10 ▫ Can you hear?

Objective
● To learn that we use our ears to hear.

RESOURCES
Range of instruments, including four drums, four tambourines and a range of beaters (including a brush and a felt beater); cardboard tubes; empty pots with lids; dried pulses and rice; gravel, sand; paints or gummed shapes; CD player and favourite CD; labels and pen.

MAIN ACTIVITY
Listen to the class's favourite CD and talk about the sounds made by the various instruments in the song: do they make loud, quiet, fast, slow, tinkly, banging or musical sounds? Give each child in turn a different musical instrument to play, asking the child to produce a given kind of sound (for example, a loud sound, a scratchy sound or a tinkling sound). Ask the children who are listening to describe the sound being made. *Which part of your body are you using to hear the sounds?* Challenge the children to listen carefully to all the instruments, then sort them into sets of instruments that make similar sounds. Ask them to label the sets according to the type of sound that they make.

Organise Group activities with adult support:
1 Work with a group of four children, using a variety of drums and beaters. Ask them to find out how many different sounds they can produce. Ask an additional adult to work with a group of four children, making as many different sounds as they can with a tambourine.
2 Leave out a range of materials for the children to make their own shakers. They should decorate the pots using gummed shapes or suitable paints. A parent helper could support this activity effectively.

ICT LINK
Set up a small group activity for the children to play along to a favourite CD with their home-made or conventional instruments.

ASSESSMENT
During the focused Group activities, note those children who are able to make a range of sounds by changing the beater or by using it differently. Note those children who talk about the sounds they have made using appropriate vocabulary. (Also see Plenary.)

PLENARY
Ask the children to show and demonstrate their shakers to the class. Encourage them to say what materials they used and how they made each shaker, as well as describing the sound it makes. Use this opportunity for further assessment of the children's understanding.

Differentiation

Support
Be sensitive to any children with a hearing impairment, as there may be certain sounds to which they are intolerant. Support children by playing a 'Follow my leader' game: beat the drum with a wooden beater and ask the children to copy your sound, then repeat with the other instruments in your collection.

Extension
Challenge children to record their sounds in a simple pictorial score.

OUTCOMES
- All children *must* know that we hear with our ears.
- Most of the children *should* be able to use the sense of hearing to compare different sounds.

- Some *could* recognise that sound comes from a variety of sources and be able to name some of these.
- A small number *could even* know how to make different sounds with the same instrument.

Lesson 11 ▪ High and low

Objectives
- To learn that different materials make different kinds of sounds.
- To explore different ways of producing high and low sounds

Vocabulary
high, low, higher, lower, highest, lowest, sound.

RESOURCES
Main activity: Wind chimes made from wood and metal in different sizes (to produce a range of notes, from low to high – make sure that it is evident which set makes the highest and which the lowest sound).
Group activities: 1 Selection of musical instruments, both pitched and unpitched. **2** Metal tubing; wooden dowelling or wooden wheels; foil; paper; strips of plastic; string or shoelaces; drawing pins; scissors; paperclips. **3** Selection of different-sized musical triangles.

PREPARATION
Drill (or ask someone to drill) a hole right through the metal tubing, about 2cm from one end, big enough to thread a lace or string through.

STARTER
Listen to the wooden wind chimes together. Ask the children to think of a few words to describe the sound they make. Repeat the activity with the metal chimes. Explain that different wind chimes make different kinds of sounds: some make low sounds and some make high sounds.

MAIN ACTIVITY
Ask the children to say which set of wind chimes makes the lowest sound, and which makes the highest sound. Put the wind chimes in order, from the lowest-sounding set to the highest-sounding set. If possible, hang them from a rail.

GROUP ACTIVITIES
1 Work with groups of six children, exploring a range of instruments to decide whether they make high or low sounds, or both. Ask the children to sort the instruments into two sets according to which type of sound they make.
2 Ask an adult helper to work with groups of four children, making wind chimes for the garden area (if you have one). They can hang pieces of metal tubing from strings attached to a piece of wooden dowelling; or cut spirals and strips of foil, paper or plastic and hang them close together from dowelling or a wheel.
3 Put out a range of musical triangles and ask the children to explore the sounds they make. Challenge them to put the triangles in order according to the note they make, from the highest to the lowest. Do they notice that the biggest triangle makes the lowest note and the smallest triangle makes the highest note?

Differentiation

Support

Be sensitive to any children with a hearing impairment. Direct children who need support in their exploration of instruments. Play a very high note on a glockenspiel and ask the children to play a high note too. Repeat the activity with very low notes and so on, until you are sure that the children can hear the difference between high and low notes.

Extension

Challenge children to explore what sounds they can make with a glockenspiel. Can they produce a high note and a lower note? Can they find other instruments that make both high and low notes?

ASSESSMENT

Make a simple tick chart to record whether the children understand the difference between high and low notes. Put an asterisk by the names of those children who can discern the difference between notes that are quite close together on the scale: these children may be ready to develop their musical skills further.

PLENARY

Listen to the wind chimes that the children have made, and decide whether they make a high or a low sound. Relate the discoveries of the group working with triangles to the sounds made by different-sized tubes in the metal wind chimes.

OUTCOMES

- All children *must* be able to explore different sounds made with instruments.
- Most of the children *should* be able to observe similarities and differences between different objects, including the sounds made with them.
- Some *could* recognise that sound comes from a variety of sources and name some of these; know the difference between high and low sounds.
- A small number *could even* know that longer tubes make lower notes.

LINKS

Across the curriculum: this lesson links with, and allows the children to attain, some of the Early Learning Goals in the area of creative development.

Lesson 12 ◘ The weather

Objectives
- To learn that sounds can be loud or quiet.
- To investigate how to make loud and quiet sounds using a range of materials.

Vocabulary
loud, quiet, soft, louder, quieter, softer, very loud, very quiet, sounds, effects, accompany

RESOURCES

Main activity: 'The Weather Song' from *Tinderbox* (A&C Black); copy of 'The weather' poem on photocopiable page 187 (also 'The weather' (red) available on the CD-ROM; watering can; water; large metal bin; large plastic sheeting.

Group activities: 1 selection of musical instruments. **2** Empty cardboard tubes; empty crisp packets; gravel in a tray. **3** Paint in a range of colours; paintbrushes; paper. **4** Commercial audio tape of the weather or other sounds. **5** Computer read-along stories such as those published by Oxford Reading Tree or Sherston (Naughty Stories), which invite the children to add sound effects at appropriate times.

PREPARATION

Cover an area of floor with plastic sheeting.

STARTER

Sing 'The Weather Song' together, adding body percussion as an accompaniment.

MAIN ACTIVITY

Read the poem about the weather on photocopiable page 187 to the children, and ask them what the first verse is all about. Talk about the sounds the rain makes. Invite the children to suggest a possible sound to accompany the first line. Will it be a quiet sound or a loud sound? Now look at the second line together and talk about the sound the rain may make. Can anyone find something to make a suitable sound to accompany this line? Read the third line of the poem and talk about the sound that water makes when it hits tin. Demonstrate this by emptying the water from the watering

Differentiation

Support

Be sensitive to any children with a hearing impairment who may be intolerant to certain sounds.

To support the activity, show the children 'The weather' (green) available on the CD-ROM, which features only the first verse of the poem. This will help children to focus their thoughts and concentrate on a smaller selection of sounds. (Please note there is no 'The weather' (blue) for this activity.)

Extension

Musicians can begin to think about how to make their sounds gradually become louder as the wind gets stronger and the rain gets heavier. After this teaching input, leave them to work together to compose their musical accompaniments to the poem.

can into a metal bin, and listening to the sound together. Decide whether it is a quiet sound or a loud sound. Finally, discuss possible sound effects for lightning and thunder; emphasise that the thunder sound must be very loud.

Talk about the need to care for our ears by not listening to very loud sounds.

GROUP ACTIVITIES

1 Work with groups of six children in turn to develop sound effects for verses 2 and 3 of the poem on photocopiable page 187, using a selection of musical instruments.

2 Ask an adult helper who has watched the Main activity to work with a group, adding sound effects to verses of the poem using everyday resources such as crisp packets, cardboard tubes, gravel and so on. The helper should reinforce the language and concepts of loud and quiet sounds, and then supervise the group as they practise their sound effects in another area of the classroom or school.

3 Set up a painting table so that the children can paint pictures of the kind of weather described in one verse of the poem. Let each group choose which verse to illustrate, but encourage them to select different verses.

4 Allow groups of four to six children to listen to a commercial audio tape or CD of the weather or other sounds. Encourage them to identify the sounds.

5 Read a computer read-along story and invite the children to add sound effects at appropriate times.

ASSESSMENT

In the Plenary session, listen to the children as they perform, to hear whether they have successfully created loud and quiet sounds in the appropriate places.

PLENARY

Allow each group to perform their sound effects for each verse of the poem in turn. Perhaps you could organise a performance in assembly.

OUTCOMES

● All children *must* be able to listen carefully to each other and work together to explore sounds; know that we use our ears to hear.
● Most of the children *should* be able to explore and change the sounds made with instruments.
● Some *could* understand what we mean by 'quiet' and 'loud' sounds.
● A small number *could even* consider how to create and change sounds to depict what is happening in a poem.

LINKS

ECM 1: Keeping healthy by making sure sounds do not damage our ears.
Across the curriculum: this lesson links to the Early Learning Goals for creative development, which include being able to recognise and explore how sounds can be changed. The children also have the opportunity to develop their knowledge and understanding of the world by carrying out simple functions on a computer.

Lesson 13 ▪ Assessment

Objectives
● To assess the children's understanding of the different sounds made by musical instruments.
● To assess the children's ability to explore a range of sounds made by a variety of materials.
● To assess the children's understanding that sounds can be changed.
● To assess the children's ability to identify objects from their sounds.

RESOURCES 💿
Main assessment activity 1: space in the classroom for the children to sit quietly; large sheet of paper; felt-tipped pen; set of 'reward' stickers.
Assessment activities: 2 Copies of a 'sounds' poem, such as 'Sounds Good' by Judith Nicholls (in *Twinkle, Twinkle, Chocolate Bar* edited by John Foster, OUP); pencils; selection of everyday objects. **3** Selection of musical instruments. **4** Range of materials for making musical instruments; scissors; adhesive; photocopiable page 188 (also 'Assessment – 1' (red) available on the CD-ROM); pencils; crayons. **5** Photocopiable page 189 (also 'Assessment – 2' (red) available on the CD-ROM); pencils; drum; wooden block and beater; set of bells; pair of maracas; musical triangle; rainstick; box with a lid or fabric cover.
ICT links: 4 'Assessment – 1?' editable, available on the CD-ROM; **5** 'Assessment – 2?' editable, available on the CD-ROM.

PREPARATION
Make enough copies of photocopiable pages 188 and 189 for all the children. Write out the poem with spaces for the children to draw pictures (see Assessment activity 2), and make copies. Put the instruments to be used in Assessment activity 5 into a box with a lid or fabric cover. Make sure that you are not going to be interrupted during the Main assessment activity, and open the classroom window.

STARTER
Gather the children together on the carpet and explain that they are going to listen to the sounds around them in the classroom and outside. They will have to sit very still and listen for two minutes. Ask them to suggest one or two sounds that they are likely to hear. Have a set of stickers ready as rewards if appropriate.

MAIN ASSESSMENT ACTIVITY
Sit very quietly for one or two minutes, listening to the sounds all around. At the end, ask the children to volunteer one sound that they heard. Make a list of these on the left-hand side of a large sheet of paper. When you have exhausted the children's ideas, go through the list again and ask the children to describe each sound in terms of how loud or quiet, fast or slow, high or low it was. The children may be creative and come up with other describing words. List the describing words on the right-hand side of the paper.

ASSESSMENT ACTIVITY 2
Ask the children to provide simple sound effects to accompany a poem read to them by yourself or an adult helper, using a selection of everyday objects. The children can draw their accompaniments as simple pictures above the appropriate words.

ASSESSMENT ACTIVITY 3
Ask groups of six children to select instruments and play a loud sound, a quiet sound, a high sound and a low sound, as well as scratchy, tinkly, musical and banging sounds.

ASSESSMENT ACTIVITY 4
Ask the children to choose from a range of materials to make an instrument. Ask them to draw their finished instruments and add suitable labels on photocopiable page 188.

ICT LINK
Display 'Assessment – 1' from the CD-ROM on an interactive whiteboard or computer. Ask the children to draw a simple picture of their instrument using the drawing tool provided. They can make their own labels to drag and drop into the appropriate place.

ASSESSMENT ACTIVITY 5
Show the children the pictures of instruments on photocopiable page 189. Remind them of the names of these instruments. You may wish to remind some children of the sounds that they make. One at a time, use each instrument to make a sound from within the box (so the children can't see) and ask the children to colour, number or tick the matching picture on the photocopiable sheet. Watch the children as they do this, and note those who are correct or incorrect (whichever group is the smaller).

ICT LINK
Display 'Assessment – 2' from the CD-ROM on an interactive whiteboard. Complete the worksheet as a whole-class; invite children to add their ideas to the board, using the drawing tool provided.

PLENARY
Invite two or three children to show, demonstrate and talk about the instruments they made in Assessment activity 4. Prompt them to describe the sound it makes in terms of how loud, high and long-lasting it is.

OUTCOMES
On completion of these Assessment activities, you should know which children have attained the following objectives linked to knowledge and understanding of the world:
- All children *must* know that we use our ears to hear and listen.
- Most of the children *should* know that sounds can be changed.
- Some *could* understand the difference between high and low sounds, and between loud and quiet sounds; recognise familiar objects by the sounds that they make.
- A small number *could even* consider how the sizes and the ways they are played create and change sounds.

Colour recognition

✓ recognises
✗ names correctly

Name	red	blue	green	yellow	orange	purple	pink	white	black	brown	grey	silver	gold

The weather

Can you hear the rain? Pitter! Patter! Pitter! Patter!

When it runs into a drain. Gurgle! Gurgle! Glug! Glug!

When it hits the old tin roof, Ting! Ting! Ting! Ting!

Thunder crashes and lightning flashes.

Can you hear the snow? Swishy! Swish! Swishy! Swish!

Falling softly to the ground. Thunk! Thunk! Thunk!

Hear it frozen, crunching underfoot. Crunch! Crunch!

Hear it turn to water when it melts. Gurgle! Gurgle!

Can you hear the wind blowing through the trees? Whoosh! Whoosh! Whoosh! Whoosh!

Rustling the leaves and blowing them to the ground. Whee! Whee! Whee! Whee!

The sun comes out, feel the heat. Phew! It's hot! Phew! It's hot!

Lovely weather we're having this week.

Illustration © Colin Shelbourn

Assessment – 1

■ Draw your instrument here.

■ Cut out the words below to describe the sound your instrument makes:

My instrument makes a _____ and _____ sound.

| low | loud | quiet | high | soft |

Assessment – 2

■ Tick ✔ the picture when you hear the sound.

1. 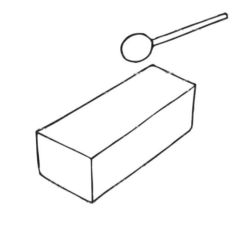	2. 
3. 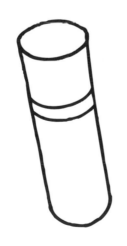	4. 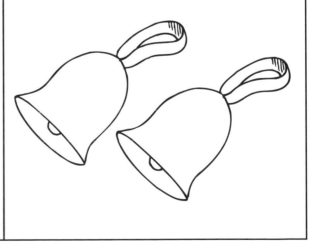
5. 	6. 

UNIT 8 · Earth and beyond

Lesson	Objectives	Main activity	Group activities	Plenary	Outcomes
Lesson 1 Up in the sky	• To learn that there are many things in the sky, some of which never fall to the ground.	List and talk about some of the things that are found in the sky.	Draw pictures of things in the sky. Sort other pictures by whether the things are always in the sky or are sometimes on the ground. Play picture dominoes. Make a display of things seen in the sky.	Talk about the things that are seen in the sky at night and in the day. Make a display of things seen in the sky during the day.	• Know that there are many things in the sky: some made by people and some there through nature. • Can sort things according to simple criteria. • Can record what they know by drawing.
Lesson 2 Rainbow	• To learn that rain and sunlight together can create a rainbow.	Create a rainbow. Talk about the colours seen and make a display. Blow bubbles and look at the colours. Add a rainbow to a picture.		Read the story of Noah's Ark. Talk about where the rainbow really is.	• Know that when it rains and the Sun is shining, a rainbow may appear. • Can communicate what they saw in an investigation.
Lesson 3 The night sky	• To learn that the sky looks different during the day and at night.	Make a list of things that can be seen in the sky at night. Talk about the shape of the Moon.	Make a display of 'The night sky'. Look for pictures of the night sky in books. Make pictures and prints for display.	Compare the displays of the sky in the day and the sky at night.	• Know that some things can be seen at night but not during the day. • Know that some things can be seen during the day but not at night.
Lesson 4 Day or night?	• To find out that objects look different during the day and at night.	Compare photographs of the same outdoor scene taken in daylight and at night.	Make the components of day and night street pictures. Make models of cars. Match pictures to day or night scenes.	Make the street pictures. Discuss the differences in colour and shade. Add light sources.	• Can identify similarities and differences between two pictures. • Can apply previous learning to a new situation. • Know that objects look different in the day and at night.
Lesson 5 Daytime sky	• To observe the changes that may occur in the sky during the day.	Look at the sky and talk about shadows. Remind the children never to look directly at the Sun. Draw pictures of the sky and play 'shadow tag'.		Compare the children's drawings of the sky at different times of the day.	• Can observe changes in the daytime sky. • Can identify similarities and differences in the appearance of the sky at different times. • Can recognise and observe shadows. • Can predict when they will see a shadow.
Lesson 6 What to do on sunny days	• To learn that the Sun can be dangerous and that we need to take care on hot sunny days.	Look at and talk about a range of items used on hot sunny days. Make a list of items the children would need. Sort the collection. Find a picnic area for role-play.		Make a list of things we need to do on hot sunny days.	• Know how to protect themselves from the Sun. • Know that it is necessary to drink plenty of water on hot days. • Are learning to consider their own needs independently.
Lesson 7 What happened?	• To learn that water apparently disappears on a hot day. • To learn that water dries up or evaporates.	Watch as puddles disappear. Talk about the changes.	Order pictures to record the changes. Investigate how long it takes for different puddles, and water pictures in different places, to dry up.	Talk about where the pictures dried up quickly and where they did not. Consider the reasons.	• Know that on a hot day, water dries up. • Can investigate, with support, how quickly water dries up on different surfaces. • Can say what happened in an investigation.

Assessment	Objectives	Main activity	Activities 2 and 3	Activity 4	Outcomes
Lesson 8	• To find out what the children know about the sky and beyond.	Draw a group picture of all the things that are seen in the sky and beyond it.	Draw a picture of a rainbow, showing how the weather would be. Draw group 'day and night' pictures. Talk about the changes.	Make posters showing the dangers of the Sun.	• Are aware that the Sun can be harmful. • Are aware of various things that can be seen in the sky. • Know that some things in the sky can only be seen at certain times.

CONTEXT

Displays

The lessons in this unit are introduced and developed through a series of displays. This is a useful tool for teaching very young children about their world, especially if the theme cannot be linked to play or first-hand experience.

Lesson 1 ▸ Up in the sky

Objective
● To learn that there are many things in the sky, some of which never fall to the ground.

Vocabulary
Sun, Moon, star, planet, cloud, lightning, rocket, aeroplane, bird, helicopter, butterfly, balloon

RESOURCES ●
Main activity: large sheet of card, light blue or grey backing paper, wide adhesive tape and display board (see Preparation); felt-tipped pen; large sheet of paper; photocopiable page 202 (also 'Up in the sky – 1' (red) available on the CD-ROM); computer or interactive whiteboard.
Group activities: 1 Paper; crayons; string. **2** Pictures cut from photocopiable page 202 (also 'Up in the sky – 1' (red) available on the CD-ROM); scissors; sorting rings. **3** Dominoes made from photocopiable page 203 (also 'Up in the sky – 2' (red) available on the CD-ROM). **4** Classroom play equipment. **5** Collage materials; templates or sponge shapes of the Moon, the Sun, the planet Saturn, stars and clouds; white and yellow paint.
ICT link: computer; internet access.
Plenary: Staple gun; thread.

PREPARATION
Cover the display board with light blue or grey paper, depending on the time of year, for an 'In the sky' display. Make a large book for the children's pictures, using a card cover and wide adhesive tape. Cut out the pictures from photocopiable page 202, then copy photocopiable page 206 on to card and cut out the dominoes. Parents or carers may be willing to lend or donate suitable objects for the display.

STARTER
Talk to the children about the dangers of looking directly at the Sun. It is very important that they know that this can damage their eyes, and that they must never do this. Make a poster, if you wish, to show next to the display – and contrary to other good practice, make the message negative by starting with the word 'NEVER'.

MAIN ACTIVITY ●
Discuss with the children all the things that they may see in the sky. You may need to negotiate some of the suggestions, as some very young children may not discriminate between things in the sky and things high up on buildings (such as television aerials). Make a list on a large sheet of paper or use the pictures from 'Up in the sky – 1' (red) on the CD-ROM displayed on a computer or interactive whiteboard, to show the pictures of things that are high in the sky and not touching the ground or a building.

GROUP ACTIVITIES
1 Ask the children to draw pictures of some of the things that are in the sky and not touching the ground or a building. Make a book of their pictures and hang it by the 'In the sky' display for the children to enjoy (and to add to if they wish).
2 Work with the children to sort the pictures from photocopiable page 202 into things that are found in the sky and things that can be seen by looking up but are attached to a person (for example, helicopter, rocket and

aeroplane). Talk about things that can be seen in the sky and also on the ground, such as aeroplanes and birds. You may wish to discuss which things are in the sky through nature and which are made by people.

3 Play the matching dominoes game from photocopiable page 203, asking the children to match identical pictures of things that are seen in the sky. Talk through the names of the things shown: 'star', 'Moon', 'cloud', 'Sun'. As the children place the dominoes, they have to say the name of the object in the picture they are matching.

4 Ask an adult to help a group of children sort through the play equipment and toys in the classroom to find models of things seen in the sky (such as birds, helicopters, aeroplanes, kites, balloons and star shapes) and add them to the display. Sort them into sets of whether they are always in the sky or only in the sky sometimes.

5 Ask a group of children to make large pictures from collage materials of the Sun, the Moon, the planet Saturn, stars and clouds. Ask them to use Sun, Moon, planet, star and cloud shapes cut from sponge to print a design on the class book cover.

ICT LINK

Look at pictures on the Internet of planets, stars and the moon. Ask the children to think of other things that can be found in the sky to 'search' on the Internet.

ASSESSMENT

Group activity 1 serves as a good initial assessment task, as it shows the children's understanding of the things that are found in the sky. The discussions during Group activity 2 will give you an insight into the children's conceptual level.

PLENARY

Talk about the large collaged Moon, stars, Sun and clouds. Discuss whether we see these things in the sky during the day or at night. Staple the Sun and clouds to the display board; attach thread to the stars and the Moon, then hang these to one side to depict the sky at night. Add the items collected during Group activity 4.

OUTCOMES

● All children *must* be able to notice things that are found in the sky and things that are not.

● Most of the children *should* be able to sort things into whether they are always found in the sky or only sometimes.
● Some *could* record what they know by drawing.
● A small number *could even* know that there are many things in the sky: some that have been made by people and some that are there through nature.

LINKS

ECM 1: Staying safe.
Between units: this lesson links to Lessons 6 and 7 in Unit 3.

Lesson 2 ◗ Rainbow

Objective
● To learn that rain and sunlight together can create a rainbow.

RESOURCES 💿

Apusskidu, edited by Beatrice Harrop (A&C Black); hosepipe attached to a tap; large space outside; bright sunshine; blank CD; squares of gummed and tissue paper in the colours of the rainbow; blue foil paper; scissors; staple gun; photocopiable page 204 (also 'Rainbow' (red) available on the CD-ROM); coloured pencils; bubble mixture and blowers; version of the story of Noah's Ark from the Bible. Make sure that you have the correct attachment to fit your hose to a tap that is close enough to your working space – this takes a lot of preparation, but the results are worth it.

MAIN ACTIVITY

Sing the song 'I can see a rainbow' from *Apusskidu*. Take the children outside and stand them where they will be able to see the rainbow you are about to make. Stand to one side of the space and ask an adult helper to turn on the tap. As the water runs freely out of the hose, either turn on the spray mechanism or place your thumb firmly over the end to produce a spray of water. Lift the hosepipe into the air so that an arc of water is created. As sunlight goes through the water, a rainbow can be seen.

Organise Group activities with adult support:
1 Talk about the colours seen in the rainbow. The children may not have clearly seen all of the colours outside, and may need a prompt for some. Conventionally, it is accepted that the colours of the rainbow are red, orange, yellow, green, blue, indigo and violet (though the existence of indigo is doubted by scientists). Use a blank CD to reflect an overhead light: it will produce the colours of the rainbow. Together, make a large rainbow with squares of gummed and tissue paper and staple it to the 'In the sky' display. Add raindrops cut from blue foil paper.
2 Give the children a copy each of photocopiable page 204 and ask them to draw the rainbow where the sunshine meets the rain.
3 Repeat the Main activity with groups of eight children. This will give them an opportunity to see the rainbow more clearly, and to talk about what they can see.
4 Put out bubble mixture and blowers. Ask an adult helper to blow large bubbles so that the children can see the colours on their surfaces clearly. Ask: *Are the colours the same as the ones you saw in the rainbow?*

ASSESSMENT

Note those children who responded to what they saw by saying (or agreeing) that they saw colours in the water. This shows that they are beginning to communicate what happens during an investigation, as well as demonstrating their observation skills.

PLENARY

Differentiation 💿
Support
To support the activity, give the children 'Rainbow' (green) from the CD-ROM and ask them to colour in the rainbow using the correct colours.
Extension
Extend the activity using 'Rainbow' (blue) from the CD-ROM. Encourage the children to draw and label a rainbow, and then add the two types of weather needed to see a rainbow in the sky.

Read the story of Noah's Ark from the Bible. Talk about where you have put the rainbow in the display. *Is it seen in the sky or on the ground?* Explain that although it appears to 'stand' on the ground, the rainbow is really hanging in the sky.

OUTCOMES

● All children *must* know that when it rains and the Sun is shining, a rainbow may appear.
● Most of the children *should* be able to look closely at the rainbow and identify some or all of the colours.
● Some *could* talk about when a rainbow appears in other things.
● A small number *could even* begin to realise that water is a prism which breaks up light into the colours of the rainbow.

Lesson 3 ▭ The night sky

Objective
● To learn that the sky looks different during the day and at night.

Vocabulary
stars, Moon, shine, twinkle, bright, clouds, planets

RESOURCES
Main activity: Picture of the sky at night (optional); large sheet of paper; marker pen; pictures of the different phases of the Moon; display board; black or dark blue backing paper.
Group activities: 1 Silver foil; white paper; thread; grey paper; scissors; adhesive. **2** Selection of story books showing the sky at night or internet access. **3** White paint; chalk or pastels; black or dark blue sugar paper. **4** Sponge star and Moon shapes; white paint; strips of black paper.
ICT link: CD-ROMs with pictures of the sky at night; computer; printer.

PREPARATION
Cover a display board with black or dark blue paper. During part of the year, it gets dark early enough for the children to see the stars and the Moon before they go to bed at night. Write to parents and carers, asking them to support the activity by taking the children outside to see the stars and the Moon before they go to bed.

STARTER
Sing 'Twinkle, twinkle, little star' with the children. Ask the children whether they have ever seen the stars at night. *What do they look like?* You may wish to use a picture of the sky at night (available as posters and on bed linens) as a stimulus.

MAIN ACTIVITY
Talk about what the children can see in the sky at night. (Take care not to refer to the Moon as a light source.) Make a list on the left-hand side of a large sheet of paper. Include stars, the Moon and clouds as well as anything else the children suggest, such as bats, birds and planets. Go through each item on your list and talk about its colour and its shape. This will lead to discussions about the Moon seeming to have different shapes at different times. Spend a few moments looking at pictures of the Moon, and respond to any questions the children may raise. Explain that the Moon's shape appears to change depending on where it is in the sky as it moves around the Earth.

GROUP ACTIVITIES
1 Work with the children to make stars from silver foil and white paper. Attach thread to some of these for mobiles. Make a large Moon from white paper, having decided with the children what shape it is going to be. Use grey paper to make several clouds. Add these to the display board to make a display of 'The night sky'.
2 Ask an adult helper to look through a selection of books or on the Internet to find and talk about pictures of the sky at night, the different Moon shapes and the stars in the sky.
3 Ask the children to make pictures of the night sky using light chalk, paint or pastels on black or very dark blue sugar paper.
4 Ask the children to use star and Moon shapes cut from sponge to print a border for the display, using white paint on black paper.

ICT LINK
Use pictures from appropriate CD-ROMs to create a picture of the night sky. Print these out and add them to the display as a frame for the larger picture.

ASSESSMENT
As the children make their stars in Group activity 1, ask them to talk about what they know about the night sky. As they refer to features such as stars,

Differentiation
Support
Support children by leading
into the theme of the night
sky with a suitable story or
poem. Talk about nocturnal
animals, and include drawings
in the display of some of the
ones that can fly .
Extension
Some children will be keen to
research the planets, as some
children have a fascination
with space. There are several
books available containing
good-quality pictures of the
planets, from which the
children will be able to draw
pictures for the display.

the Moon and clouds, add these to the display. Talk about things that can be
seen at night at some times but not at others, such as aeroplanes and bats.
Note those children who know what things can be seen in the night sky.

PLENARY
Compare the two displays you have made so far (from Lessons 1 and 2 of
this unit). Look at the things that can be seen during the day, and then at
the things that can be seen at night. Invite the children to name all the
things that are in both pictures and all the things that are only in one.

OUTCOMES
- All children *must* know that the sky looks different at night.
- Most of the children *should* know that some things can be seen at night
but not during the day and that some things can be seen during the day but
not at night.
- Some *could* recognise that light at night comes from a
range of sources and name some of these.
- A small number *could even* use simple texts to find
information.

LINKS
Between units: this lesson links to Unit 7, Lessons 7
and 8.

Lesson 4 Day or night?

Objective
- To find out that objects look
different during the day and at
night.

Vocabulary
darker, light, lighter,
headlights, same, different

RESOURCES
Main activity: Two photographs of the same place, one taken during the
day and the other at night; copy of *Can't You Sleep, Little Bear?* by Martin
Waddell (Walker Books); display board divided down the middle, one side in
bright blue backing paper and the other in a darker colour (see Preparation).
Group activities: 1-4 Templates of cars, houses, streetlights and people;
squares of tracing paper; strips of grey or dark green paper; scissors;
adhesive; paint in a range of colours. **5** Recycled materials; adhesive; paints.
6 Photocopiable page 205 (also 'Day or night?' (red) available on the CD-
ROM); pencils.
ICT link: 'Day or night?' interactive available on the CD-ROM
Plenary: Staple gun; squares and strips of yellow paper; templates of stars.

PREPARATION
Take two photographs of an outdoor scene, one by day and one by night,
otherwise as similar as possible. Cover the display board so that the side
representing daytime is a brighter blue or lighter than the side representing
night-time.

STARTER
Read the story *Can't You Sleep, Little Bear?* and talk about how it gets dark
at night-time. Ask the children what happens when it gets dark at home. *Do
you switch on the lights? Why?*

MAIN ACTIVITY
Show the children your two photographs and talk about the things that are
the same and the things that are different. Talk about the time when the
children went into a dark place to look at coloured shapes (see Unit 7,
Lesson 8). How many children remember that colours looked darker or less
bright? Ask the children whether they think the colours look the same at
night or look darker. Remind the children how you made the colours look

darker when you mixed black paint with them.

Explain that you are going to make a display of the street where you live. Tell them about the houses in your street, the cars and the street-lamps. You are going to make two pictures: one to show what your street looks like during the day, and another to show what it looks like at night. The children are going to work in groups to make these pictures.

GROUP ACTIVITIES

1 Work with children to make a row of houses for the daytime picture. Explain that your house has a red front door and a neighbour's house has a green one. Ask two children to paint the correctly coloured doors on two copies of the house template. When they have finished, talk about the colours of the windows during the day. If necessary, take the children outside to look. Stick the windows (squares of tracing paper) into place.

2 Repeat the activity with another group, making the colours of the doors darker by mixing a little black paint into the red and green paint. Invite four children to do the same for the four cars from Group activity 3.

3 Invite a group of four children to paint four cars for the daytime picture in yellow, red, green and blue.

4 Ask an adult helper to work with a group of eight children, making street-lights with thin strips of grey or dark green paper.

5 Working with groups of six children at a time, make models of cars from recycled materials. Ask them to paint the cars for either the daytime or the night-time picture.

6 Ask the children to complete photocopiable page 205 by drawing lines to match the objects to the picture (daytime or night-time) in which they belong.

ICT LINK

Using 'Day or night?' interactive from the CD-ROM, encourage the children to drag and drop the pictures into the correct 'day' or 'night' scene.

ASSESSMENT

During the Plenary session, invite different children to add to the display at different times. This will give you the opportunity to talk about the similarities and differences between the two pictures with small groups of children. photocopiable page 205 can also be used to assess the children's understanding of the differences between how a street appears by day and how it appears by night.

PLENARY

With a group of children who may need support, watching and helping, staple the cars, street-lights and houses onto the display board before talking about how the colours of the objects in the two pictures are different. Refer back to the children turning on their lights at night so that they can see. Show the children the squares of yellow paper and stick these to the night-time picture to show that the lights in the houses have been turned on. Now invite the children to say how the cars will look different at night. Invite another group to join you, and ask them to stick strips of yellow paper to the cars to represent the light coming from the headlights. Ask the children to say why the cars have their lights on. Ask another group to repeat this task with the street-lights, giving the ones in the night-time picture rays of light. Remove the stars and the Moon from the night-time picture of photocopiable page 205 and add them to the night-time display. Invite these groups to go and make more stars for the sky, using the star templates. Extend the activity with a group of children by attaching pictures of people, dark and light, to the correct pictures. Ask them to give reasons for their decisions. Finally, add any further stars.

OUTCOMES

● All children *must* notice that there are differences between daytime and night-time.
● Most of the children *should* be able to identify similarities and differences between two pictures.
● Some *could* know that objects look different in the day and at night.
● A small number *could even* compare the brightness of light in the day and night-time pictures.

LINKS

Between units: this lesson links with Unit 7, Lesson 8.
Across the curriculum: read rhymes and stories about night-time during literacy activities.

Lesson 5 ▣ Daytime sky

Objective
● To observe the changes that may occur in the sky during the day.

RESOURCES

Large sheets of paper; pencils; access to sunshine, shadows and clouds. Watch the weather forecast for a changeable day, or be ready to teach this lesson when the conditions are right.

MAIN ACTIVITY

Talk about the sky on a 'normal' day: whether there are always clouds in the sky, whether the Sun is shining, whether the sky is blue or grey, and so on. Relate the discussion to the weather information you collected in Unit 3.

Take the children outside and remind them about not looking directly at the Sun. Ask an adult helper to watch the children and make sure that they do not do this. Ask the children to stand with their backs to the Sun and look at the clouds in the sky. *What do the clouds remind you of? How much blue sky can you see between the clouds?* Talk about whether the Sun feels hot on their backs. *Can you see a shadow just in front of you? What does it look like? Is it the same size as you, or is it smaller or bigger? Can you see any other shadows on the ground?* Go on a 'shadow hunt' if appropriate.

Organise Group activities with adult support:
1 Ask an adult helper to work with groups of six children in turn, drawing an accurate group picture of the sky as they can see it. They should decide how many clouds to add to the picture, and whether to show the Sun behind the clouds or in the middle of a blue area. The helper should number the pictures and write the time that each recording was made.
2 Go outside with a group of ten children and play 'shadow tag'. When they are standing on a shadow, they cannot be tagged. If someone jumps on their shadow, they are 'it'.
3 Repeat the activities several times during the day.

ASSESSMENT

When the activities are repeated, ask the children to predict whether they will see any changes in the sky. *Do you think there will be more clouds? Why do you think that? Do you think you will be able to see your shadow?* Note the children's responses.

PLENARY

Compare the group pictures, noting similarities and differences. Invite the children to evaluate some of the observations: *Was Dave right? How do you know?* Ask them to watch the weather forecast later and predict whether the sky will be different tomorrow.

Differentiation
Organise the children into mixed-ability groups, so that children who need support can be helped by other children.

Challenge the children to draw around shadows of each other and encourage them to observe how their shadows change size and position during the day.

OUTCOMES
● All children *must* be able to look for and notice shadows.
● Most of the children *should* be able to think of similarities and differences in their observations at different times of the day.
● Some *could* talk about observations and begin to understand that all solid objects have a shadow.
● A small number *could even* begin to understand that shadows are formed when light is blocked by a solid object and use the information to predict when they will see a shadow and when they will not.

Lesson 6 ▷ What to do on sunny days

Objective
● To learn that the Sun can be dangerous and that we need to take care in order to keep safe on hot sunny days.

RESOURCES ◉
Collection of sun hats, parasols, sunglasses and bottles of sun cream; photocopiable page 206 (also 'What to do on sunny days' (red) available on the CD-ROM); pencils; paints; paper; garden umbrella and base; cups; water.

MAIN ACTIVITY
Send a letter home to parents and carers, explaining that you are setting up a display to show the dangers of the Sun and the need to take care on hot sunny days. Ask them to reinforce this message at home.

Look at the sunglasses and talk about how they are different from ordinary spectacles. Point out the darker lenses, and explain that these are special glasses for helping to protect the eyes. Emphasise that it is still not safe to look at the Sun even when wearing sunglasses: they are not that good at protecting the eyes. Talk about the other things in your collection. *Why do we put sun cream on? Why is it important to wear a sun hat? Why do we need to drink plenty of water in hot weather?*

Organise Group activities with adult support:
1 Ask a group, working together, to complete the sentences of all the things that we need to do to keep safe on a hot day, using the writing frame on photocopiable page 208
2 Ask the children to arrange the collection of items on a display surface, grouping items of the same kind together.
3 Set up a painting table and ask the children to paint pictures of the things they like to do on sunny days.
4 Go outside on a hot day and find a shady spot for storytelling or a picnic lunch. Make the preparations first: wearing sun hats, putting on sun cream and so on.
5 Set up a garden umbrella or pagoda and resources for a play picnic (including cups of water) for the children to access.

ASSESSMENT
Use the children's lists of dos and don'ts to assess their understanding of what they need to use to protect themselves from the Sun. Note those children who have a good awareness of the issues; reinforce the message individually every day with those who do not.

PLENARY
Make a list of all the things we have to remember to do on hot sunny days. You may think it appropriate to list all the things that the children should *not* do: stay in the sunlight for too long, stay thirsty and so on. Display the list(s) prominently by your display.

OUTCOMES
● All of the children *must* know that they should protect themselves from the Sun.

- Most of the children *should* know how to protect themselves from the Sun.
- Some *could* know the importance of drinking plenty of water on hot sunny days.
- A small number *could even* consider their own needs independently.

CONTEXT Summer rain

The idea for the following lesson was inspired by watching the playground dry up quickly on a wet day under the strong rays of the summer Sun. The view is magnificent and exciting. Much discussion of where the water is going can take place, allowing you to challenge some groups without confusing the other children. As far as some children are concerned, if they can't see the water any more then it doesn't exist.

Lesson 7 ◘ What happened?

Objectives
- To learn that water apparently disappears on a hot day.
- To learn that water dries up or evaporates.

Vocabulary
dry up, evaporate

RESOURCES
Main activity: Hot sunny day; two half-litre containers of water; chalk.
Group activities: 1 photocopiable page 207 (also 'What happened?' (red) available on the CD-ROM); scissors; adhesive sticks; paper. **2** Water; cups; chalk; broom. **3 and 4** Paintbrushes; pots of water.

PREPARATION
Watch the weather forecast and choose a hot sunny day.

STARTER
Ask the children to tell you what happens to an ice cream on a hot day. What about an ice lolly? When you are sure the children realise that these things melt because of the heat of the Sun, tell them that the Sun also makes something happen to water. Explain that you are going to explore what happens to water on a hot day.

MAIN ACTIVITY
Go outside on a hot day and pour half a litre of water to make a puddle in the middle of the playground. Wait for the water to soak into the ground before drawing around the outside with a piece of chalk. Ask an adult helper to pour another half-litre of water to make a puddle in another part of the playground with a different group of children, and to draw around the edge of this puddle. After a while, return to the puddles to see whether anything has happened. What do the children notice about the size of the puddles? Draw round the puddles again. Repeat this action until the puddles have both dried up.

Differentiation
Support
Let children who need support explore this activity, rather than carry out a structured investigation. They should learn that on a hot day, water dries up.
Extension
Challenge the children, using 'What happened?' (blue) from the CD-ROM, to write a sentence to describe what has happened in each picture, before they stick them down into the correct order.

Back in the classroom, talk to the children to find out what they think has happened to the water. How many of them think the puddle has disappeared completely, and how many think that it has dried up? Explain that the water has *dried up* or *evaporated*. It has become part of the air and gone up into the sky.

GROUP ACTIVITIES

1 Give the children a copy each of photocopiable page 207. Ask them to cut out the pictures and put them in the correct order to show the changes they have just seen, then stick them down on paper as a record.

2 With a group, set up an investigation to compare whether a deeper puddle dries up faster than one that has been spread out. Tell them that they should use the same amount of water to make two puddles, then spread out one of the puddles with a broom.

3 Give the children pots of water and let them go outside and paint water pictures. Invite them to work with their friends, starting at the same time, to paint similar-sized pictures on the bricks, paving slabs and playground. Challenge them to find out on which surface the picture dries up the fastest.

4 Challenge the children to find a place where their picture does not dry up too quickly.

ASSESSMENT

Keep the ordered pictures as evidence of the children's knowledge of how the puddle dried up.

PLENARY

Talk about the places where the children chose to do their paintings. Did some paintings dry up or evaporate faster than others? Did anyone find a good place where the painting did not dry up so quickly? Where was this place? Can the children explain why this place is better? (The water will dry more slowly on an uneven surface, and in the shade.) Relate the learning to the previous lesson, which told the children to drink plenty of water on hot sunny days. Ask the children whether they can now give a reason why they need to do this.

OUTCOMES

● All children *must* notice that the water dries up.
● Most of the children *should* know that on a hot day water dries up and be able to ask questions about why puddles dry up and where the water goes.
● Some *could* notice that water dries up faster on some surfaces.
● A small number *could even* respond to suggestions about how to find out which puddle dries up the fastest and so say what happened in an investigation.

LINKS

Across the curriculum: this lesson develops the children's early skills in thinking and scientific enquiry.

Lesson 8 ▪ Assessment

Objective
● To find out what the children know about the sky and beyond.

RESOURCES

Main assessment activity: large sheet of paper; felt-tipped pens in a range of colours.
Assessment activities: 2-4 A3 paper; crayons in various colours; pencils.
4 Computer (optional).

MAIN ASSESSMENT ACTIVITY

Tell the children that you are going to make a picture of all the things they can think of that are seen in the sky and beyond it. As they make suggestions, choose an appropriate-coloured pen and draw the things they suggest. Then talk about all the things in the finished picture. Note those children who suggest planets, stars and the Moon as well as things such as clouds, the Sun and rainbows. Separate your paper into day and night areas if you wish.

ASSESSMENT ACTIVITY 2

Ask the children to draw picture of a rainbow, and to show what the weather would have to be like for the rainbow to appear.

ASSESSMENT ACTIVITY 3

Fold a sheet of A3 paper in half and work with a group of children at a time, recording their suggestions about the changes in the sky during the day and at night. Ask: *Would some things be seen at night but not in the day? Would some things be seen in the day but not at night?* Ask them when they would see shadows and when they would not. *When would you see a rainbow? Would you see one at night? Why not?* Ask them whether clouds always look the same shape and colour. Remind them of the dangers of looking directly at the Sun.

ASSESSMENT ACTIVITY 4

Ask the children to make a poster showing the dangers of the Sun. Talk with them first about all the things in the Sun awareness display, and remind them of some of the activities they did in that lesson (Lesson 6). Use a computer for this activity if you wish, using images and words for the children to select from.

PLENARY

Share some of the pictures with the children and play 'Spot the differences', identifying all of the things included on some pictures and not on others.

ASSESSMENT OUTCOMES

On completion of these Assessment activities, you should know which children have attained the following objectives linked to knowledge and understanding of the world:
● All the children *must* be aware that the Sun can be harmful to our health.
● Most of the children *should* know that rain and sunshine are needed to make a rainbow.
● Some *could* know that some things can be seen at night but not during the day and that some things can be seen during the day but not at night.
● A small number *could even* show that they are aware of how to look after their own needs independently on a hot day.

PHOTOCOPIABLE

Up in the sky – 1

Illustration © Colin Shelbourn

SCHOLASTIC

Up in the sky – 2

Illustration © Colin Shelbourn

PHOTOCOPIABLE

Rainbow

■ Draw a rainbow in this picture.

Illustration © Colin Shelbourn

◣ SCHOLASTIC

Day or night?

Illustration © Colin Shelbourn

What to do on sunny days

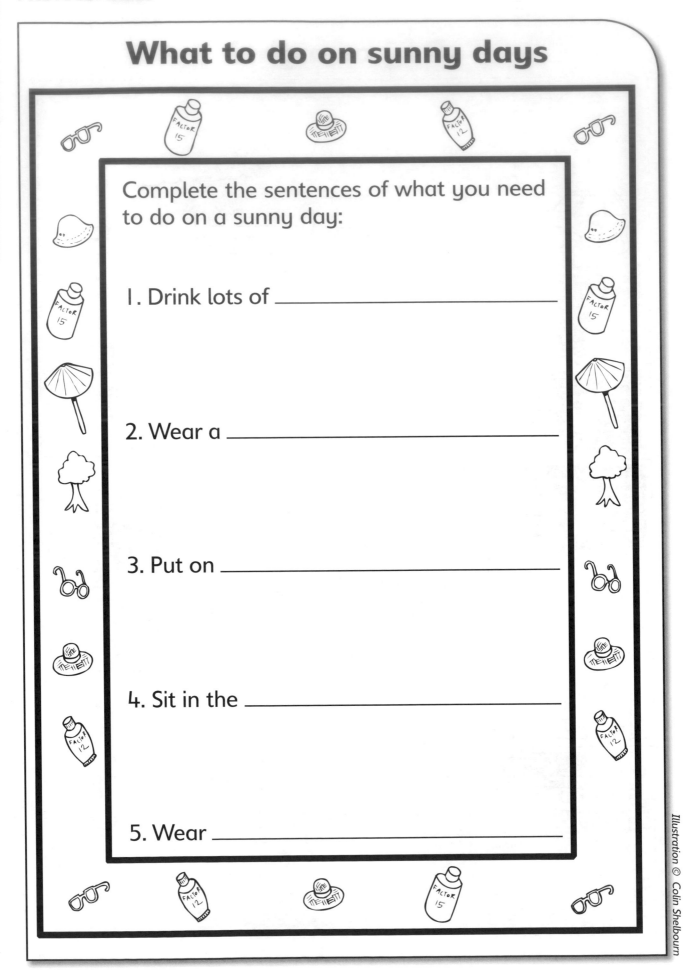

Complete the sentences of what you need to do on a sunny day:

1. Drink lots of _____

2. Wear a _____

3. Put on _____

4. Sit in the _____

5. Wear _____

Illustration © Colin Shelbourn

What happened?

■ Place these pictures in the correct order

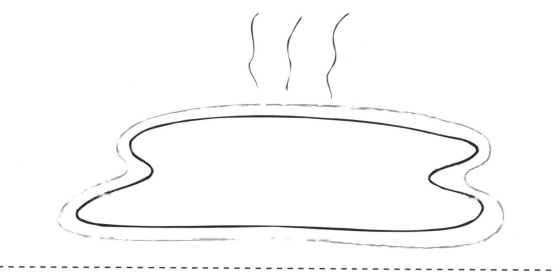

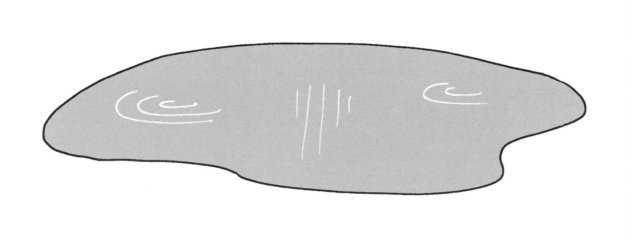

Illustration © Colin Shelbourn

SCHOLASTIC

In this series:

ISBN 978-0439-94502-8

ISBN 978-0439-94503-5

ISBN 978-0439-94504-2

ISBN 978-0439-94505-9

ISBN 978-0439-94506-6

ISBN 978-0439-94507-3

ISBN 978-0439-94508-0

To find out more, call: 0845 603 9091
or visit our website www.scholastic.co.uk